GAY PLAYS
VOLUME THREE

Cock & Bull Story *by Richard Crowe and Richard Zajdlic*, Terminal Bar *by Paul Selig*, Levitation *by Timothy Mason*, The Prisoners of War *by J.R. Ackerley*.

Male sexuality and the machismo of the boxing ring are the ingredients of Crowe and Zajdlic's unusual *Cock & Bull Story*, while American Paul Selig's *Terminal Bar* is an abandoned club in New York's red-light district where schoolboy Dwayne finds himself in the company of a streetwalker and a runaway housewife. By contrast Timothy Mason's brilliant *Levitation* (also American) discovers a family gathering by moonlight in the garden in front of their house and treading carefully on their past, present and future. Included with these three contemporary plays, J.R. Ackerley's *The Prisoners of War* was first performed in 1925 and was described by Siegfreid Sassoon as 'painful but impressive'. Begun while Ackerley was himself a prisoner in Germany in 1918, the play is about confinement and repression and the way in which the enforced proximity of the prisoners can heighten and distort emotion. While the homosexual theme may appear blatant to readers today, the play is a fascinating example of the kind of work which evaded the Lord Chamberlain's veto.

This, the third anthology in the *Gay Plays* series, is selected once again by playwright Michael Wilcox, whose work includes *Rents*, *Lent* and, most recently, *Massage*.

SIXTEEN
GAY PLAYS

Volume Three

COCK & BULL STORY
by
Richard Crowe and Richard Zajdlic

TERMINAL BAR
by
Paul Selig

LEVITATION
by
Timothy Mason

THE PRISONERS OF WAR
by
J.R. Ackerley

Edited and introduced by
Michael Wilcox

METHUEN DRAMA

A METHUEN NEW THEATRESCRIPT

This volume first published as a Methuen New Theatrescript in 1988 by
Methuen Drama, Michelin House, 81 Fulham Road, London SW3 6RB, and
distributed in the United States of America by HEB Inc, 70 Court Street,
Portsmouth, New Hampshire 03801, USA.

British Library Cataloguing in Publication Data

Gay plays. — (A Methuen theatrescript).
  Vol. 3
  1. Drama in English, 1900- Special
  subject: Homosexuality – Anthologies
  I. Wilcox, Michael, *1943-*
822′.912′080353

ISBN 0-413-14740-1

Printed in Great Britain by Richard Clay, Bungay, Suffolk.

CONTENTS

INTRODUCTION

The Giant Homophobia is alive and well in Britain. It is busily reclaiming lost territory, so keenly won by countless activists of many generations. Thatcher's parliament, supported, to its eternal shame, by the Opposition Labour front bench, voted in favour of making it an offence for local authorities to promote positive images of homosexuality. This ruling is the notorious Section (formerly Clause) 28. Exactly how this will be put into practice remains to be seen. In Britain, local authorities have responsibility, among other things, for schools, colleges, libraries and many social welfare organisations. It could mean that students will not be allowed to read novels and plays in which homosexuality is treated at all sympathetically which, I suppose, will exclude this volume from school, college and public libraries. It could mean that *all* work by homosexual authors will be removed from the shelves. There are many local authorities throughout the land and each will interpret the new legislation as it pleases. This might mean that books available in one part of the country are not available in another. It may well become illegal for Gay support groups to be funded in any way by local authorities. And what of E.M. Forster, Oscar Wilde, Tennessee Williams and the rest? Will sixth-form students be allowed to read Marlowe's *Edward II*? The vague wording of Section 28 will allow manifold interpretations, at the whim of homophobic councillors. Where will it end?

And all this at a time when condoms and 'safe sex' are freely advertised and promoted, very sensibly, by a worthy (if late) AIDS awareness campaign, run . . . yes . . . by the same Thatcher Government! So school students can watch an Agony Aunt on television giving us a demo of how to put on a condom (she used an uncomfortable looking wooden penis, to the merriment of a few million teenagers), but it may be an offence (depending on how the new legislation is interpreted) for those same students to have an open discussion that includes homosexuality at their schools and colleges. Teachers may be committing a criminal offence by discussing homosexuality (except, presumably, in the most derogatory terms) with their students.

The achievements of homosexual writers, painters, film-makers and composers are surely a positive affirmation of gayness? No government, however homophobic, should be allowed to deprive its citizens, of whatever age, of a vital, pulsating part of their culture.

Anyone seeking an example of what homophobia can do to people should read *Cock and Bull Story*. The sexual ambiguity of two young East End lads lets loose fear and violence. Travis and Jacko have become profoundly disturbed in their search for a machismo that is acceptable to their mates and to themselves. Their attitude towards women is cruel and thoughtless. Subtleties of affection and respect for the plurality of humankind are not admitted into their world. The love of man for man can only be expressed through aggression, whether in brutal street fights, or homoerotic clinches in the boxing ring. Add to this the culturally imperative alcohol abuse, and you have an explosive mixture. There is, I contend, a link between homophobia and violence (murder even) on the football terraces and in the streets of Britain. This unusual play deserves wide attention. It contains a warning of the direction in which the Government's legislation against homosexuals will surely lead.

Two plays in this volume come from across the Atlantic. *Terminal Bar* is set in the near future in plague-stricken New York. Two women in a heterosexual bar are surrounded by death and decomposition. A 16-year-old boy from the gay bar next door, who blames his survival on his extreme unattractiveness, has been cruising a guy who turns out to be dead. The humour is chilling. The concept and execution of the play are extraordinarily accomplished. It consists of a single act of, I guess, just over an hour, and is the assured and imaginative achievement of a young American dramatist, Paul Selig. I have read another of his plays, *Body Parts*, which I also commend to your attention. I await his future work keenly.

The second play from America, *Levitation* by Timothy Mason (whose *Bearclaw* is in *Gay Plays: Volume Two*), is also partly about death, although the effect is not numbing but (forgive me) uplifting. This beautiful play is brim full of magic. Are these characters really living on the same planet as those distressed East End lads? Timothy Mason exercises such perfect stagecraft, controlling the proceedings with wizardry. Metaphysical? Surreal? Ghostly? The loves and fears of earthlings set against the immensity of the heavens.

Positive images of homosexuality, certainly. How dare Thatcher give local authorities the power to ban this play from our schools and colleges? What madness is overtaking us? One might also ask why a play of such quality, first staged in 1984 in the USA, has not been produced by one of our national theatre companies. When reviewing *Terminal Bar* on the Fringe of the 1985 Edinburgh Festival, Nicholas de Jongh wrote in the *Guardian* of 'our two homophobic national theatre companies', by which I presume he meant The National Theatre and the Royal Shakespeare Company. I wish one of them would produce *Levitation* and make sure there would be an abundance of school matinées. Would their funding be put at risk?

After three contemporary plays, how distant the world of J.R. Ackerley's *The Prisoners of War* at first seems. The first draft was written while Ackerley was a prisoner of war himself in 1918. Like the main character, Captain Conrad, Ackerley was interned eventually in Switzerland. Prisoners with servants? Hotel accommodation? Switzerland? Yes, indeed! Officers were officers, a class apart. First over the top in the trenches, waving revolvers, the most vulnerable in the horror of combat, then, for those who survived the battle, relative luxury and privilege. The officers in the play grumble like mad, address each other in the curious lingo of the period, and, for all the appalling experiences of war, seem like emotionally stunted and overgrown children. That, of course, is the point. Behind the racist and sexist banter, and the war-scarred personalities, lie scarcely expressed, homosexual tensions, especially between Conrad and young Second Lieutenant Grayle, the much quested for, but never achieved, 'holy' object of desire. This 'crush' is the true cause of Conrad's apparent insanity at the end of the play. In the wonderful *My Father and Myself* (The Bodley Head, 1968) Ackerley describes how he was attracted to two young men during his internment, but how guilt and fear caused him to closet his passions in the privacy of his notebooks and the first draft of this script. By projecting his own 'unresponsiveness to love' onto Grayle, Ackerley was expressing his own fear of sexual contact (thoroughly exorcized in years to come!). Thus the pressures of society's homophobia leads to misery and insanity.

I guess that the only reason *The Prisoners of War*, with its (to us) blatantly homosexual theme, was allowed to be performed was due partly to the topicality of the predicament of the young soldiers, and partly that the Lord Chamberlain, in whose office it lay to grant the play a performing license, was a clueless, old dodderer. 'You see, Captain Conrad,' says Mme Louis, 'I heard you do not greatly care for the fair sex.' 'The fair sex?' replies Conrad. 'Which sex is that?' Gays of the time received such lines with glee. But such sentiments also spoke to heterosexual men who had lived and suffered with comrades of all types and classes. If young soldiers (and the not so young) had gone to the front with Housman's *A Shropshire Lad* in their pockets, what awaited them, in the theatre at least, was R.C. Sherriff's *Journey's End*, and, some years before that fine play, Ackerley's *The Prisoners of War*. On consideration, does the distress and violence promoted by homophobia seem so distant a theme?

Michael Wilcox
July, 1988

COCK & BULL STORY

RICHARD CROWE and **RICHARD ZAJDLIC** became involved in acting, writing and directing while at Southampton University, and founded the Ratskins Theatre Company in 1983. They wrote, performed and directed *Cock & Bull Story* in 1985 and have toured the play both in and outside London. They also wrote, performed and directed *Cannibal* (another 2-hander) which was produced at the Warehouse Theatre, Croydon in February 1987. Both *Cock & Bull Story* and *Cannibal* were performed by Crowe and Zajdlic at the Lyric Studio, Hammersmith in May 1988.

Cock & Bull Story

Starting from the original theme of male sexuality and 'machismo', the script of *Cock & Bull Story* evolved over a period of eight months through intense, recorded improvisation.

We began with two extremes – a homosexual and a rapist – and a metaphor – boxing. The intention was to investigate the 'macho' image that pressurizes men into adopting a stereotype often alien to their true natures and feelings.

Our first task was to develop two credible characters, which we began with an almost blasé attitude and false confidence. We soon found, however, that Jacko and Travis quickly left their black/white extremes to be drawn together into a murky grey. The parallels between ourselves and Jacko and Travis became actually real as we were forced, inevitably, to confront our own paranoia, fear, guilt and hostility.

This specifically heightened the aggression and authenticity of the piece, and made rehearsal prior to scripting both dangerously exciting and, at times, unbearably tense. The subsequent collaboration on the script became a nerve-shredding test of will, requiring a self-conscious return to a detached objectivity neither of us now felt.

Perhaps the power of this intensely subjective confrontation explains much of the play's success – that it does appear to challenge those same blasé attitudes and probe the insecurities of its audience.

The play does not seek to dictate, however, there is no 'message' as such, nor should there be any bias of sympathy – Travis is no more a hero than Jacko. The 'truth' in the play is wholly dependent on each individual's response. Sexual paranoia is a universal experience – as the fascinating, widely differing and extremely personal stories related to us in the bar after performances has testified.

Richard Crowe & Richard Zajdlic

RICHARD CROWE and **RICHARD ZAJDLIC** became involved in acting, writing and directing while at Southampton University, and founded the Ratskins Theatre Company in 1983. They wrote, performed and directed *Cock & Bull Story* in 1985 and have toured the play both in and outside London. They also wrote, performed and directed *Cannibal* (another 2-hander) which was produced at the Warehouse Theatre, Croydon in February 1987. Both *Cock & Bull Story* and *Cannibal* were performed by Crowe and Zajdlic at the Lyric Studio, Hammersmith in May 1988.

Cock & Bull Story was first performed at the Plaza Theatre, Romsey on April 25th 1985, by Ratskins Theatre Company with the following cast:

RUPERT TRAVIS	Richard Zajdlic
JACKO FOSTER	Richard Crowe

RUPERT TRAVIS	eighteen years old, a successful amateur boxer otherwise unemployed with aspirations to turn professional and go to London.
JOHN 'JACKO' FOSTER	twenty years old, Travis's mate, unemployed and aimless. Frequently in trouble with the police for fighting. He wants to go to London with Travis.

The play is set in the changing room of a gym in a provincial town in the south of England, on the night of an important boxing match. Should Travis win against his old rival, Sangster, he will turn professional.

Jacko is there to help Travis prepare for the fight and to celebrate his anticipated victory.

The first act takes place before, the second act after the match. Access to the changing room is on stage left, beyond which is the hall in which the match will be fought.

A wooden chair and milk crate are all that is required on stage. This may be supplemented, however, with a gym bench, punch bag, lockers, posters and so on.

The opening of the play: When the audience are in and seated, the following song is played through the PA into the auditorium.

Mates

JACKO: Who's gonna walk you home tonight
After the party after the fight?
Who's gonna make sure you're all right?
Who's gonna walk you home?

JACKO: 'Ello, darlin'.

TRAVIS: Jacko!

JACKO: All right then, son?

TRAVIS: Magic, mate.

JACKO: Who's always with ya to see you win
Down at the ringside down at the gym?
Who's always with you through thick and thin?
Who's gonna walk you home?

TRAVIS: You are Jacko.

JACKO: That's right, mate.

TRAVIS: Where we going now then?

JACKO: Pick up a bird.

TRAVIS: Up the disco?

JACKO: No mate – Kentucky Fried!

BOTH: We'll be together side by side
We'll be together till we die.
We're the boys, we're the lads
We are mates, mates, mates.

TRAVIS: Who's gonna get you home tonight
Another Friday, another fight,
Who's gonna make sure you're all right?
Who's gonna get you home?

TRAVIS: Look at the state of ya.

JACKO: Bastard jumped me.

TRAVIS: What ya gonna tell ya mum this time?

JACKO: You'll think of something.

TRAVIS: Me?

JACKO: You're me best mate, ain't ya?

TRAVIS: I'm your only bleeding mate –
Who else'd hang around with a bastard like you?

JACKO: You love me really.

TRAVIS: Yeah.

TRAVIS: Who's always with you when you get stick
Round at your mum's place, round the nick?
Who's always with you through thin and thick?
Who's gonna get you home?

JACKO: You are Travis.

TRAVIS: Almost there, mate.

JACKO: Home sweet home.

TRAVIS: You ain't half a bleeding weight.

BOTH: We'll be together side by side
We'll be together till we die.
We're the boys, we're the lads
We are mates, mates, mates.

JACKO: Bastard, I'll have him next time.

TRAVIS: How'd it happen anyway?

JACKO: He jumped me, didn't he?

TRAVIS: He jumped ya?

JACKO: Hiding behind a bleeding telephone box!

TRAVIS: What, a Mill boy? Bunch of fairies!

JACKO: Too bloody right. Sholey Mill.

BOTH: Sholey, Sholey, Sholey Mill.
Sholey Mill. Sholey Mill.
Sholey, Sholey, Sholey Mill. Sholey, Sholey Mill.
Wank, wank, wank, wank, wank, wank –

VOICE: Oi! You two, piss off and go home!

ACT ONE

Lights come up on TRAVIS *alone on stage, stripped to the waist. He is sitting on a simple, wooden chair, upstage right. By the chair is his kit bag, containing his boxing gear and two pairs of bagmits. Sparring pads, boxing gloves, boots and skipping rope are scattered around the chair.*

On the back wall, tatty posters announcing boxing contests; against the wall, a low bench, various bits of broken boxing paraphernalia strewn on or around it.

Downstage left, as if creating a second corner of an imaginary boxing ring with the chair, is a plastic beer crate.

The song Mates, *pre-recorded, can be heard in the auditorium.* TRAVIS *sits through it, obviously apprehensive. It is about an hour before his match and* JACKO *is not yet there.*

The song ends.

TRAVIS: No. No, not me. Why me? I can't do it.
Beat Sangster tonight. Beat him and you've won. Beat it. I *can't*. Can't. Scared. What if I can't? What if it happens again?
They're all watching me. Everyone watching me. Staring. Why me? Always me. Why? What can they see? Stop! Stop staring at me.
Rocky staring at me. Rocky Marciano – the living legend. Forty nine fights. Forty nine wins. He never gave up. Always won. He's the best – the winner.
I ain't like you. I *can't* do it!
The clinch, Travis. No. The clinch – smashing them, killing them. Your power, your strength. Just like Rocky, same as Rocky. Rocky. Rocky!
Can Sangster beat Rocky? Can he, Travis? Can he? No! Then smash Sangster. Kill him. Clinch him, Travis – clinch him!
No. Don't let it happen again. It ain't gonna be like last time. Ain't gonna be like that. Not tonight. Not ever. They're all watching me. Everyone staring at me.

Well, watch me smash him. Beat him. Watch me win. Always.
One thought. One word – kill.
Kill, kill, kill, kill, kill, kill, kill, kill! Rocky!

Lights down. JACKO *enters in the darkness.*

TRAVIS: Bloody hell, what's going on?

JACKO (*whispering*): Give us a touch of your willy!

TRAVIS: Jacko!

JACKO: Keep it down, will ya!

TRAVIS: What, me willy?

JACKO: No. Your mouth, stupid.

TRAVIS: Where the bloody hell've you been? I thought you weren't coming.

JACKO: Couldn't miss this one, could I.

TRAVIS: Almost bleeding did. Not long now, Jacko –

JACKO: Oi, not so loud, eh. No one around, is there?

TRAVIS: Only you and me.

JACKO: Oh, we're all alone then.

TRAVIS: 'Ere, turn them bleeding lights on.

JACKO *is quiet, moving around the stage, sneaking up on* TRAVIS, *who still can't see anything.*

TRAVIS: Jacko? . . . Jacko? . . . Jacko! Oi, gerroff!

Lights up. JACKO *has grabbed* TRAVIS *and pulled him onto his knees.* JACKO *is dressed-up, ready for a night on the town, but his clothes have become messed-up and there is a rip in his jacket.*

JACKO: 'Ello darling!

TRAVIS (*getting free*): Piss off, Jacko. Where'd you spring from?

JACKO: Window out the back.

TRAVIS: You what?

JACKO: Wanted to surprise you.

TRAVIS: Nearly shit meself. Thought I'd gone blind.

JACKO: Too much of that, mate!

TRAVIS: 'Ere, what you been doing?

JACKO: How d'ya mean?

TRAVIS: The state of you. That rip in your jacket.

JACKO: Oh, yeah. Done it getting in.

TRAVIS: Looks like you've been in a fight.

JACKO: No. I was climbing in through the bog window and I slipped. Ended up with me head down the bleeding bowl!

TRAVIS: I always said you was full of shit.

JACKO: Yeah. Ripped me jacket and everything.

TRAVIS: I thought you weren't gonna make it.

JACKO: Me? I had to be here – get ya ready, psyche you up. Couldn't miss this, not tonight.

TRAVIS: Yeah, tonight's the night, eh Jacko! London here we come!

JACKO: The birds!

TRAVIS: The flat!

JACKO: The team!

TRAVIS: Yeah!

JACKO: Living in London, mate. I wouldn't miss it for the world. All them birds!

JACKO *removes his jacket and throws it onto the bench.* TRAVIS *puts his tee shirt on.*

JACKO: So, how d'you feel?

TRAVIS: Fighting fit – can't wait to get in there, Jacko.

JACKO: Yeah. Smash him, son.

TRAVIS: I'll kill him. Be all over in the first round. I'll move so bleeding fast, Sangster won't know what hit him.

JACKO: Not like last time.

TRAVIS: No way. Just think of that, eh, Jacko – me a pro boxer.

JACKO: Yeah, just think of that. You could've been one months ago!

TRAVIS: Well, after tonight, eh. He's here, Jacko – the boss man. No bleeding talent scout this time.

JACKO: What! Charlie-bleeding-Murray?

TRAVIS: The man himself. Biggest thing since Terry Lawless, and he's come to see me.

JACKO: Brilliant! You seen him yet?

TRAVIS: Seen him? I spoke to him! Shook his hand and everything. Course, old Pascoe done most of the talking. Me, I was just stood there, trying not to fart!

JACKO: Bloody hell. What a night this is gonna be.

TRAVIS: Yeah.

JACKO: Townpark – pride of the South!

BOTH: Sholey Mill eat shit!

TRAVIS: They've had this coming for a long time.

JACKO: Too bleeding long.

TRAVIS: I hate all them bastards.

JACKO: Thing that really sticks in my guts.

TRAVIS: What's that?

JACKO: Thing I hate, is the way they been mouthing off lately. You know what I saw on the way here?

TRAVIS: No. What?

JACKO: TRAVIS IS A QUEER BOY. Signed Sholey Mill. Sprayed all over the walls of the multi-storey.

TRAVIS: Yeah, and who better to know, eh – bunch of bum bandits the lot of them!

JACKO: Cocky bastards.

TRAVIS: Yeah, and they're saying you're so scared of Baker, you ain't even gonna turn up tonight. Be two empty places, ringside, where you and your old man oughta be.

JACKO: Piss off! Only one person gonna be missing tonight, mate. And that's Baker.

TRAVIS: You what?

JACKO: He won't be here.

TRAVIS: Course he will. Bleeding hero since he done you over. King of Sholey.

JACKO: Done *me* over! What a load of shit.

TRAVIS: How d'ya mean?

JACKO: Oh, come on, Travis – that weren't a fight. Ain't a fight when someone jumps you. He was hiding behind a bleeding telephone box with a piece of wood. Got me one in the guts before I'd even seen him, the bastard. And anyway, I was pissed an'all. Elaine was walking me home.

TRAVIS: He reckons he beat you fair and square, face-to-face, like.

JACKO: Be a different story tomorrow.

TRAVIS: You still gonna get him tonight, then?

JACKO: Oh, yeah. I'll find him, don't you worry.

TRAVIS: He'll have a knife, Jacko.

JACKO: So, he'll have a knife.

TRAVIS: Yeah, but he knows you're after him. He's been going round with an armed escort since he done you over. You won't get a chance to get him alone – he'll have at least two of his mates with him.

JACKO: Fine.

TRAVIS: You bleeding nutter – fine.

JACKO: No problem.

TRAVIS: Three?

JACKO: Not when you know they're there – you can see them coming, face-to-face.

TRAVIS: What, with no back-up or nothing? You reckon you could take them?

JACKO: I know it, mate.

TRAVIS: You done it before? Three, I mean.

JACKO: Yeah – once.

TRAVIS: Want me along?

JACKO: Just leave it to me, eh.

TRAVIS: It ain't gonna be that easy.

JACKO: You don't know nothing.

TRAVIS: Oh, yeah. So what d'you know that I don't.

JACKO: Plenty, mate.

TRAVIS: Like what?

JACKO: Like not stopping for some bleeding bell for a start!

TRAVIS: Rules is rules, Jacko.

JACKO: Yeah, I know. All of you prancing around with some prick in a dickie bow making sure no one gets hurt – piss off!

TRAVIS: No one gets hurt! Sangster was dying –

JACKO: Yeah, and Baker's dead, mate. Listen, when he goes down, I'll boot him in the face again and again. What he done to me! Rules is rules! There are no fucking rules – not for me.

TRAVIS: You're beautiful when you're angry.

JACKO: Piss off. Listen, mate, don't you worry about Baker. I mean, I ain't gonna be with you in the ring when you get Sangster, am I?

TRAVIS: Oh, yeah – ref'd love that. See you getting in the ring – oh, that's all right, he's just me mate come to help me out. Sholey Mill'd go mad, all be piling in.

TRAVIS *throws the crate at JACKO who catches it.*

TRAVIS: Here, your old man coming tonight?

JACKO: Course – he wouldn't miss this for the world. Townpark versus Sholey Mill!

JACKO *puts the crate down, centre stage, and sits on it.*

He'll be in that front row, bumming cigars off old Charlie Murray.

TRAVIS: Whole place'll go wild when I win.

JACKO: Yeah, punch-ups in that crowd.

TRAVIS: 'Ere, you make sure old Tom protects Murray. Don't want him getting done in by that load of yobs.

JACKO: He'll be all right with Tom. Sholey boys don't dare go near him.

TRAVIS: Bleeding nutter your dad.

JACKO: Bleeding hero, mate. He could take them all on.

TRAVIS: Whole of bleeding Sholey – piss off.

JACKO: No problem.

TRAVIS: Yeah.

JACKO: How many was it in the Red Lion?

TRAVIS: Fifteen years ago, Jacko.

JACKO: In their own pub.

TRAVIS: Three or four, weren't it?

JACKO: Ten. Ten blokes.

TRAVIS: Ten?

JACKO *gets up from the crate, TRAVIS sits on it. They begin to go into the first of many 'set routines', using the audience to pick out members of the Sholey Mill gang.*

JACKO: Archie Taylor and his lot – all twelve of them.

TRAVIS: 'Ere we go.

JACKO: Tom Foster versus fourteen blokes. On his own too.

TRAVIS: No back-up or nothing –

JACKO: No back-up or nothing. Twenty of you Mill boys –

TRAVIS: And my old man steaming into ya –

JACKO (*standing on the crate behind TRAVIS*): And my old man steaming into ya. One, two, three, you're next –

TRAVIS: Through the window –

JACKO: Through the window. Then you –

TRAVIS: The bar –

JACKO: Over the bar –

TRAVIS: Bodies flying everywhere –

JACKO: Bodies flying everywhere. Eleven, twelve. And my old man, he's getting more and more wild –

TRAVIS: And there's not a mark on him –

JACKO: And there's not a mark on him. Twenty-nine, thirty.

BOTH: Saving Taylor till last!

TRAVIS: Fifteen years ago, Jacko!

JACKO: Yeah, but they're still talking about it. Even tonight, Tom in that crowd, and we'll all be there, giving it –

JACKO *begins to sing, TRAVIS joining in after a few lines:*

We are the Townpark, the pride of the South,
We got all the boot and we got all the mouth.
We look at your birds and their knickers come down –
The Townpark boys are in town!

They begin to repeat the song, JACKO breaking off halfway through, picking on a member of the audience, pointing threateningly.

JACKO: Oi, what you fucking looking at? Come on then, wanker!

TRAVIS (*trying to restrain him*): Oi!

JACKO (*pushing TRAVIS away*): I'll bleeding have you!

They snap out of the 'set routine'.

TRAVIS: Bleeding nutter, your Dad, and you're the same.

JACKO: Yeah, well, family tradition, innit.

TRAVIS: What, kicking people's heads in?

JACKO: Yeah.

TRAVIS: Lovely. Different now though, innit. Taylor's mob never carried blades. Not like Baker and his dagger boys.

JACKO: What's different? – It's all Sholey, innit.

TRAVIS: *Blades*, Jacko. And Baker had you last time.

JACKO: My turn now then, innit. Look, don't you worry about Baker. You just worry about what you gotta do.

TRAVIS: I don't need to worry about Sangster.

JACKO: No? So what went wrong last time?

TRAVIS: I dunno.

JACKO: Come on, Travis – we don't wanna make the same mistakes again. So, what was the problem?

TRAVIS: I dunno. S'pose I just froze, that's all.

JACKO: You can do better than that.

TRAVIS: Nervous like, that talent scout being there. London contract if I won, whole of bleeding Townpark turning up to see me. Big night, weren't it.

JACKO: Even bigger night tonight, mate. You ain't gonna freeze again, are ya?

TRAVIS: Course I ain't. Know what to do this time, don't I?

JACKO: Knew what to do last time.

TRAVIS: I just froze that's all. Like I said –

JACKO: It was easy.

TRAVIS: Course it was easy. I know that now. Found that out in the last twenty seconds.

JACKO: So why didn't you do that before? Come on, you know what works for you – clinch. Always gets you wound up, gets you going. So why leave it till the third round?

TRAVIS: I dunno.

JACKO: First round you didn't, second round you didn't. Why not?

TRAVIS: Couldn't get near the bastard, that's all.

JACKO: Couldn't get near him?

TRAVIS: He was controlling the fight, making me do what he wanted –

JACKO: That's your job!

TRAVIS: I know –

JACKO: Make him do what you want. You should've controlled it.

TRAVIS: Well he was that time, all right?

JACKO: So how? Why? Look, come on Travis!

TRAVIS: I weren't right! I weren't ready that's all. I weren't ready when I got in the ring.

JACKO: You weren't ready? We did everything right, didn't we, same as we always do? I spent hours psyching you up.

TRAVIS: Yeah, yeah, it was great.

JACKO: You looked brilliant when you went out there, really steaming, raring to go.

TRAVIS: Felt brilliant –

JACKO: So?

TRAVIS: It was just seeing him.

JACKO: Sangster?

TRAVIS: Yeah, Sangster.

JACKO: How d'ya mean?

TRAVIS: Seen him earlier that evening, hadn't I? Only, I never knew it was him them. See, I'd never seen Sangster before, just heard a lot about him. Good boxer, really fast with his hands. But I didn't know what he looked like.

JACKO: Pascoe's bum-hole, so?

TRAVIS: So I was in the bog, having a slash, when Pascoe's bum-hole walked in.

JACKO: You what?

TRAVIS: Remember going through the routine before the first fight, and I had to dive out for a slash?

JACKO: Yeah.

TRAVIS (*beginning to act out the scene*): Well, in I go, no-one else around, so it's jocks down, plonker out –

JACKO: That's a bit hard with your gloves on, innit?

TRAVIS: Not half, I was standing there on tiptoe, trying to flip it into the bowl. When in walks this bloke. He comes in, an' closes the door. An' then he starts staring at me. Staring at me like some bird or something –

JACKO: How d'ya mean, like some bird?

TRAVIS: Look, I'll show ya.

TRAVIS *positions* JACKO *as if he is* TRAVIS *in the toilet. They play out the scene,* TRAVIS *as Sangster.*

TRAVIS: Right, now you're me, and you're standing there in the bogs, having a slash.

JACKO *is reluctant.* TRAVIS *positions him again.*

TRAVIS: In the bogs, having a slash.

JACKO: Okay.

TRAVIS: And there's this bloke, staring at ya. And then he starts walking towards ya.

JACKO (*breaking his position*): Oi, leave it out.

TRAVIS: You're still slashing, mind.

JACKO *moves back into position.*

TRAVIS: Walking towards ya, he is, and staring the whole time. Walks right up behind yer, and . . . Wha-hey.

TRAVIS *grabs* JACKO's *buttocks.*

JACKO: Sod off!

TRAVIS: I ain't finished yet.

JACKO (*moving away*): Well I bleeding have.

TRAVIS *goes after* JACKO, *taking up a position next to him, again as if standing in the toilet.*

TRAVIS: Come on, Jacko! So he's standing next to me, smiling, and then he gives me this wink.

JACKO: He what?

TRAVIS: Mmm, Big Boy!

JACKO: He said that?

TRAVIS: Yeah, looking like he fancied me. I thought he was gonna grab me cock or something.

JACKO: I'd have kicked his teeth in. Cut his hand off and shoved it up his bleeding arse!

TRAVIS: I had the fight to think about! But I'd clocked him, hadn't I. Wouldn't forget his face. Thought, afterwards, find him, you and me – smash his bleeding head in.

JACKO: And this bloke was Sangster?

TRAVIS: Yeah, but I didn't know that, did I – not till I got in the ring.

TRAVIS *sets up the ring, simply by moving the crate upstage left, opposite the chair. Through the description of the match, he uses it as his corner stool.*

TRAVIS: Ref called us over, and he was walking towards me – Sangster. And it was him – the bloke in the bogs. Staring at me, he was, and smiling.

JACKO: Jesus!

TRAVIS: Well, you know how I control a fight.

JACKO: Yeah.

TRAVIS: Straight in there, into the clinch. Only this bloke's a bleeding queer boy!

JACKO: So, you didn't want it – right?

TRAVIS: Didn't wanna get anywhere near the bastard. I wanted to get out of there. Wanted to go up to Pascoe and say, I ain't fighting that bloke. You get me someone else. You get me someone who's a boxer – not some poof! All set though, weren't it. And it blew me just like that. I weren't getting into no clinch with him – fucking queer!

JACKO: I thought you was scared of him.

TRAVIS: Two rounds. Two rounds of me running away. And I thought, I'm losing it – Murray, London, everything. I weren't gonna throw London away – not for some bleeding arse bandit, I weren't!

JACKO: So, then what happened?

TRAVIS: Sitting in me corner, end of round two, Pascoe rubbing me down with a towel. What's wrong with you, he goes. I just looked across – saw Sangster there, still smiling. There's nothing wrong with me. Nothing! So I went for it. Final round – the clinch. Way behind on points. Had to be a knockout. Only I left it too late.

JACKO: Got him in the clinch, though.

TRAVIS: Yeah, and he loved it.

JACKO: Did he?

TRAVIS: Course he did. 'S what he wanted all along.

JACKO: So, what happened?

TRAVIS: You saw what happened. Had him trapped in the corner – final round – smashing him –

JACKO: No, no. Not then. In this clinch. How did you *know* he loved it?

TRAVIS: Way he was holding me . . . like some bird . . . You know! Like you've got hold of some bird on the dance floor, and you're pulling her in, nice and close . . . Way she touches ya, pushes herself against ya . . . enjoys feeling ya, feeling what she's doing to ya. Only, this was a bloke, this was Sangster –

JACKO: You mean he had a hard-on!

TRAVIS: Bleeding queer!

JACKO: Did he?

TRAVIS: Yeah, yeah, he did. And that's why he's going down tonight. Round one. No fucking about this time.

JACKO: But this is brilliant! Why didn't ya tell me?

TRAVIS: Brilliant!

JACKO: Yeah.

TRAVIS: You ever been in a clinch with a queer boy?

JACKO: Yeah, but Travis, think about it. Sholey Mill's top fighter a bleeding bum bandit! You wait till the lads hear about this –

TRAVIS: No, Jacko. You ain't gonna tell them nothing.

JACKO: You what? After all they've said about us! Travis is a queer boy.

TRAVIS: No. I ain't having people saying he was just a poof. I get a London contract out of this, turn pro cause I beat the best there is amateur level. I ain't having no one say I was nursed through to the big time beating up powder puffs anyone could smash in. That bloke's gotta be good. I don't want no one to know he's queer. Everyone's gotta know him for a bleeding good fighter, and I beat him!

JACKO: Wish you'd told me before.

TRAVIS: See why I couldn't though, don't ya?

JACKO: Yeah. Little boy, see, Travis.

TRAVIS: Gerroff!

JACKO (*pinching* TRAVIS's *bottom*): Nothing like a little boy to warm your hands on!

TRAVIS: I ain't a little boy – twelve inches at least!

JACKO: Yeah, but you don't use it as a rule.

TRAVIS: Good one, Jacko.

JACKO: It's true, though, that about little boys. That night we was up 'Spiro's'.

TRAVIS: Oh, leave it out.

They begin to play out the scene inside 'Spiro's', a nightclub, and later in the alley, using the audience to pick out particular characters – the 'virgins' and Ralph.

JACKO: There we were, me and you stood by the dance floor, chatting away – sussing out who was the virgins.

TRAVIS: Oh, yeah. She was. And her.

JACKO: Cor – she definitely ain't!

TRAVIS (*approaching her*): Hello darling.

JACKO (*pulling* TRAVIS *back*): And there was that bloke – eyeing you up.

TRAVIS: What bloke?

JACKO: Over there – started turning away.

TRAVIS: Oh, yeah, looking really embarassed.

JACKO: I wanted to sort him out there and then.

TRAVIS: In the disco! Bouncers would've had words to say about that.

JACKO: So, I went up and had words with him.

TRAVIS: What exactly did you say?

JACKO: You don't wanna know.

TRAVIS: Yeah, I do. I thought you told him you was gonna do him in.

JACKO: Not *exactly*.

TRAVIS: Well, what – exactly?

JACKO (*moving off and addressing* Ralph): Well, I went up to him, didn't I, said – Hello, you look like a nice boy. What's your name? Oh, Ralph, he goes. Nice. Well, I tell you what Ralphy, my mate little Rupert over there, says he likes the look of you –

TRAVIS: You sod!

JACKO: Says he'll meet you in the back alley. Ten minutes – okay?

TRAVIS: You bastard, Foster, and you told me you'd got a coupla birds lined up for us!

JACKO: Did you see the speed old Ralph buggered off at. Really excited he was!

TRAVIS: And there's me, stood in the alley, expecting the redhead with the tits.

JACKO: Should've seen your face when old Ralph turned up. It was brilliant!

TRAVIS: You mean you was watching!

JACKO: Course I was. I weren't gonna miss that. Me, I was hid up the fire escape.

JACKO steps onto the crate.

JACKO: Couldn't hear nothing, but I could see it all –

TRAVIS: You shit!

JACKO: You two yakking away, getting really involved. You was at it a good ten minutes.

TRAVIS: I couldn't get away.

JACKO: I'm surprised you could stand it.

TRAVIS: What?

JACKO: Just being that close to him. Why didn't ya do him in?

TRAVIS: I ain't gonna beat up some bloke in a back alley. Gotta protect me knuckles. What if they got cut-up?

JACKO: So, why stick around?

TRAVIS: I was waiting for you, ya bastard. You and the redhead with the tits. Anyway, I never knew that bloke was queer.

JACKO: Never knew he was queer! – Stuck out a mile.

TRAVIS: Blimey. That one of the signs, is it?

JACKO (*getting off crate and walking over to* TRAVIS): Course it is. I mean, some bloke starts walking toward ya with this bleeding great bulge in his trousers – what ya s'posed to think? 'Ello, that's a funny place to keep a budgie.

TRAVIS: I dunno. Anyway I never noticed no bulge.

JACKO: No, you wouldn't. So, what did he say, eh?

TRAVIS: Flashed the ash, didn't he.

JACKO: Ay, ay.

TRAVIS: What's that s'posed to mean?

JACKO: Sure sign, innit.

TRAVIS: Eh?

JACKO: Fag, see. *Fag.* Do you wanna fag?

TRAVIS (*perplexed*): Oh, right.

JACKO: The bulge, the fag, the walk an'all. Look, this is what you should've done. Now, I'm you, right, down the end of this alley, and you're this bloke, Ralph. First thing is – you suss out the walk. Right, now, walk towards me.

TRAVIS walks over to JACKO.

JACKO: Brilliant, Travis! Now, think about it. Poofs don't walk like that. How do poofs walk? Now, go back and nance it up a bit.

JACKO illustrates how TRAVIS should walk. TRAVIS reproduces JACKO's movements awkwardly.

JACKO: That's better. Now, what did he say.

TRAVIS: Hello, my name's Ralph.

JACKO: Travis! Queers don't talk like that. Like this –

JACKO adopts a ridiculously camp voice, which TRAVIS again tries to imitate.

JACKO: Hello, my name's Ralph and I'm a homo. Now you.

TRAVIS: But he never –

JACKO: Come on!

TRAVIS: Hello, my name's Ralph and I'm a homo.

JACKO: Ooh, Travis – Saggitairyarse.

TRAVIS: Very funny.

JACKO: Now, flash us the ash.

TRAVIS: Do you wanna fag?

JACKO: Oh, come on, Travis. Like this – Do-you-want-a-fag?

TRAVIS: Do-you-want-a-fag?

JACKO: That's much better. Then, you shoulda gone –

JACKO *grabs* TRAVIS *violently.*

JACKO: You want your teeth shoved up your arse, you bent bastard.

TRAVIS: Piss off!

JACKO: But you didn't, did ya. What *did* you say?

TRAVIS: Told him I couldn't, cos of me training.

JACKO: Oh, no. You pillock! You never told him you was a boxer!

TRAVIS: Yeah, really interested, he was.

JACKO: Yeah, don't tell me. He was a bodybuilder, right?

TRAVIS: Yeah! How did you know?

JACKO: Oh, come on, Travis – they *all* are! What did he do next, offer to show you his collection of muscle mags?

TRAVIS: Eh?

JACKO: Well, think about it, will ya. *Boxer* – well, what's that bring to mind? Rippling muscles, sweaty bodies, naked blokes in the showers. It drives them wild!

TRAVIS: Oh.

JACKO: Well, come on, Ralph – drives you wild.

TRAVIS (*ineffectually*): Oooh!

JACKO: Brilliant, Trav. Look, more like this. Rippling muscles, sweaty bodies –

JACKO *puts his arms around* TRAVIS *suggestively.*

JACKO: You make a lovely queer, Travis.

TRAVIS: You ain't so bad yourself.

JACKO: But have you got the bulge?

JACKO *gropes* TRAVIS.

TRAVIS: Look, piss off! You're bloody stupid, you are. Signs, fags – he never touched me. He laid one finger on me, I'd have battered him!

JACKO: But you didn't, did ya. Just left it to me to do him in.

TRAVIS: Bleeding head-case, you are.

JACKO: You didn't even put the boot-in when he was down.

TRAVIS: Weren't nothing left to put the boot-in on. I was about to go, no trouble, just walk away. And then you come steaming in from nowhere.

JACKO: You can't do that, Travis. Once you've clocked a queer, you can't just walk away. You gotta batter the bastard! Kick his bleeding head in!

TRAVIS: He ended up in hospital.

JACKO: Yeah? Well that's just where he oughta be – sick, see. 'S where all queers oughta be.

TRAVIS: Bastard – setting me up like that.

JACKO: 'S only a laugh.

TRAVIS: Laugh! Telling a queer I fancied him?

JACKO: I done you a favour, mate. Giving you a queer to bash – you oughta thank me.

TRAVIS: I'd rather have had the redhead with the tits.

JACKO: Yeah, well, turns out that was a bit of a mistake. See, she fancied me really.

TRAVIS: Yeah, don't every bird.

JACKO: You've noticed, then.

TRAVIS: Yeah. Surprised they didn't put you down for that.

JACKO: He wanted to – Fletcher.

TRAVIS: Bastard.

JACKO: Had me down that nick two days asking questions.

TRAVIS: Lucky bastard!

JACKO: Me? I never done nothing.

TRAVIS: And he believed ya.

JACKO: Don't you?

TRAVIS: Oh, yeah.

JACKO: See – and *you* was there.

TRAVIS: Very persuasive, Jacko.

JACKO: Bloody queers. Ain't natural.

TRAVIS: Course it ain't. If it was natural, God would've made Adam and Bruce.

JACKO: Or Rupert and Ralph.

TRAVIS: Can't say nothing about me, mate – birds I've had.

JACKO: Oh, yeah. How many?

TRAVIS: Can't count past sixty.

JACKO: Sixty!

TRAVIS: And that's just today.

JACKO: You like chicken, do ya?

TRAVIS: Wait till London, mate. Be sixty birds in the first week!

JACKO: Gotta get there first, pal.

TRAVIS: Sangster? Anyone trying to stop me getting sixty birds is in for a right pasting. He'll be stretchered home after the fight!

JACKO: And we'll be off to –

BOTH: London!

TRAVIS: Can't wait! What a time. What a time we're gonna have – all them birds!

JACKO: Yeah. You know, I wouldn't be at all surprised if some of them London birds are almost as experienced as me. I'm probably being advertised up there, right now – Main attraction! Coming to London! Sex maniac – Jacko Foster!

TRAVIS: Yeah, and one about me an'all – Coming to London –

JACKO: Big Pillock, Rupert Travis. Two inches – any offers?

TRAVIS: Piss off! They'll all be queuing up for me.

JACKO: Yeah. First night up there, we'll do it all – everything.

They begin to act out their fantasies of London life.

TRAVIS: Dump the bags. Steam into the nearest pub.

JACKO: Wait for me! Twenty pints of London Pride.

TRAVIS: Seventeen –

BOTH: Eighteen, nineteen, twenty!

TRAVIS: And then where?

JACKO: On to one of those big London nightclubs. 'Open eight till late – strictly over twenty-ones!'

TRAVIS: What's that – inches?

JACKO: Jesus. You'll have no chance.

TRAVIS: Sod off!

JACKO (*sticking his arm between TRAVIS's legs*): You'll have to show them mine!

TRAVIS: All right girls?

JACKO (*withdrawing his arm*): No, mate, once you're in you're on your own. Oh, look, Trav – all them birds!

TRAVIS: Yeah. Leather minis, fishnet stockings – tits bobbing up and down on the dance floor!

TRAVIS dancing opposite JACKO who has his fists up his jumper.

TRAVIS: Hello darling. Trav.

JACKO: Lorraine.

TRAVIS: Fancy a dance?

JACKO (*jumping into his arms*): No, I wanna screw!

BOTH: Yeah!

TRAVIS (*throwing him off*): Real class birds.

JACKO: Pick up a coupla birds each, then back to our place.

TRAVIS: What – you, me, and four birds?

JACKO: What's wrong with that? You do your own and then swap over.

TRAVIS: That's four. Four times!

JACKO: So?

TRAVIS: In one night?

JACKO: Well?

TRAVIS: Well, I was just thinking. Four. Four, first night – well, that ain't enough, is it.

JACKO: That ain't enough! More times than you've ever done it in your life.

TRAVIS: Piss off is it!

JACKO: Birds'll be queuing up! One comes anywhere near you, you'll run a mile.

TRAVIS: Me?

JACKO: What about that stag night up the Docker's club – Delicious Dolores and her bowl of fruit?

TRAVIS: I weren't hungry, was I.

JACKO: Sex on a plate and you bottled it!

TRAVIS: Bleeding hundreds of blokes watching. I weren't gonna do it in front of all them blokes!

JACKO: I did.

TRAVIS: You'd do it anywhere.

JACKO: I have too – Debenham's bogs, bus shelters. 'Ere, you ever done it in a bath?

TRAVIS: You ain't gonna do it in the bath when we get our flat.

JACKO: Why not?

TRAVIS: Eugh! I wanna wash in water.

JACKO: Have to get two baths then.

TRAVIS: Two baths! What sort of place you got in mind?

JACKO: Nothing very much. I thought – a nice little pad somewhere. Coupla bedrooms, bathroom *each*, nice big lounge. Colour T.V., video, toaster – the lot!

TRAVIS: I've heard there's this place called the Ritz going, Jacko.

JACKO: Perfect, old boy. Cocktails on the balcony.

TRAVIS: Gobbing at the punters below.

JACKO: Yeah! What d'ya reckon, tenner a week?

TRAVIS: More like a thousand.

JACKO: That's all right – social'll pay. Social'll pay for everything. Me – I'm gonna have a chauffeured limo to sign on.

TRAVIS: All right for some.

JACKO: You can come with me.

TRAVIS: Leave it out! I won't be able to bum around with you all day. Be a pro boxer then. Gotta discipline myself.

JACKO: Get pissed in Soho on me own then.

TRAVIS: Well, I might –

JACKO: Oh, no, Travis. You're a pro boxer now, ain't ya? Gotta discipline yourself. That's no birds, no booze, no late nights. Good times is over for you, Trav, boy. They'll work your balls off!

TRAVIS: That's what I want.

JACKO: What, to be in bed by eight?

TRAVIS: Tucked-up with some beautiful blonde – not half!

JACKO: Bollocks. You'll be so knackered you won't be able to raise a smile, let alone anything else!

TRAVIS: I'll be so fit, I'll be able to go on all night.

JACKO: All night!

TRAVIS: All night, mate. They'll soon get tired of four minute Foster!

JACKO: You'll see. After a week up there, you'll be so knackered, you'll be pleading to come back here.

TRAVIS: No way. I've been to the place, Jacko. I loved it. It's bleeding huge. You wanna see the ring they got there. And this big wall covered with mirrors! And the smell of the place – gets right inside ya. I was just walking around, watching Max Lewis on the bags, Carl Chase an' all – real pros. Pro fighters working out with pro trainers – bang, bang, bang! One, two, three. Brilliant! You'll see what I mean when we get there. When you're stood there watching me. Once you got the atmosphere of the place, you won't be able to keep away.

JACKO: Me? I ain't going anywhere near the bleeding place.

TRAVIS: Eh?

JACKO: Ain't exactly my idea of a good time – spending yer whole life in a boxing ring.

TRAVIS (*moving across stage to exit, left*): Why're you coming up then?

JACKO: Dunno. Bit of a change I s'pose. Oi! Where you off to?

TRAVIS (*going off*): See what's happening.

JACKO (*urgent*): Well don't leave the door! Travis – the door!

JACKO *left alone on stage, agitated.*

JACKO: Fuck it!

TRAVIS (*running in*): Just seen Pascoe – time to move!

JACKO: You never told him I was in here?

TRAVIS: Course not.

TRAVIS *starts getting boxing gear out of his bag.*

TRAVIS: Oughta see it, Jacko. Filling up out there, 's like the bleeding Albert Hall.

JACKO: Not long now, then.

TRAVIS: Don't you ever dream about it, though – what you can do in London?

JACKO: The birds, you mean?

TRAVIS: No, not just the birds. Get your bleeding mind off your cock, Foster. I mean, what d'ya *think* about? Dreams I've had!

JACKO: Yeah, and the sheets in the morning. Eugh!

TRAVIS: No. What about a job?

JACKO: Yeah, sure.

TRAVIS: Yeah. Just something, eh.

JACKO: Yeah. Just so long as I got a few quid in me back pocket. I mean, I don't wanna be a bleeding brain surgeon, do I!

Having got all his boxing gear ready, TRAVIS *now begins to strip off.*

JACKO: What you gonna do about Lynsey when we go to London, Travis?

TRAVIS: Eh?

JACKO: All this talk about birds and that – what about Lyns?

TRAVIS: Don't remind me. She wanted to come tonight.

JACKO: She here?

TRAVIS: No, she ain't. Couldn't have that, could I – she'd be hanging around afterwards.

JACKO: Nice one, Trav.

TRAVIS: When I told her she couldn't come here, she wanted to know if I was going round her place afterwards.

JACKO: And are ya?

TRAVIS: Like hell, am I! Told her I'd be going out on the piss with the lads. She goes – you'll behave yourself, won't you. You won't get off with some other bird? Me? Course not, I go.

JACKO: You what?

TRAVIS: Two birds, though. That's another story.

JACKO: Yeah!

TRAVIS: Can't wait, mate.

JACKO: Big celebration, eh.

TRAVIS: Bleeding right!

JACKO: You know last time, when you said you hadn't – you know, with Lynsey yet – and I had to go out and buy those johnnies for ya. Did ya?

TRAVIS: I bleeding wasted them, didn't I – whole packet of three!

JACKO: How d'you manage that?

TRAVIS: Well, I'd never used one before, had I?

JACKO: You what?

TRAVIS: I'd never . . . aw, you knew that!

JACKO: I knew you'd never bought any.

TRAVIS: Never used one neither. Gill was always on the pill.

JACKO: Lucky boy.

TRAVIS: Well, I had to see what one looked like, didn't I. You know, try it on, see how it worked.

JACKO: You mean you'd never done that?

TRAVIS: No.

JACKO: Blimey.

TRAVIS: So, that wasted one of them.

JACKO: Good was it?

TRAVIS (*now naked, playing out the scene*): Didn't get a chance. Bleeding standing there, bollock naked, with this Durex on me cock, when me Mum walked in!

JACKO: You're kidding!

TRAVIS: No.

JACKO: What did ya say?

TRAVIS (*running on the spot*): Told her I was going out for a run.

JACKO: What – with one of them on?

TRAVIS: Well, it was raining out.

JACKO: Did she see it?

TRAVIS: Bleeding must've done. I was standing there with this in one hand and a mag in the other I'd fished-out from under me Dad's bed –

JACKO: Jesus!

TRAVIS: The best bit was her bombing off downstairs and getting straight on the phone to the old man.

JACKO: She never told him.

TRAVIS: No, she didn't give a toss about me. It was him that got the bollocking – she never knew he read those mags.

JACKO: Yeah – you're pulling my bleeding leg!

TRAVIS: No, straight up. I did try one on, and she did walk in.

JACKO: What a waste! So that was the first one, what about the rest?

TRAVIS (*pulling on his jock strap*): Bust one of them.

JACKO: How d'ya manage that?

TRAVIS: Old Percy here – too big.

JACKO: Bollocks!

TRAVIS: I stuck them in an'all. Didn't half hurt!

JACKO: You prat.

TRAVIS: No. I was showing Lyns.

JACKO: Showing Lyns what?

TRAVIS: She'd never seen one before. Thought they was really funny. So I was telling her all the things you could do with them.

JACKO: Like what?

TRAVIS: Blowing them up like balloons! We was just mucking about, stretching one – and it snapped!

JACKO: Bloody hell.

TRAVIS: 'Ere, had you fixed them or something?

JACKO: Had I hell! They were sealed, weren't they.

TRAVIS: That wouldn't stop you.

JACKO: Thanks, mate.

TRAVIS: So, I only had one left.

JACKO: And what d'you do with that – fill it up with water and chuck it at your old man?

TRAVIS: No. We used that one.

JACKO: So, ya did?

TRAVIS: Well, not exactly.

JACKO: Well what? *Exactly*.

TRAVIS: Well, she rolled it on for me, you know, like it says on the packet – 'to improve the quality of your lovemaking.' Bleeding lovely, it was.

JACKO: So, what happened?

TRAVIS: I blew it, didn't I. There I was – on the job. No complaints from her, bleeding loving it, she was. When, all of a sudden, it felt different.

JACKO: Eh?

TRAVIS: You know – different. Like when you lose ya trunks in the swimming pool.

JACKO: Oh, no – it didn't!

TRAVIS: It did, it bleeding did! I pulled out – oh, no! What's up, she goes. It's gone!

JACKO: You bleeding prat!

TRAVIS: Well, where is it? She's going – Where is it? I just pissed meself. She went wild – kicked me out!

JACKO: I don't believe a word of this!

TRAVIS: It's true!

JACKO: So, you still haven't had her yet?

TRAVIS: I stuck it in.

JACKO: Stuck it in! That ain't nothing, mate.

TRAVIS: Left something up there, didn't I.

JACKO: Yeah, lovely. Nine months time and she'll give birth to a bleeding rubber plant!

TRAVIS *continues getting changed into vest, shorts, boots throughout the next section.*

JACKO: Bleeding hell, Travis – that's two months, two months you been going out with her and you *still* ain't done it yet!

TRAVIS: Bleeding laugh, though, Jacko.

JACKO: So, you still only got two notches on your nob.

TRAVIS: Number of birds you're supposed to have had – you wouldn't have a cock left with the notches on it!

JACKO: So, what are you gonna do when we go to London?

TRAVIS: 'S gonna be tricky, innit.

JACKO: Yeah.

TRAVIS: Got one thing in me favour, though.

JACKO: What's that?

TRAVIS: She loves me.

JACKO: She loves ya!

TRAVIS: That's what she reckons.

JACKO: *So* – What you gonna do about it?

TRAVIS: Well, the way I see it – just invite her up for a coupla weekends.

JACKO: I see.

TRAVIS: Well, she wants to stay up there.

JACKO: What, *live* there?

TRAVIS: So she says.

JACKO: In *our* flat?

TRAVIS: Yeah.

JACKO: Well, you can count me out for a start!

TRAVIS: Don't worry about it. It's all under control. Like I said, just a coupla weekends.

JACKO: You're pretty serious about her, ain't ya?

TRAVIS: Course I ain't.

JACKO: 'I love you, Travis.'

TRAVIS: Sod off!

JACKO (*grabbing* TRAVIS): Here, is it love? Blimey – you're burning-up! Open your mouth – say 'ah!'

TRAVIS: Piss off, Jacko! Besides, that's your department – you and Elaine.

JACKO: Yeah, well that's all over now, innit.

TRAVIS: Yeah, but when it was on, eh – way you two walked into the pub together. Violins going, staring in to each other's eyes! Me and the lads used to puke-up!

JACKO: You was just jealous, mate. Wanted it for yourselves.

TRAVIS: Yeah? Well, she's free now – and who's made a grab for her? No one.

JACKO: She wouldn't bleeding have you, mate – that's why! Not after me.

TRAVIS: I wouldn't touch anything after you'd had it, Foster!

JACKO: No? Well, that don't give you much of a choice then, does it –

BOTH: Birds I've had.

TRAVIS: My arse!

JACKO: So, you ain't gonna drop it when we go to London?

TRAVIS: I don't reckon, Jacko – I do like her.

JACKO: Must be something pretty serious. I mean – two months and you're still hanging-out for it!

TRAVIS: Ain't just about that, though, is it.

JACKO: Ain't it?

TRAVIS: No.

JACKO: Right – you ready?

TRAVIS: No. I'm going home.

JACKO: Time to move. Let's go!

JACKO *throws* TRAVIS *a skipping rope and they begin to go through their warm-up routine,* JACKO *adopting the role of trainer.*

JACKO: All right – thinking about the fight, beginning to get that adrenalin going, legs moving. Feeling that strength, that power beginning to go through.

TRAVIS *begins to skip, on* JACKO's *command, 'ten',* TRAVIS *skips at double speed for ten seconds, on the command, 'normal', returning to his original pace.*

JACKO: Right – time to get those legs moving. Come on now. Ten! Come on, let's move those legs, higher, faster, more! Right – normal. Okay, Travis – Sangster. There's just him between you and London, mate. You're a pro boxer after tonight and what's he? – Just some Sholey Mill fairy! Ten! Come on, move those bleeding legs you lazy bastard. Higher, faster, move it, more! Right – normal. He's gonna reckon you're scared after the last fight. But you show him – bleeding queer! One thought, one word – kill! Kill that bastard. Take him by surprise – straight in there – into the clinch!

TRAVIS: Clinch him!

TRAVIS *throws the skipping rope down and moves to the chair, where he begins to bind his hands with bandages.*

TRAVIS: I can beat anyone after a clinch. I'll smash anyone.

JACKO: You *can*? Oh, you have, mate, you *have*. Hamilton, Royce, Chivers, Greene – we've beat them all. Even bleeding Skids – you look what you done to him.

TRAVIS: Said he was the best, best in the club. That's what he reckoned – old Pascoe an' all.

JACKO: But you beat him. You smashed him. You showed them who's best.

TRAVIS: Trapping him in the corner – smashing into him!

JACKO: And you was only sparring!

TRAVIS: Sparring! What's that? Practice for the real thing! – everything's the real thing. Gotta win all the time!

JACKO: All the time. Every time. Unbeatable. Winner!

TRAVIS: The best. I'm the best.

JACKO: *We're* the best – J/T magic!

TRAVIS: The team!

JACKO *kneeling in front of* TRAVIS *putting his boxing gloves on and a ribbon round his waist.*

JACKO: Trapping Skids on the ropes –

TRAVIS: Him grabbing me –

JACKO: Going into the clinch!

TRAVIS: And all of a sudden, feeling it burning through me. That power – shooting through!

JACKO: Like someone's stuck a bleeding battery up your arse!

TRAVIS: Then smashing him! Killing him! Into his guts. Into his face!

JACKO: And we all thought Skids was your mate.

TRAVIS: Mates don't come into it. Skids, Sangster – 's all the same. Could've been anyone. Could've been you, Foster.

JACKO: Oi! Rules of the game.

TRAVIS: There's only one rule – gotta win all the time!

JACKO: But he was your mate.

TRAVIS: Fuck it!

JACKO: You don't touch your mates, Travis.

TRAVIS: Don't matter, don't mean a thing. I got no mates in the ring.

JACKO: You ain't got many outside it! Just one clinch with you and old Skids don't dare come near ya!

TRAVIS: Good.

JACKO: Good. The clinch, Travis. What happens in the clinch?

TRAVIS: Feel brilliant. Feel alive!

JACKO: The adrenalin. That power.

TRAVIS: Power shooting through ya – tearing through! Through your arms, your legs – your whole body alive!

JACKO: In the ring, with Skids – the clinch!

TRAVIS: You can feel him with all of you. Your arms locked, his body against mine – smelling his sweat, his breath. Feeling his power, strength – and he ain't as strong as me!

JACKO: Rocky's power!

TRAVIS: Rocky!

JACKO: Rocky versus Jersey Joe Walcott.

JACKO *turns to the chair, puts on the sparring pads.*

TRAVIS: That poster I got – Rocky versus Jersey Joe. One punch – bang! And that's it. That look in Jersey Joe's eyes – dead. Nothing left. Nothing. And old Rocky, his bleeding eyes, they're burning. Power in his body just flooding out. Hitting Skids and watching all the life draining out of him. He was Jersey Joe then and I was Rocky –

JACKO (*holding up the left hand pad*): And I'm Napoleon bleeding Bonaparte.

TRAVIS (*hitting the pad*): Sod off! I was alive and he was dead, and that's the best feeling in the world.

JACKO: You bleeding nutter!

TRAVIS: Yeah, and I love it.

JACKO holds up both pads, TRAVIS jabbing at both as he speaks.

TRAVIS: All that counts is winning and feeling like that!

JACKO: All right – let's go.

They go through a routine with the pads, practising first jabs, then hooks, then upper-cuts, JACKO holding the pads up and shouting instructions, wheeling round the stage during the jabs, standing still for the hooks and upper-cuts.

JACKO: One. One. Come on, Travis, it's Sangster. One, two, Harder! One, two, three. And again – one, two, three. Right – hook. Again, again again. Upper, upper, upper, upper. Come on! One. One. That's better. And again – one, two. Good. One, two, three.

TRAVIS: Sangster!

JACKO throws off the pads and goes to TRAVIS. They kneel, centre stage, staring into the audience, as if in their corner of the ring looking across at Sangster.

JACKO: Okay, Travis. You're looking good, boy – looking sharp. In that ring, you and Sangster, just the two of you. You're gonna have him tonight, gonna smash him, finish him!
   All of us lot with ya – whole of bleeding Townpark, cheering you on, boy. Forward, forward, you keep going

forward – straight in there and keep the pressure on him! We're gonna show them Mill boys – bunch of fairies! Gonna show Murray something special. Show him who's the best, the winner. *Always.* Even last time, Travis – you won. We all saw that, we all *knew* that. So, you have him tonight. You smash him, finish him, kill him!

TRAVIS: Sangster!

JACKO: Nothing can stop you. No one can beat you. Round one – the clinch. The clinch – round one. Clinch him. Smash him!
   One thought, one word – kill! Kill the queer bastard! Feel your power, your strength. Rocky's strength shooting through you, Travis. Rocky, Travis – you're the same as Rocky –

TRAVIS: Rocky, Rocky.

JACKO: Can Sangster beat Rocky, Travis? Can he? Can Sangster beat Rocky?

TRAVIS (*standing up*): No!

JACKO (*standing up, moving behind TRAVIS*): Then smash Sangster tonight. Kill him!

TRAVIS: Kill!

JACKO: Had him last time, ain't gonna let him get away this time – lucky queer!

TRAVIS: Queer bastard!

JACKO: Let's finish him, Travis.

TRAVIS: Finish it.

JACKO: In that ring – ripping him apart. One thought. One word.

TRAVIS: Kill!

JACKO: One name. One fighter

TRAVIS: Rocky!

JACKO: Who's dead?

TRAVIS: Sangster.

JACKO: Sangster.

TRAVIS: Bastard!

JACKO: Sangster.

TRAVIS: Smash him!

JACKO: Sangster.

TRAVIS: Kill him!

JACKO: He's yours Travis!

TRAVIS: KILL HIM!

JACKO: Murray out there.

TRAVIS: Watch me, Murray. Watch me.

JACKO: Gonna make him sit up and watch you, boy.

TRAVIS: Gonna make them all sit up and watch me.

JACKO: Every-bleeding-one! Let's go. Let's show them all – Kill, kill, kill –

BOTH: Kill, kill, kill, kill, kill, kill, kill –

TRAVIS: ROCKY!

Lights down.

ACT TWO

Lights up on JACKO, *alone on stage. After the match. The crate has been returned to its original position, the skipping rope and sparring pads have been put with the general paraphernalia around the bench. A clean set of casual clothes for* TRAVIS *are on the chair.*

TRAVIS (*off*): Jacko!

JACKO: Here mate! I'm in here.

TRAVIS *enters, euphoric. He is wet, having come from the shower, and is dressed only in a towelling robe. He is carrying a towel.*

TRAVIS: I won!

JACKO: I know, mate. I know.

TRAVIS: I won, Jacko. I bleeding won! Winner!

JACKO: Unbeatable!

TRAVIS: Unstoppable. No one can beat me. Not now. Not ever! I won, Jacko. I won. We're going to London!

JACKO: We're going to London.

TRAVIS: You and me. Let's pack our bags – now, tonight. London!

JACKO: Great!

TRAVIS: Oh, and the way I won, Jacko. The way I won. Ain't no one ever gonna forget that. Not for a long time. Sangster – their top bleeding fighter! He's shit.

BOTH: Sholey Mill shit!

TRAVIS: You ain't gonna forget it, are ya Jacko? You ain't never gonna forget that one, are ya?

JACKO: No, mate. I'm never gonna forget it.

TRAVIS: And none of them will, neither. None of them. *Travis* – you fucking remember me! Every single-bleeding-one of ya!

JACKO: Oh, they'll remember you all right.

TRAVIS: Too right they will. I gotta say it, Jacko – I was fucking magic tonight!

JACKO: Yeah. Course you were, mate.

TRAVIS: Brilliant! I done something good out there.

JACKO: Yeah. You won!

TRAVIS: But more than that. More than just winning –

JACKO: You smashed him. You killed him!

TRAVIS: No – way I felt. Way I won. Beating everything, smashing it down – coming out a winner. I can beat anything now. Nothing can stop me. Well, what did you think?

JACKO: It was a bloody good match.

TRAVIS: More than that, Jacko.

JACKO: Yeah, it was brilliant!

TRAVIS: The bleeding best, don't ya reckon. Best match I've had. Best match I've ever fought.

JACKO: Yeah. I reckon it probably was.

TRAVIS: Probably!

JACKO: Well –

TRAVIS: Well, what?

JACKO: Well – the way you feel about it, I'd say it was the best match you'd had.

TRAVIS: It was! Come on, Jacko!

JACKO: Oh, fuck it. I didn't see it.

TRAVIS: You what?

JACKO: I didn't see it. I couldn't see it.

TRAVIS: Couldn't?

JACKO: No, see. I stuck me head round the door, but there was this bleeding great crowd in front of me. I couldn't see a bloody thing.

TRAVIS: So what! So-bloody-what! Big crowd in front of ya – well, push through them, push through to the front!

JACKO: They was all packed tight together –

TRAVIS: Well, push through them anyway! Crowd! Crowd in front of *you*!

JACKO: Look, I know what happened, know everything that went on. Sort of had this running commentary from the bloke in front –

TRAVIS: But you didn't see it! You didn't see me beat him. You didn't see how I beat him!

JACKO: Well, is that *important*?

TRAVIS: Yes it is *important*, how I fucking beat him!

JACKO: I'm sorry. Glad you won, though, eh.

TRAVIS: Yeah, me too.

JACKO: I am! Look – I couldn't go out there. I couldn't be seen, right.

TRAVIS: Why not?

JACKO: I just couldn't, that's all.

TRAVIS: What, Jacko?

JACKO: I just didn't want anyone to see me tonight.

TRAVIS: You ain't that ugly.

JACKO: That's not what I mean.

TRAVIS: You done something?

JACKO: No, I ain't done nothing.

TRAVIS: You have, ain't ya.

JACKO: Look, just drop it, eh.

TRAVIS: You ain't been beating up queers again, have ya?

JACKO: No! Look, Travis, I'm sorry I didn't see ya match. I'd have given anything to've been out there – but I couldn't. Right?

TRAVIS: So, why you holding out on me – I'm your mate, ain't I?

JACKO: Yeah, course you're me mate. You're me best bleeding mate.

TRAVIS: I'm your *only* bleeding mate. Who else'd hang out with a bastard like you?

JACKO: Yeah. I just didn't wanna be seen, right.

TRAVIS: But why?

JACKO: It's not important. Look, I'm sorry I missed your match, but –

TRAVIS: Yeah, all right. You said.

JACKO: Well, tell us what happened, then.

TRAVIS: Sod it, Jacko, ya bastard! I wanted you to see that one.

JACKO: I *wanted* to see it.

TRAVIS: More than anything – that one was important.

JACKO: There'll be other matches.

TRAVIS: Not like that one –

JACKO: Oh, come on Travis –

TRAVIS: All right, all right.

JACKO: When you're champion of the bleeding world, you'll have forgotten all about this fight. Won't matter a toss I weren't there.

TRAVIS: No.

JACKO: Anyway, I was with you before – getting you ready, psyching you up. Unbeatable!

TRAVIS: The team!

JACKO: J/T magic, eh.

TRAVIS: Yeah.

JACKO: So – how many rounds?

TRAVIS: Not even one.

JACKO: I thought you was a bit quick. What was it – a knockout?

TRAVIS: No.

JACKO: Ref stopped it?

TRAVIS: He did, an'all.

JACKO: He thought Sangster was gonna get killed, right?

TRAVIS: Yeah. Old Pascoe thought I was gonna get disqualified.

JACKO: Disqualified!

TRAVIS: That's what he said afterwards. You should've seen him, though, Jacko. Old Pascoe, even Pascoe, really pleased for me he was. Grinning all over, tears in his eyes –

JACKO: He was probably sitting on a carrot.

TRAVIS: Sod off, Foster! He was a good bloke. Should've seen him. Really pleased.

JACKO: You made his day, eh.

TRAVIS: You should've heard that crowd, an'all. That roar at the end – like they was all smelling blood or something. All going for the kill with you.

JACKO: Brilliant!

TRAVIS: He thought I'd be scared cause of losing last time – hang back, bide me time. But I just steamed in. Grabbed him –

JACKO: Straight in there, then – like *I* told you.

TRAVIS: Yeah. The *clinch*.

JACKO: No hanging about.

TRAVIS: Trapping him on the ropes – hands like that – back against the post. It was like hitting a bleeding punch-bag. Punch, punch, punch – queer bastard!
    But the best thing, Jacko, the best thing was old Sangster looking at me, and his eyes dying – looking at me. And then hitting him. Just one more time. Hard as rock.

JACKO: Brilliant. 'Ere, did he get turned-on like last time?

TRAVIS: Who cares, Jacko? I won, that's the thing.

JACKO: Yeah. Glad you won.

TRAVIS: London, eh, Jacko.

JACKO: *London.*

TRAVIS: The flat! The team!

JACKO: The birds!

TRAVIS: Charlie Murray!

JACKO: Charlie Murray?

TRAVIS: Oh, and them birds. Them gorgeous London birds!

TRAVIS *jumps onto* JACKO, *singing: 'Here we go, here we go, here we go!' etc . . .* JACKO *joining in, then suddenly throwing* TRAVIS *off.*

JACKO: Piss off!

TRAVIS: What a night! What a night we're gonna have. Spoilt for bleeding choice, ain't we. I reckon Baker oughta be first.

JACKO: Yeah. Maybe.

TRAVIS: Then getting pissed. Getting bleeding rat-arsed and then picking up a bird –

JACKO: Oi! You're a pro now – you gotta discipline yourself.

TRAVIS: Not till I've signed the

contract. Murray's bringing it round me house tomorrow so me old man can look at it.

JACKO: Your old man – didn't know he could read!

TRAVIS: He'd sign anything that got me out of the house

JACKO: Lovely.

TRAVIS *now by the chair beginning to change into his casual clothes.*

TRAVIS: So, we got tonight to do it all – everything, first night in London job. So, where we going first?

JACKO: Dunno. It's up to you. Where d'you wanna go?

TRAVIS: Up to me? I thought you'd be working it out. Bleeding hell, Jacko, – you've had hours!

JACKO: Hadn't really thought about it.

TRAVIS: You've had the whole bleeding evening!

JACKO: Oh, yeah!

TRAVIS: Yeah. That's right. What you been doing in here – picking your arse or something, while I've been out there earning a living?

JACKO: Look, I didn't know you'd wanna make a move straightaway. You're the one normally likes to sit around for hours and soak-up the bleeding atmosphere!

TRAVIS: Soak-up the bleeding atmosphere! Tonight?

JACKO: Even more reason, innit? This is the last fight you're gonna have here – do you realize that? Could be the last time you'll be in this room. Don't that mean nothing?

TRAVIS: Gonna be in a bleeding gym for the rest of me life.

JACKO: Yeah, but not *this* one.

TRAVIS: No, I s'pose not. But I wanna be *in* something else tonight.

JACKO: Yeah. Well we can do that later.

TRAVIS: Later!

JACKO: Yeah – bomb up the club. Pick up a coupla tarts.

TRAVIS: What about before that? What about now? Get the beers in, round-up the lads.

JACKO: Yeah, we could do.

TRAVIS: What! Ain't you really sorted it all out?

JACKO: Jesus Christ, Travis – what d'your last bleeding slave die of, eh? I ain't your sodding manager – old Murray is. You want a big celebration laid on, you get *him* to do it.

TRAVIS: He's been drawing-up my contract, watching me fight. I've been smashing Sangster. *You* ain't had bugger-all to do, Foster.

JACKO: All right, then, Travis – well, where d'you wanna go?

TRAVIS: I dunno. Hadn't thought.

JACKO: Yeah, well, hang around a bit, maybe you'll make up your mind.

TRAVIS: Hang around a bit! We gotta be out, mate – big night!

JACKO: I know it's a big night.

TRAVIS: The biggest! I was thinking about it as Sangster was going down. Thought about going up the club, seeing if that bird's there, you know – the really gorgeous one with the red hair and the tits.

JACKO: I thought you might fancy something quite quiet tonight. You know, like just you and Lyns.

TRAVIS: Something quiet? Anyway, I told ya – not Lyns tonight. Used up all them johnnies, didn't I.

JACKO: I've got a few. You can borrow them if you like.

TRAVIS: Want them back afterwards, do ya?

JACKO: You could use my place. Take her round there. I'll bomb off and see Elaine.

TRAVIS: You gotta be kidding!

JACKO: Yeah. Just winding you up.

TRAVIS: Winding-me-up! You was serious, weren't ya? What – *Elaine* and *Lyns*?

JACKO: Well, why not?

TRAVIS: I thought you'd finished with her for good.

JACKO: Yeah, well, I have sort of.

TRAVIS: 'Ere, what's up? What's got into you tonight? No cans, no nothing and now all this Elaine shit. You all right?

JACKO: Fine. Look, I just didn't want to push you into anything, that's all. Didn't know what you'd want.

TRAVIS: Booze and birds, mate. Booze and birds! That's what I want. That's what we been saying all along. Look – you got something on your mind?

JACKO: No. Just thinking, that's all.

TRAVIS: About Baker?

JACKO: No. About birds actually.

TRAVIS: What about Baker? When you gonna fit him in?

JACKO: I dunno. Sometime.

TRAVIS: I thought you'd have made plans.

JACKO: No, I haven't made any bleeding plans!

TRAVIS: Thought tonight was the night.

JACKO: It is.

TRAVIS: Here, you're not scared are ya? Not bottling it?

JACKO: I told ya – Baker's dead, Travis.

TRAVIS: Yeah, but when, Jacko?

JACKO: From the moment he laid a bleeding finger on me. Now drop it Travis!

TRAVIS (*now changed and ready to go*): All right. All right. I just wanna get out there, Jacko. Wanna go. All them birds just waiting for us – Let's go!

JACKO: When I'm ready.

TRAVIS: But –

JACKO: I said, when I'm ready.

TRAVIS: And when's that gonna be? I'm dying for a bird!

JACKO: Oh, yeah. And who's that gonna be?

TRAVIS: Anyone who offers.

JACKO: Anyone who offers! What, like that stripper at the stag night?

TRAVIS: Yeah. Maybe.

JACKO: Like last time – oh, don't make me laugh!

TRAVIS: Well, maybe someone else then –

JACKO: If you bottled that, mate, you'll bottle anything!

TRAVIS: Well, let's just see, eh, Jacko. Let's just bloody see –

JACKO: That comedian had it right about you, didn't he?

TRAVIS: Come on. Are you coming or not? –

JACKO: Picking on you, when you went out for a slash.

TRAVIS: Yeah, real clever bastard. Well I'm going –

As TRAVIS makes his way to the door, JACKO picks up the crate and throws it at him, yelling 'Oi!' as he does so. TRAVIS turns and catches the crate. JACKO grabs it and, turning TRAVIS round, pushes him back into the room.

JACKO: And when he found out your name was Rupert!

TRAVIS (*hurling crate back to JACKO, who catches it*): You told him ya sod.

JACKO begins to act out what happened at the Dockers' club with the Irish comedian and, later, Dolores, the stripper, trying to cajole a relucant TRAVIS into staying. TRAVIS just wants to go. JACKO puts the crate down, blocking the exit, stands on it and begins to imitate the comedian, physically preventing TRAVIS from leaving by grabbing him.

JACKO: Oh, it's Rupert, is it? What a lovely name.

TRAVIS: Look, are you coming out then?

JACKO: So, dere I was, in de little boys' room, not half an hour ago – when in walks young Rupert here. Oh, I said to him, will you be staying for de strippers later? Oh, no, he said, dat I will not. And I couldn't believe my ears! But it was den I noticed de packet of Planters on his wee willy dere. Oh, to be sure, I tought – dat must be de reason. De poor lad's focking nuts!

TRAVIS (*breaking from* JACKO): Yeah, made me look a right prick, didn't he.

JACKO (*stepping off the crate, joining* TRAVIS): What a night, though, eh. All them strippers, cheap booze.

TRAVIS: Free tickets an'all.

JACKO: Hundreds of blokes there. Every bloke in town, I reckon. Including two of Baker's boys – Mug Lugs and that black bastard, Eroll.

TRAVIS: See – nutter. S'posed to be having a laugh, just a good night out –

JACKO: We did, didn't we?

TRAVIS: Oh yeah, really funny what you did to Eroll in the bogs!

JACKO: Just give him a message for Baker.

TRAVIS: And the rest.

JACKO: Really funny that was. Went in there, all nice and quiet. And there's old Eroll, having a slash, talking away to himself. Didn't understand a bleeding word –

TRAVIS: Yeah, yeah. I'm going –

JACKO *grabs* TRAVIS's *arm and pushes it up behind his back, at the same time grabbing his chin, acting out what happened with Eroll and again, physically preventing* TRAVIS *from leaving.*

JACKO: Listen, blackhead – got a message for Baker. You tell him, Mr Foster says he's dead. You got that?

TRAVIS (*in pain*): You're breaking me bleeding arm!

JACKO: Yeah? And you're pissing down the front of your trousers!

TRAVIS: Let go, Jacko.

JACKO: Let's hear the message first.

TRAVIS: Mr Foster says you're dead. Now, piss off!

TRAVIS *struggles free, obviously genuinely hurt.*

JACKO: I'm sorry, mate.

TRAVIS: Nearly broke me bleeding arm.

JACKO: Just got a bit carried away, that's all.

TRAVIS: No wonder they scarpered after that!

JACKO: Yeah. Missed all the action, didn't they. It was just then old Dolores come on with her bowl of fruit –

TRAVIS: Oh, her. Yeah. Come on –

JACKO: Oh, she was gorgeous.

JACKO *begins to sing 'The Stripper', raucously, imitating Dolores as she slinks towards* TRAVIS, *again preventing him from leaving. This time* TRAVIS *getting caught-up in the action, laughing as* JACKO *dances lewdly round him, giving him a wolf whistle.*

JACKO (*shouts out, as if to Dolores from the crowd*): Come on, darling. Over here. Get them off!

TRAVIS *joins in.* JACKO *reverts to imitating Dolores, groping* TRAVIS, *managing to undo his trousers.*

TRAVIS (*holding his trousers up*): Oi! Gerroff!

JACKO (*kneeling*): Sex on a plate.

TRAVIS: Why'd she pick me, eh? I mean, why's it always me?

JACKO: Little boy, see, Travis. She couldn't believe anyone was that small –

JACKO *suddenly pulls* TRAVIS's *trousers down.*

JACKO: Wanted to see it for herself!

TRAVIS: I couldn't handle it.

JACKO: That was her job.

TRAVIS (*hitching his trousers up and moving away*): It was too much for me.

JACKO: So, you hitched up your trousers and ran – you prat! You know what she was gonna do?

TRAVIS: Course I know.

JACKO: Well, didn't you want it?

TRAVIS: Course I wanted it.

JACKO: So? What was up then?

TRAVIS: Nothing was *up* – not with all them blokes watching, it weren't.

JACKO: You mean you couldn't?

TRAVIS: Not exactly.

JACKO: Well, *what* – exactly?

TRAVIS: Well, you know . . . it's like when you wanna slash.

JACKO: Eh?

TRAVIS: When you wanna go . . . only you can't cos there's other blokes there.

JACKO: It's never happened to me.

TRAVIS: Happens to everyone!

JACKO: Not me, it don't.

TRAVIS: No, it bleeding wouldn't. Nothing ever happens to you.

JACKO (*getting up*): I don't know about that – old Dolores enjoyed herself in the end.

TRAVIS: Trouble with you, Foster – you ain't got no pride.

JACKO: You what?

TRAVIS: Letting her get you up on that stage. Tying you up an' all!

JACKO: 'Ello, I thought, a pervert! I could get into this.

TRAVIS: And when she stuck that pineapple ring over your nob!

JACKO: Gorgeous!

TRAVIS: I'll never touch fruit again.

JACKO: I felt a right prick in the end, though. Stuck up there with me trousers round me ankles, arms tied like this – I couldn't bleeding move!

TRAVIS: I should've left you there.

JACKO: Oh, thanks, mate.

TRAVIS: You'd have done it to me.

JACKO: So?

TRAVIS: Brilliant night, though, eh, Jacko?

JACKO: *I* enjoyed myself.

TRAVIS (*making a move to go again*): Yeah, so what we doing talking about it? We oughta be going –

JACKO (*grabbing his arm*): Best bit was afterwards, seeing that message from Baker, sprayed all over the wall –

TRAVIS: Yeah, I know. I'm going –

JACKO (*still holding him*): 'J.F. – Message received. Baker rises from the grave!'

JACKO screams and jumps into TRAVIS's arms.

TRAVIS: Oi! Leave it out.

JACKO: And then that copper coming round the corner – and you and me like this.
'Evening, boys – consenting adults, are we?'

TRAVIS: Yeah, and you giving our names as –

JACKO (*adopting a camp voice*): Wupert and Walph?

TRAVIS (*throwing JACKO onto the floor*): Piss off!

JACKO: Bloody pigs – fancy pulling us in for that. Drunk and disorderly!

TRAVIS: It's your fault, Foster – they'll nick you any excuse, you know that.

JACKO: Yeah, but what a way to end the evening, though.

TRAVIS: Old Fletcher, standing over you –

JACKO still sat on the floor, TRAVIS standing over him, imitating Fletcher.

TRAVIS: You again, Foster? You again? Well, let me warn you, lad – next time, I'll have you. Don't matter what it is. Just one foot out of line and I'll put you away for good. Do I make myself clear?

JACKO: Crystal.

TRAVIS: I never knew his name was Crystal.

JACKO: Yeah. Almost as bad as Rupert, eh!

TRAVIS: Look, piss off, *Johnny* – least I ain't named after a Durex!

JACKO: Least I know how to use one.

TRAVIS: Always a first time.

JACKO: Oh, yeah. And when's that gonna be?

TRAVIS: Tonight. Gonna need them. Got fifty pee?

JACKO: What for?

TRAVIS: Quick, ain't ya? Machine in the bogs at the Waggon. Reckon that's our first stop. You coming?

JACKO (*throwing a packet of condoms on the floor*): 'Ere, use these.

TRAVIS (*going and picking them up*): Cheers, mate, but I'll need more than three!

JACKO: Well, I ain't going to the Waggon – I hate that pub.

TRAVIS: All right. The Nelson, then.

JACKO: Thought this was s'posed to be special – we drink there every night.

TRAVIS: You do.

JACKO: Anyway, I thought you was after birds tonight?

TRAVIS: I am.

JACKO: Well, then . . . I thought we might try Franky's.

TRAVIS: Franky's! All bleeding dogs in there! Besides, it's miles away.

JACKO: Nice and quiet.

TRAVIS: Like a graveyard.

JACKO: We'll liven it up.

TRAVIS: Sod off, Jacko!

JACKO: What?

TRAVIS: Sod off! What's up with you? 'I don't wanna go to the Waggon, we drink all the time in the Nelson.' And now all this Franky's crap!

JACKO: Well, if you don't wanna go.

TRAVIS: No, mate, it's not me that don't wanna go.

JACKO: I dunno what you mean! Look, I thought you was after birds tonight –

TRAVIS: Yeah.

JACKO: Yeah. Well, last time I was up Franky's they was falling all over me!

TRAVIS: Yeah! That's what you say about every bird, Foster. You reckon every bird fancies you!

JACKO: Well, it ain't far off, is it –

TRAVIS: Walk down the bleeding High Street with you, and it's – That one fancies me. That one's got her eye on me –

JACKO: All right, Travis. What about you, eh? All these birds s'posed to be outside queuing up for you – how many you actually had, eh?

TRAVIS: Can't count past sixty.

JACKO: Bollocks! I can count the birds you've had on two fingers, mate – Gill and Charlene.

TRAVIS: What about Lynsey?

JACKO: Lynsey?

TRAVIS: I stuck it in!

JACKO: Jesus Christ – if you count that you might as well count a wank!

TRAVIS: It's way past sixty then.

JACKO: Yeah. It would be.

TRAVIS: But I go for class birds, Foster. Not like you – any old dog'll do.

JACKO: Old dog! You name one, Travis. You name one I've been with.

TRAVIS: What about Jane Lawrence?

JACKO: She was okay.

TRAVIS: Okay?

JACKO: Yeah . . . not stunning . . . no bleeding model. But she weren't a dog.

TRAVIS: Only a dog'd let you do it to her in a ditch!

JACKO: Oh, come on, Travis. That was me first time. I was only thirteen.

TRAVIS: Thirteen?

JACKO: Yeah.

TRAVIS: Bollocks!

JACKO: Yeah?

TRAVIS: You was knocking birds off at thirteen?

JACKO: I was knocking Jane Lawrence off at thirteen.

TRAVIS: When d'you start on birds?

JACKO: Before you had your first wank, mate.

TRAVIS: Bullshit, Foster!

JACKO: Yeah?

TRAVIS: All right, then. What about

now – tonight? All this mouth. All this lip about birds and that. Well prove it, Foster. You and me on the hunt – tonight.

JACKO: All right.

TRAVIS: Now.

JACKO: Later.

TRAVIS: What's wrong with now?

JACKO: Nothing – you go on if you wanna go. I ain't stopping ya.

TRAVIS: And what you gonna do – sit here and toss yourself off?

JACKO: It's all you'll be doing tonight, mate.

TRAVIS: I'm gonna get a bird.

JACKO: Yeah! Course you are, Travis.

TRAVIS: Well, at least I'm gonna try.

JACKO: Well, you don't want me there then, do ya? I mean, if you're gonna go out and pick up some classy tart, you don't want me around cramping your bleeding style.

TRAVIS: Thanks, Jacko. Thanks a lot. We're meant to be going out. What a night we are gonna have – piss-up with all the lads. Muff-hunt with me best mate. Now all of a sudden I'm having a big celebration on me bleeding own. Cheers, Jacko, mate!

JACKO: Well, celebrate with Lyns.

TRAVIS: Why not you? Oh no, cause you wanna stay here, yak away about old times – well you can piss off!

Again TRAVIS *moves off towards the exit.*

JACKO: Oi!

TRAVIS: What?

JACKO: I am coming with ya.

TRAVIS: When?

JACKO: Tonight.

TRAVIS: Yeah, but when?

JACKO: *Tonight.*

TRAVIS: You see! Look, Jacko, I wanna get a bird. You're always going on about it. Me not having enough. Me not getting enough. The dust on my cock. And why is that, Jacko?

Cause you're always fucking it up for me – that's why.

JACKO: I'm always fucking it up for ya! Who bottled Dolores, Travis? You ran, mate. Not me. Jesus Christ, you don't need me with you when you go on a muff hunt – all you need's a pair of running shoes!

TRAVIS: You're beginning to make me bleeding laugh, Foster.

JACKO: Yeah?

TRAVIS: All this talk about getting Baker. It's you who needs the bleeding running shoes, mate.

JACKO: What are you trying to say, Travis?

TRAVIS: 'Oh, I'm gonna get you Baker, you're dead. Mr Foster says, you're dead' – bleeding hell!

JACKO: Makes you laugh, does it?

TRAVIS: Bloody right, it does. Going on about it all night.

TRAVIS *jumps onto the crate.*

TRAVIS: 'From the moment he laid a finger on me'. From the moment he laid a finger on you, you ain't been able to get off the bog!

JACKO *pushes* TRAVIS *off the crate, kicking it out of the way.*

JACKO: Don't fucking push it, Travis. I'll get him when I'm ready, when I want.

TRAVIS: And when's that gonna be?

JACKO: What's that to you? Wanna come along and watch, do ya?

TRAVIS: No, I wanna help.

JACKO (*grabbing* TRAVIS's *right hand*): You wanna help! You might cut your precious bleeding knuckles –

JACKO *pulls* TRAVIS *away from the exit into centre stage, pursuing him.*

JACKO: Charlie Murray wouldn't like that, would he?

TRAVIS: I just don't want you to be jumped again, that's all.

JACKO: And what you gonna do about it if I am? You wouldn't even beat up that bleeding queer in the alley.

TRAVIS: What's that got to do with it?

JACKO: Just watched me, didn't ya? Just left it to me.

TRAVIS: So?

JACKO (*pushing* TRAVIS *around, kicking his shins*): Didn't even put the boot in when he was down. Just watched me piling in.

TRAVIS: Sod off, Jacko. What's eating you?

JACKO: Always bleeding watching me, ain't ya? Watching me beat up queers, watching me with birds. What you trying to do, sonny, pick up tips? Ain't you got nothing better to do? Ain't you got nothing to do with your own bird?

TRAVIS: Yeah.

JACKO: Yeah?

TRAVIS: Yeah!

JACKO: With Lynsey?

TRAVIS: Yeah. Maybe.

JACKO: Oh, I'm sorry, I forgot, ya don't do ya? Well you better get a move on, son. You're going to London, and you still ain't done it yet.

TRAVIS: That's all right, Jacko. Ten years time she'll still be around, and you'll still be mouthing off about Baker. Still be saying he's gonna die!

JACKO: You reckon?

TRAVIS: He must be pissing himself laughing.

JACKO: Maybe, Travis, maybe.

TRAVIS: So why aren't you going for him, Jacko?

JACKO: Just waiting, that's all.

TRAVIS: You're just waiting? Waiting for what?

JACKO: I don't wanna rush things.

TRAVIS: Well I wanna rush things!

JACKO: Well piss off and go then!

TRAVIS: What, and leave you here all alone, mate? Someone's gotta walk you home, hold your little hand across the green. After all, nasty Baker might be out there with his little piece of wood.

JACKO: You shut your fucking mouth!

TRAVIS: Or is that what you want? Is that why you're hiding in here, Jacko? Cause you're scared, scared you'll get beaten up again. Scared Baker will get you down and have you whimpering like some bleeding poof!

JACKO *hits* TRAVIS *in the face.*

JACKO: Fuck you!

TRAVIS (*moving away*): Fuck Baker, Jacko, not me. What you hiding in here for? You get out there and smash Baker. You kill him.

JACKO: All right Travis, if that's the way you want it.

JACKO *goes to* TRAVIS's *kit bag. Pulling out a pair of bagmits, he throws them at* TRAVIS's *feet.*

JACKO: We'll do it your way, like we was in the ring. But no one calls me a bleeding poof!

TRAVIS: I ain't gonna fight ya Jacko.

JACKO *pulls a second pair of bagmits from the bag.*

JACKO: Scared?

TRAVIS: I just wanna go out.

JACKO: Later.

TRAVIS: Later! With you it's always later!

JACKO: Right after this.

TRAVIS: I ain't gonna fight ya.

JACKO: You fucking will!

TRAVIS: This is stupid. You're me mate.

JACKO (*putting on the bagmits*): Mates don't come into it – your words.

TRAVIS: Don't touch your mates – yours.

JACKO: You fought Skids.

TRAVIS: Yeah, and look what I done to him.

JACKO: Right, he don't come near ya now, does he Rupert?

TRAVIS: Fucking right he don't.

JACKO: So what's the problem? I can beat anyone after a clinch, I'll smash anyone.

TRAVIS: Yeah, that's right.

JACKO: Me an' all, Rupert?

TRAVIS: Shut up.

JACKO: Come on, Rupert

TRAVIS: Fucking shut up!

JACKO: Shut up, shut up – that all you can say? You fucking poof!

TRAVIS (*picking up the bagmits*): Fuck you!

JACKO: That's better, come on.

TRAVIS: I don't wanna fight ya, Jacko.

JACKO (*mocking*): 'I don't wanna fight ya, Jacko.' That's it, innit. You're just a fucking poof!

JACKO hits TRAVIS, who manages to block the blow. Seeing no way out of fighting JACKO, he struggles to put the bagmits on.

JACKO: A bleeding nancy boy.

JACKO again hits out at TRAVIS, who blocks the blow, backing away. JACKO pursues TRAVIS, hitting out, but each time being blocked. Eventually JACKO stops and drops his guard.

JACKO: Come on, Travis, I'm an open target. Hit me. Hit me!

JACKO hits out at TRAVIS, who again blocks the blow.

JACKO: You're supposed to be the big bleeding boxer, ya wanker!

Again JACKO hits out, again TRAVIS blocks and dodges away.

JACKO (*walking towards TRAVIS slowly*): Why won't you fight me, Travis?

TRAVIS: Cause you're me mate. This is stupid, Jacko.

JACKO (*raising his fist, then gently tapping TRAVIS's gloves*): Yeah, it's bleeding daft.

JACKO turns away from TRAVIS, the fight apparently over, and walks across stage, his back to TRAVIS. TRAVIS pursues.

TRAVIS: Yeah. Bloody right it is. Look, what's all this about –

TRAVIS grabs JACKO's arm and

swings him round, as he does so JACKO *punches* TRAVIS *in the gut.* TRAVIS *doubles over,* JACKO *grabs him, raising his head and spitting at him, before knocking him over onto the floor.* JACKO *walks round to the other side of* TRAVIS, *who gets up, furious.* TRAVIS *the boxer takes over, hitting out at* JACKO *pushing him back across the stage. Eventually* JACKO *grabs* TRAVIS *and they go into a clinch.*

TRAVIS (*in the clinch*): No!

JACKO (*pushing him off and kneeing TRAVIS in the groin*): You fucking queer!

TRAVIS (*on the ground*): It ain't what you think.

JACKO: Keep away from me, Travis.

TRAVIS: It's not what you're thinking. It ain't that.

JACKO: Ain't that?

TRAVIS: No.

JACKO: I bleeding felt it, Travis.

TRAVIS: Felt what?

JACKO: You fucking loved it, didn't you?

TRAVIS: I didn't. I didn't love it. I hate it. I hate liking it. It ain't what you think.

JACKO: No?

TRAVIS: It's just then, just in the clinch. Never any other time. You can't help it. You're all psyched-up, all parts of you, Jacko, excited –

JACKO: Including ya bleeding cock?

TRAVIS: Every part of ya, what's wrong with that? Yeah, me cock, but other parts as well, like me legs, me arms. That don't make me queer.

JACKO: I don't feel like that. I ain't never felt like that! Why? Why me?

TRAVIS (*getting up*): That's how I win. That's how I win all me fights.

JACKO (*taking off his bagmits and throwing them down*): I'm ya best mate!

TRAVIS (*throwing his bagmits down*): I could've killed you, Jacko! You look what I done to Skids!

JACKO: You fucking watch it. You're lucky I didn't break your bleeding neck!

TRAVIS: So why didn't you. Cause ya don't believe it, cause it ain't true, that's why. Well, ain't that it?

JACKO: It ain't just me, son, it ain't just me saying it.

TRAVIS: What you talking about?

JACKO: I wanted to set it all straight tonight. All them lies, all that crap Sholey Mill been coming out with. And now look what you done!

TRAVIS: I done my bit.

JACKO: Yeah.

TRAVIS: Yeah, I done my bit. I smashed Sangster's head in. What about you, eh! What you hiding in here for? Why aren't you out there, smashing Baker.

JACKO: He's finished.

TRAVIS: So I been hearing all bloody night.

JACKO: I got him on the way here. Him and two of his dagger boys. All of them leaning over the side of the multi-storey, calling out, asking me how my fucking boyfriend was – You! Spraying it all over the walls – TRAVIS IS A QUEER BOY. JACKO LOVES TRAVIS. See – they're all saying it. All saying you're a bleeding queer.

TRAVIS: And what you do about it?

JACKO: What d'you think I done about it?

TRAVIS: I don't know anymore.

JACKO: I went in there and I got them. All of them, all coming at me, asking how my little bender buddy was – calling me a bleeding queer! If I'd had any sense I would've got out of there, run. But I didn't, I went wild, and I smashed them, all of them. And all I had was a piece of old exhaust.

TRAVIS: Well ain't you the fucking hero!

JACKO: Just watch it! Calling me a fucking queer!

TRAVIS: Look, what's it matter? What do we call them? The Sholey Mill bum bandits! What's it fucking matter?

JACKO: Just what Baker said –

TRAVIS: What?

JACKO: Sangster told them. It was you in that last fight, you in the clinch. You fancied him, wanted to touch him up.

TRAVIS: You was smashing his bleeding head in. He'd have said anything.

JACKO: Just then, Travis, in that clinch, you had a bleeding hard-on. That's just what Sangster told Baker. In the clinch you had a hard-on.

TRAVIS: He's the bleeding queer and look what I done to him!

JACKO: What's it matter what you done to him?

TRAVIS: It means I win, Jacko. Means I beat it. Means I don't want it, and I don't ever want it.

JACKO turns and walks away from him.

I shut it out. It don't ever happen, apart from in the ring, apart from the clinch, when every part of me feels like that, not just that one.

JACKO (his back to TRAVIS): All the times we been together.

TRAVIS: So? I don't wanna touch ya. I don't fancy ya. I ain't never thought anything like that. Ere, how many times you touched my arse, Foster?

He jokingly touches JACKO's buttocks. JACKO swings round and hits out, TRAVIS ducking and moving away.

JACKO: Yeah, just mucking about, nothing in it!

TRAVIS: No? So why d'ya do it? Give you a laugh, does it, Jacko? That make you feel good does it?

JACKO: You fucking watch it!

TRAVIS: There ain't no difference!

JACKO: No, only we weren't having a laugh. We weren't mucking about!

TRAVIS: I don't muck around in the ring!

JACKO: No. Right. It was dead serious. You felt like that!

TRAVIS: I didn't want it. I wanted to go out. I tried my hardest not to fight you. It was all over Baker. All cause I said you was scared, that you was hiding from him. What? – And you'd already bleeding got him.

You wanted it, didn't ya? Wanted a fight, wanted a clinch. You bastard. You believed him.

JACKO: No. No, I didn't believe him, not then. But afterwards, thinking about what he said.

TRAVIS: What?

JACKO: Sangster was pissing all over ya –

TRAVIS: Queer bastard!

JACKO: You only beat them after the clinch –

TRAVIS: I told ya why –

JACKO: Skids an' all.

TRAVIS: So?

JACKO: All your fights –

TRAVIS: Shut up –

JACKO: It's only after the clinch –

TRAVIS: Shut it, Jacko –

JACKO: You go wild –

TRAVIS: It's the power, innit –

JACKO: Sangster don't reckon so.

TRAVIS: Queer bastard!

JACKO: Are they all queer, Travis?

TRAVIS: Meaning what?

JACKO: I dunno.

TRAVIS: You dunno.

JACKO: No!

TRAVIS: And why?

Indicating the place where they had the clinch.

TRAVIS: Cause that don't mean nothing, that's why!

JACKO: That don't mean nothing? Course that means something! Means something to me!

TRAVIS: What?

JACKO: Well it means Sangster was right for a start. And all that crap you come out with about him in the bogs, before the first match – touching your arse. Well, what is that – little fantasy of yours? Like some bird on the dance floor – is that how you felt?

TRAVIS: And you had to know, didn't ya? Had to find out for yourself, wanted to feel it for yourself, didn't ya? Well, are you happy now then? D'you enjoy feeling my fucking hard-on?

JACKO (*grabbing* TRAVIS): I'll fucking kill you!

TRAVIS: Jacko, I'm ya mate. I ain't no different, I'm the same as I ever was.

JACKO (*throwing* TRAVIS *to the ground*): Are ya?

TRAVIS: We're mates. We're going to London. Gonna get that flat. All them London birds, that's all we've been talking about all evening.

TRAVIS gets up.

TRAVIS: Muff-hunting, screwing birds, it's all we've talked about for years!

JACKO: It's just talk, Travis. It's just talk. Everybody talks about getting birds – even bleeding queers.

TRAVIS: What, and screw them too? Queers don't screw birds. I was gonna screw a bird tonight, we both was. What I gotta do to convince ya, call you in when I'm on the job?

JACKO: I've seen you on the job, Travis. I seen you try it on with Dolores, and you just bleeding ran.

TRAVIS: I told you why – all them blokes watching!

JACKO: So?

TRAVIS: So I was scared, scared in case I couldn't. Not cause I'm queer, but just . . . everyone watching. Well ain't you ever worried about getting it up?

JACKO: No, I bleeding ain't.

TRAVIS: No, you're the fucking super-cock, ain't ya?

JACKO: Yeah, if you like.

TRAVIS: You're full of shit, Foster.

JACKO: And you're so fit you can go on all night! No wonder Lynsey's looking so bleeding happy –

TRAVIS: You leave Lynsey out of this –

JACKO: Why ain't you screwed her yet, Travis?

TRAVIS: I have.

JACKO: Oh yeah, ya stuck it in!

TRAVIS: It's different with Lynsey. I like her, Jacko, like her a lot. She don't wanna go to bed, wants to take it nice and easy. I don't mind, 's what I want too. I don't want it to go wrong. Don't want it all fucked up like you and Elaine.

JACKO: How sweet. Well why don't you go and live in London together then –

TRAVIS: Cause we're gonna get a flat. I thought that's what you wanted, thought you was keen. Way you talked about it before the fight, I thought you couldn't wait. Or was that just talk? Just bullshit?

JACKO: Yeah, maybe. Well think about it – London, living together, you and me. Well I had to know, didn't I?

TRAVIS: So why wait till now? Why not before the fight, why didn't you do all this then?

JACKO (turning away from TRAVIS): Cause I didn't want to fuck it up for ya, just have a bit of a laugh, that's all.

TRAVIS: You cunt. Didn't want to fuck the fight up for me? Just have a bit of a laugh? It weren't just then, in the clinch. You been at it all evening, ain't ya? Talking about Dolores, you bringing up Lynsey – asking me all them questions, like, have you screwed her yet, Travis? Ever since you got here you been trying to suss it out, suss out if I was queer – if ya best mate's queer? Well, you made your mind up yet? You fucking cunt.

JACKO: Yeah, that's right. Oh, Jesus Christ, Travis, what d'you expect me to do – come running in here, say, 'ere Trav, rumour has it you're a queer, are ya? I told ya – I had to know. London, living together, just being mates.

TRAVIS: So?

JACKO: So I had to know. I mean, with that bender Ralph, why didn't you do him in? Why'd you just leave it to me to do? Way he was looking at you, Travis, like he knew he had it made.

TRAVIS: Don't you think I saw that? I saw. Scared me bleeding shitless that did. Yeah, big laugh setting Travis up with a queer. But it's always me. They all go for me. Why? Makes you think, what can they see in me? What's wrong with me? It makes me scared, Jacko.

JACKO: Scared?

TRAVIS: Yeah, I'm scared. Course I'm scared. In the ring, feeling like that, smashing someone, winning – that's brilliant. But later, afterwards . . . yeah, I'm scared. Scared of what happens. I get in a clinch, I'm so close I can . . .
I like it. It turns me on. But I don't want that. I ain't like that. So I fight against it – hit him, smash him, kill him. Anything, just to get away.
That's how I win, Jacko. Fighting against it, beating it. And I win every time.
Like I said, you was lucky I didn't finish the job.

JACKO: Like I said, Travis, you was lucky I didn't break your bleeding neck.

Pause. JACKO goes and sits down on the chair, upstage right.

TRAVIS: All right. Okay. Let's go out now, pick up a coupla birds. You can see for yourself then. I'll show you what I like.

JACKO: I can't.

TRAVIS: We can go up the club.

JACKO: I can't, can I?

TRAVIS: I ain't queer!

JACKO: That's not what I mean. I told ya, I got Baker and two of his boys.

TRAVIS: So?

JACKO: So use ya fucking nounce, will ya? How long before the pigs find out. I'm surprised they ain't sussed yet.

TRAVIS: What?

JACKO: Me hiding in here.

TRAVIS: That why ya didn't see me match?

JACKO: Didn't want no one to know I was around, did I?

TRAVIS: Load of pigs out front. I thought they was expecting trouble.

JACKO: No, that's all over now – Sangster, Baker – Sholey Mill eat shit, eh?

TRAVIS: Come on, let's go out. We can risk it.

JACKO: No.

TRAVIS: You ain't scared of the pigs, are ya?

JACKO: No point.

TRAVIS: I wanna show ya, Jacko.

JACKO: Show me what? There ain't nothing to prove, is there. You just said it all.

TRAVIS: You staying put?

JACKO: Nowhere else to bleeding go.

TRAVIS: I could nip out, get some cans –

JACKO: No, cheers, but –

TRAVIS: No, right.

Pause. TRAVIS *goes and picks up his jacket.*

TRAVIS: I think I'll make a move then, Jacko.

JACKO: Yeah, all right.

TRAVIS: Wanna get up the club, see. Got it all sussed. Now I'm a pro, that redhead with the tits – she'll be all over me.

JACKO: Yeah.

TRAVIS: Think I'll go for her tonight.

JACKO: Yeah, well, make good use of me johnnies, eh.

TRAVIS: I know what to do with them now. I'll get her to roll one on. Won't that be something? Call round for you tomorrow, then?

JACKO: No. No, there's no point. I'll still be down the nick.

TRAVIS: Oh yeah – getting grilled by Fletcher.

JACKO: Yeah. Just leave it, eh? I'll call on you sometime, when I get out.

TRAVIS: You'll get out of it. You always do.

JACKO: Yeah.

TRAVIS (*going*): Right, I'll be off then.

JACKO: Look – Ah, look, just give us a whistle if the pigs are outside, will ya?

TRAVIS: Yeah. See ya.

TRAVIS *exits.* JACKO *alone on stage, sitting in the chair. Very quietly the last two verses and chorus of the opening song,* 'Mates', *is heard in the auditorium. Lights go slowly down on* JACKO.

Curtain.

TERMINAL BAR

In memory of Mr Bunny Lake

'Only those who still have hope can benefit from tears.'
Nathanael West, *The Day of the Locust*

PAUL SELIG was born in New York City in 1961 and is a recent graduate of the Yale School of Drama. *Terminal Bar* was premièred at the Edinburgh Fringe Festival in 1985 and subsequently toured the UK. In 1987 the play was performed by En Garde Arts in New York. His other work includes: *Body Parts*, produced in New York at the Ohio Theatre; *Long Island Dreamer*, a mini-musical written on commission for the New York Shakespeare Festival; *The Pompeii Travelling Show*, presented in workshop at the San Diego Repertory Theater; and *Moon City*. Paul Selig has been playwright-in-residence at the Poetry Center in New York.

Terminal Bar
I returned to live in New York when I was seventeen, eager to immerse myself in a lifestyle I had heard only faint, uncomfortable whisperings about in the small New England town where I was raised. The sexual revolution that had taken hold several years earlier had reached a fever pitch, and I found myself, naive and full of awe, in the throes of a bacchanalia with great expectations and no set of instructions.

It was a time for me when sex, by its nature, was something bleary, hungry and nameless, and there was solace to be found in it, some hope for romance. The bars were bastions of beauty where, from my corner stool, life and love would begin to unfold for me sometime after the fourth drink. I imagine *Terminal Bar* is as much an ode to my own longings, my own misconceptions of a lifestyle that I knew was on the brink of disappearing as it is an exorcism of my panic in the face of what (at the time) was an unnamed epidemic that seemed to lift people from their bar-stools into hospital with 'They Can't Seem To Find What's Wrong.'

In retrospect, it's frightening to me how prophetic the play is. When *Terminal Bar* was first performed at the end of 1983, the audience was quite confused as to the nature of the plague described in the text. By the time of its New York première three years later, there could be no doubt in anyone's mind.

The bars and backrooms that Dwayne refers to have been deserted by their patrons or padlocked by the board of health, and what little remains of what used to be called 'The New Freedom' is essentially underground, and there is no pretext of romance or love, only a desperate denial of the inherent possibility of death.

I recall being in such a place as Dwayne describes in his monologue at precisely his age; a backroom bookstore where men would saunter around in a circle surrounded by dark cubicles, staring at one another and possibly coupling off. The jukebox I leaned against played a 1950's love song, 'Johnny Angel, How I love him . . .' and suddenly it all became a dance, a lush and sexual prom for all of us who had never been to one. I have always referred to *Terminal Bar* as a romantic play, and I think the romance is precisely the romance of yearning, Holly's, Martinelle's and Dwayne's, contradicted by the grim reality that houses such a simple longing.

Paul Selig

Terminal Bar was first performed at the Edinburgh Festival in 1985 by Magnet Productions with the following cast:

MARTINELLE *25, A streetwalker*   Michele Costa
HOLLY *30, A runaway housewife*   Alice Arnold
DWAYNE *17, A schoolboy*   Martin Burrell

and the voices of LENNIE and BERNICE, read by the actors portraying DWAYNE and HOLLY

PROLOGUE

Music plays in the darkness. It is gentle, futuristic, slightly mournful. It continues quietly throughout the prologue.

MARTINELLE *sits isolated in a pool of light. She is twenty-five years old and vaguely attractive. She wears a fake fur chubby, a mini-skirt, and sequined platform shoes. She holds a large portable radio in her lap. A price tag hangs from it.*

MARTINELLE *fiddles with the radio. It broadcasts static.*

MARTINELLE (*to someone off-stage*): So there I am, standin' in the ruins of the Crazy Eddie Christmas window holding on to this t.v. for dear life, an' I am dealing with this PERSON who is trying to pry it outa my arms. So I tell him, 'What do I look like to you that allows for you to treat me in such a manner? I'm no refugee. You don't see me dragging my mattress along the highway.' But he wasn't buying. So I say, 'YOU take the radio an' give ME the damn t.v.' . . . Charlie? You get through to Staten Island or you still loving yourself in the mirror? Anyways, I told this guy he'd look real sharp walking around the streets with a radio. He said it was a basic look an' he was not a basic person. I told him to look on the positive. Fact that anybody's still walkin' the streets at all is cause for a party. 'Radio'd add a bit of class,' I said. 'Like being in your own parade.' Then he says to ME, 'All's fair in love an' looting,' an' he dances out the window with the freakin' tube . . . I'm not getting any stations on this. How's that for fun, huh Charlie? I spray painted lips on the hole in the wall. It's a big kiss from me to you . . . Charlie?

MARTINELLE *goes back to examining the radio. She remains dimly lit throughout the following. Lights up to reveal* HOLLY *on another part of the stage. She is thirty years old, southern, and very pregnant. She has an enormous teased hairdo. She packs a suitcase with miscellaneous items: baby bottles, a camera, etc.* DWAYNE, *in darkness, is the voice of* LENNIE.

HOLLY: Lennie? I'm upstairs. Earth to Lennie.

LENNIE: What is it?

HOLLY: I feel like hell an' I ain't hung over. You doing somebody?

LENNIE: Yes.

HOLLY: I can sniff the formaldehyde all the way up here. Who you doing, Lennie?

LENNIE: Ricky Jordon.

HOLLY: Alice Jordon's son? He wasn't but a child. What happened to him?

LENNIE: Plague.

HOLLY (*excitedly waving an American flag from suitcase*): THAT'S THREE, LENNIE. THAT'S THREE FOR AURORA.

LENNIE: He'd been to Houston with the chorale from the high school.

HOLLY: I helped out at his party when he turned nine. I remember that day because people were actually saying it might snow. It didn't after all, but I remember wishing it had. Still, a fine time was had by all.

LENNIE: You frightened people.

HOLLY (*packing liquor*): I don't like kids. Kids don't drink. We never had any kids before 'cause they'd all suffocate.

LENNIE: What are you talking about now, Holly?

HOLLY: In the closet. You keep the cleaner's plastic in the closet. Folks know you use it for embalming?

LENNIE: Does it matter?

HOLLY: To me it does. It's distressing to get a dress back an' know the plastic's gonna be wrapping a cadaver. You get to my favourite part yet?

LENNIE: No.

HOLLY: Well, tell me when you do 'cause I don't wanna miss it. Tell me how it works, Lennie.

LENNIE: They let out a breath . . .

HOLLY: So you stick a feather on their

lips so you can see when the time comes.

Laughs.

That's my favourite part 'cause it's the most unnatural thing you do. I tell about it at parties.

Pause.

Maybe I got the plague, Lennie.

LENNIE: Don't be a fool.

HOLLY: Maybe I do. TURN THE DISHWASHER TO BOIL. BURN THE SHEETS. HOLLY'S GOT THE PLAGUE.

LENNIE: You couldn't have it.

HOLLY: I most certainly could. I know what's going on in our country's urban centres. I read the magazines.

LENNIE: You couldn't have it. You're a Christian. Alice Jordon is very ashamed right now.

HOLLY: I don't believe it's true what they say. I think it's carried on the air. Like snowflakes, only invisible.

Pauses, rubs belly.

Maybe it's just my condition. Lennie?

LENNIE: What are you talking about?

HOLLY: Jesus H. Christ. MY CONDITION.

Pause.

I went down to the room yesterday

LENNIE: Did you wear a mask?

HOLLY: I didn't know that was Ricky Jordon on the table. He developed just fine. Pretty as his mama. I went into the closet an' played with the plastic.

LENNIE: Did you wear a mask when you went into the room?

HOLLY: I shaped the plastic into a body. Do you know what that body turned out to be, Lennie? A woman. I thought that was sorta strange. I laid down next to it anyway.

LENNIE: Long as you wore a mask.

HOLLY: I THOUGHT about wrapping myself up in it. But I ain't lived yet.

LENNIE: Jordon boy used to come swim in our pool.

HOLLY (*closing suitcase*): I'm leaving you, Lennie. I'd rather be embalmed by a stranger.

LENNIE: Well, will you look at that. There it goes. There goes the feather.

LENNIE *laughs.*

HOLLY (*to herself*): I ain't even seen snow . . .

Lights dim on HOLLY. MARTINELLE *still examines the radio. More static.*

MARTINELLE: Charlie? I stuck my head through the hole in the wall an' said our names together. They echoed around the entire room. Charlie an' Martinelle. Martinelle an' Charlie.

Pause.

Charlie?

Lights up on DWAYNE *on another area of the stage. He is seventeen years old, homely, and wears a parochial school uniform. He is coatless and obviously freezing.* HOLLY, *in darkness, is the voice of* BERNICE.

DWAYNE: HELLO? HELLO, MOM? I'M DOWNSTAIRS.

BERNICE: What?

DWAYNE: Under the window. Downstairs.

BERNICE: WHAT YOU WANT, WHITE BOY?

DWAYNE: Bernice?

BERNICE: DWAYNE? IS THAT YOU, DWAYNE?

To someone inside.

It's the Copeland boy, Dwayne. WHAT YOU WANT, DWAYNE?

DWAYNE: I can't get in the apartment.

BERNICE: I CHANGED THE LOCKS.

DWAYNE: What?

BERNICE: I CHANGED THE LOCKS.

DWAYNE: Where's my parents?

BERNICE: THEY'S EVACUATED.

DWAYNE: Can I have my coat?

BERNICE (*inside*): He wants his coat.

DWAYNE: I'M COLD.

BERNICE: YOU CRAZY, DWAYNE? YOU THINK I'M GONNA RUMMAGE THROUGH THAT FILTHY ROOM OF YOURS ON MY NEWLY FOUND LEISURE TIME?

In.

Leave me be, Roscoe. Quit futzing with my hairpiece.

DWAYNE: I WANT MY COAT. I'M COLD.

BERNICE: YOU BRINGIN' ME DOWN. DWAYNE. YOU BRINGIN' ME DOWN AN' I'M HAVIN' A PARTY. WE'RE DRINKING THE NIQUIL OFFA YOUR BUREAU.

In.

What?

Out.

DWAYNE? ROSCOE WANTS TO KNOW DID YOU TAKE IT FROM THE LITTLE CUP THEY GIVE YOU OR PUT YOUR MOUTH ON THE BOTTLE?

DWAYNE: I . . . I don't remember.

BERNICE: WELL, THINK. THINK. 'CAUSE YOU'RE THAT WAY, AREN'T YOU DWAYNE? YOU'RE THAT WAY. ROSCOE SAYS YOU TRIED TO TOUCH HIM THROUGH HIS PANTS WHEN HE WAS TAKING YOU UP IN THE ELEVATOR, AN' I FOUND MATCHBOOKS IN YOUR LAUNDRY. YOU'RE A CARRIER.

DWAYNE: GIVE ME MY COAT.

BERNICE: TELL BERNICE THE TRUTH, NOW. TELL ME SO'S I'LL KNOW TO THROW MYSELF OUT THE WINDOW AFTER WE KILL OFF THE BOTTLE.

In.

I know what floor we're on, Roscoe. It's the sentiment, that's all. The sentiment.

Out.

TELL ME YOU'RE A BOIL ON THE MEMORY OF YOUR PARENTS AN' THE FAITHFUL MAID THEY LEFT BEHIND.

YOUR MAMA LEFT BEHIND HER FURS. YOU THINK I LOOK PRETTY, DWAYNE? THEY LEFT A MESSAGE FOR YOU.

DWAYNE: What? What is it?

BERNICE: SAYS, 'NURSE CALLED TO SAY YOUR ORTHODONTIST DIED.' FROM STICKIN' HIS FINGERS IN YOUR MOUTH, I EXPECT. YOU AIN'T NEVER GONNA GET THOSE BRACES OFF NOW, DWAYNE, AN' YOU WAS UGLY TO BEGIN WITH. PREPARE YOURSELF FOR A LIFE OF MISERY.

DWAYNE *begins to cry freely.*

BERNICE (*shrieking*): IT'S THE END OF THE WORLD. IT'S THE END OF THE WORLD.

In.

What? How am I supposed to know where they kept any damn candles? They was all slobs.

Out.

I NEVER LIKED ANY OF YOU, DWAYNE. DID YOU KNOW THAT? THIRTEEN YEARS AN' I NEVER LIKED ANY OF YOU. YOUR MAMA USED TO MEASURE THE LIQUOR. GO BACK TO THAT PLACE ON YOUR MATCHBOOKS IF THE NUNS AIN'T BURNED IT YET. GO AWAY.

DWAYNE *sobs.*

BERNICE: Hey, Roscoe. Copeland boy's crying. No it ain't. I take no responsibility.

Out, concerned.

YOU CRYING, DWAYNE? YOU CRYING OUT THERE?

DWAYNE *turns away from her.*

BERNICE: WELL THAT'S JUST FINE. CRY ALL YOU WANT TO CRY. WE'RE ALL GONNA BE DEAD SOON ENOUGH ANYWAYS. SHED A FEW TEARS FOR BERNICE WHILE YOU'RE AT IT. BERNICE WHO'S GONNA BE LEFT ALONE AN' DEAD IN THE DARK.

In.

Roscoe? Smile for Bernice so she can see where you are . . .

Lights fade from DWAYNE. *Prologue music fades.* MARTINELLE *rises. Thumps the radio.*

RADIO ANNOUNCER: . . . REPEAT, THIS IS *NOT* A TEST . . .

MARTINELLE *hurriedly switches stations. More static. Finally, music.* MARTINELLE *hugs the radio.*

MARTINELLE: CHARLIE. I THINK I GOT PENNSYLVANIA. LATER ON WE CAN DANCE. WE COULD DO IT IN FRONT OF THE MIRROR. PRETEND WE'RE IN A CROWD. Dance and not cope with anything . . .

Glass shatters off-stage.

MARTINELLE (*frightened*): CHARLIE?

Blackout. Music blares in the darkness. End Prologue.

Lights up on the Terminal Bar, an abandoned club in New York's red-light district. A table, barstools, a bar. Also a huge hole in the plaster of one wall with red lips spray-painted around it. The bar has been decorated for Christmas, and there is a warmth, a beauty to the decay.

HOLLY *stands, dripping wet from the rain. She has a Polaroid camera around her neck and clutches a soggy paper bag and an equally soggy map. Her suitcase sits open on a barstool, an 'I Love New York' sticker peeling from it.*

MARTINELLE *sits at the table. It is littered with cosmetics and she daintily paints her fingernails. A suitcase rests on the floor beside her. She is dressed as before, only her stockings are torn and her make-up is caked.*

MARTINELLE: . . . So I tell him, 'Fine, Charlie. Fine. Get on the telephone. I'm happy to work. Fine. You do your business in there on the phone an' I'll do mine right here on my stool.' That's it over there. Charlie carved my name in the seat with his knife. Stuffing pops out an' it's like I'm sitting on angel hair. Tammy an' Elvira used to work the all-night news-stand on thirty-ninth. Charlie sent 'em there 'cause they was both illiterate. That's what kind of man he is. Had them both stretch out on the sidewalk an' he spray-painted their outlines on the cement, then put in their names, the hours they worked, an' the number here at the bar in case of emergency. Tammy was just thrilled about the whole thing. Used to hang out on her paintmarks all the time. Off hours an' everything. Not working. Just lying there so's people'd know she belonged someplace. Used to go out in the blizzards and shovel snow from it. Charlie was touched. I thought she was being a deal.

HOLLY: I was worried you might be angry with me.

MARTINELLE (*ignoring her, with growing menace*): Tammy never did learn to read. Used to look at the pictures in Good Housekeeping. Elvira, on the other hand, got real hooked on Ebony an' changed her name to something African I can't pronounce right. So I used to call her Girlie. That's what Charlie called the ones whose names he couldn't remember. The lesser ones. Everything was, 'Hi, Girlie, how's your health?' or 'Hi, Girlie, I hate your shoes.' New chick with a Jewish name was Girlieberg. She had only one ear an' coveted my good pumps, but everybody's gotta be someplace, right? Like, now you're here, an' a little while ago you was irritating people somewhere else in our fair city. FINE. Tammy an' Elvira evacuated a while ago to Pennsylvania where the air's still good. Moved in with an Amish family. Sent Charlie a snapshot of themselves both wearing bonnets. Just like you'd hope to see in a margarine commercial, except they was black. Just like both your eyes woulda been if you'd been five minutes longer getting your ass back here you bitch.

HOLLY: I . . .

MARTINELLE: You pregnant bitch. What is it makes you think you can leave me alone for so long? You think I'm common or something? You think I'm a common streetwalker? Well, maybe I was, but I ain't anymore. I am the only one left an' I am THRILLED about it. I am a harem unto myself.

HOLLY: I got lost.

MARTINELLE: I have been sitting here painting my fingernails since three o'clock this afternoon.

HOLLY: An' they're very attractive.

MARTINELLE: They're like BRICKS. You could break every damn window in New York with my fingernails.

HOLLY: Coulda started on your toes.

MARTINELLE: Hick.

HOLLY: I must say I'm flattered. I didn't think you'd miss me so much.

MARTINELLE: I didn't miss you. I've been entertaining myself.

HOLLY: An' you got Charlie here.

MARTINELLE: HE'S ON THE TELEPHONE.

HOLLY: Still?

MARTINELLE: YES. STILL.

HOLLY puts paper bag on MARTINELLE 's table.

HOLLY: Must have the mint in quarters is all I can say.

MARTINELLE: I just got so shattered about your not showing up I was getting ready to slit my wrists.

MARTINELLE slashes her wrists with nailpolish. Holds them out.

An' what makes this REAL tragic is I'm all outa red polish an' I gotta slit 'em in pink. I may be a lotta things, but I ain't pink.

HOLLY (*drying herself off*): Well I am very sorry, Martinelle. I hope you know I wouldn't do nothing to upset you intentionally. I plain got lost.

MARTINELLE: You don't get lost with a map.

HOLLY: It got soggy an' the streets started to run together. An' as I personally do not have the finest sense of direction in the world, I was using the Empire State Building as my point of reference. Then I looked up one second an' it just wasn't there no more.

MARTINELLE: What?

HOLLY: Lights went out. POOF.

MARTINELLE: We could be in Detroit for all we know.

HOLLY: I agree with you entirely.

Wiping feet on map.

SO MUCH FOR NEW YORK. You know, I have this unChristian part of me wants to get on the horn an' tell all the folks back home I finally been to see the lights of fourteenth street, only there wasn't any.

HOLLY *turns on the radio, and joins in on 'purplish'.*

RADIO: . . . symptoms which may include recently appearing or slowly enlarging purplish nodules on or beneath the skin, rapid and otherwise unexplained hair loss, a dry, persistant cough not caused by smoking, night sweats, weight loss of more than ten pounds in one month.

HOLLY (*blithely joining in*): Purplish

nodules on or beneath the skin, rapid and otherwise unexplained hair loss, a dry, persistant cough not caused by . . .

MARTINELLE (*speaking over final words of radio announcer*): I don't want to cope with the news.

HOLLY: What is it you expect of me, Martinelle?

MARTINELLE: CHANGE THE CHANNEL.

MARTINELLE *throws nailpolish at HOLLY, streaking her dress.*

HOLLY: MARTINELLE. I AM SHOCKED.

MARTINELLE (*miserably*): So what. So what.

HOLLY (*turns off radio*): Now my dress reflects my bleeding heart.

Goes to bar and pours herself the first of many huge drinks.

You'd think this rain'd turn to something more inspiring. I'm soaked clear through.

Pause, seductive.

I could take off all my clothes, I guess. Put 'em by the radiator. If I had a hanger I would do that.

MARTINELLE: You shoulda thought about the hanger nine months ago.

HOLLY (*giggling*): Stop that. Life's precious.

Drinks.

Oh, I do enjoy retainin' fluids. Models sleep sittin' up. I read it in a magazine. Sleep sittin' up so's all the fluids'll drain from their heads an' they'll have cheekbones. What price beauty. I was to sleep sittin' up I'd drown the kid.

MARTINELLE: You're such a deal.

HOLLY: I am not a deal.

MARTINELLE: Holly's a deal. Remind me later an' I'll spray paint it on the wall next to the lips.

HOLLY: A great big kiss from you to Charlie.

MARTINELLE: Hole looked naked. I got tired of staring at it.

HOLLY: Well, it's very attractive.

MARTINELLE: Don't try to be nice to me. I ain't forgiven you yet.

HOLLY (*exasperated*): I had to go all the way to the Indian Deli. Little Calcutta. They're foreigners an' don't know about the plague. I think it's what they're used to. Nasty boy in a turban kept trying to get me to buy coffee. I told him I didn't care to stay awake. I've SEEN just about everything. He wouldn't give me your boiled water for free. I had to buy a teabag with it. I told him I don't drink tea. I told him my girlfriend, who's an exotic named Martinelle, don't drink tea neither. There was this old woman in the corner sitting on a milk crate. She had a dot on her forehead. It coulda been a lesion.

MARTINELLE: Did you get me a mirror?

HOLLY (*cheerfully*): You know the one's I passed was all broken?

MARTINELLE: Quit smiling.

HOLLY: I was voted most cheerful of my high school class.

MARTINELLE: You married a mortician.

HOLLY: Well, he had an above-ground pool.

Catches her reflection in drink.

OH MY HAIR. MY HAIR.

Takes camera from around her neck, smiles broadly, takes a flash picture of herself, then aims camera at stomach.

SMILE, PRECIOUS.

Snaps picture of stomach.

Mommy loves you.

MARTINELLE: He's gonna be a poster child. I can feel it.

HOLLY (*removing hairspray from suitcase*): Your water's catching germs.

MARTINELLE *dips a napkin in the coffee container, removing her makeup.*

I ain't had my face off in a week.

HOLLY: I fail to see what is so

frightening about the ladies' room.

MARTINELLE: Girlieberg's in there. She's been in there a month.

HOLLY (*fixing hair with snapshot as mirror*): Doing what?

MARTINELLE: Last I heard she wasn't feeling so hot.

HOLLY: I swear, if I was drunk I'd cry.

Uncapping hairspray.

MARTINELLE: I hate that stuff.

HOLLY: Well I hate things with moveable parts. One of the many reasons I left my husband.

Sprays hair.

They say this stuff eats away at the Ozone Layer. Ozone's what stops the moon falling down on us an' making us go squish. Neighbours back home had two teenagers used to come skinny-dip in our pool when Lennie an' me was sleeping. They kept threatening to picket my hair.

Sprays room.

MY CONTRIBUTION TO THE WORLD OF TOMORROW.

Laughs.

MARTINELLE: You're such a tourist.

HOLLY: What of it. Maybe later you can show me some prostitution beauty tips. Maybe I can go to the bar next door an' practise soliciting in your shoes.

MARTINELLE: Charlie always said to be sure your shoes matched your makeup. That's 'cause johns always look at your feet first 'cause they're too embarrassed to look you in the face. Be sure they matched, so it don't come as such a shock going from foot to face.

HOLLY: I adore those shoes.

MARTINELLE: They're mine.

HOLLY: And you're the loveliest woman I've ever seen.

MARTINELLE: Yeah.

HOLLY: So maybe later you can show us how you do our national monuments.

MARTINELLE: I don't do that for fun.

HOLLY: Well, we're gettin' to be friends an' there's no t.v.

MARTINELLE: I only do it for Mr. Greenberg.

HOLLY: Ain't the Statue of Liberty a sort of unnatural thing to desire?

MARTINELLE: It's a free country. He's a Russian Jew who landed on Ellis Island an' I remind him of his mother. He used to be in a wheelchair an' I'd just have to stand there with the torch while he rolled towards me an' rocked himself back an' forth to get that seasick feeling. Now he's bedridden I go towards him an' he just rolls his eyes.

HOLLY: Sounds real patriotic.

MARTINELLE: Charlie wouldn't approve of my doing it for free.

HOLLY: You'd do it for a girlfriend. We are girlfriends.

MARTINELLE: Not quite.

HOLLY: Well, we're gettin' to be an' I'm a laugh riot after I've had a few. Only reason Lennie an' me ever got invited out. I was the fun half of the couple.

MARTINELLE: Precious there your first?

HOLLY (*proudly*): Yes. He's my one.

Bellowing at stomach.

YOU'RE MY ONE.

Waving flag from suitcase.

FIRST AURORA BABY TO BE CONCEIVED AFTER THE PLAGUE.

MARTINELLE: You got the plague in Aurora?

HOLLY: Yes we do. Three cases documented. Lennie buried 'em all.

MARTINELLE: You never touched any of 'em.

HOLLY: Well . . . no. Why would I do that? I hardly even let Lennie touch me. He was about as much fun as pressin' fat into a halfslip.

Sighs.

Maybe it's just men on the whole. First thing I said to him once we got married was, 'Lennie, get me a vodka an' a single bed. I'm not sure I like you enough'.

MARTINELLE: How do you account for precious?

HOLLY: I don't rightly know.

To stomach.

YOU'RE AN ACCIDENT. YOU CAME FROM THE POOL. I'm convinced. It was one of them naked neighbour boys relieving himself of his male instincts into the chlorine. Picture me, if you would. Picture me floatin' flat on my back whilst I'm being attacked from all sides by these teenaged sperm cells. Like Jaws. Bouncing offa my artichoke bathing cap an' taking big hefty bits outa my private parts.

MARTINELLE: An' Lennie bought that?

HOLLY: He never was one to notice a person's appearance. Finally one day when I was stickin' out to here an' he still hadn't got the picture I figured it was time to go. An' here I arrive in the wicked city of steel an' glass just like Marlo Thomas in the opening of That Girl, only them folks I was hoping to sing my theme song's all dead.

MARTINELLE: Chill out.

HOLLY: Oh, quit being such an ostrich. How should I react? OH NO. Cover my face? OH NO. There ain't nothin' wrong out there. It's always five in the a.m. Stations are always signed off. Everybody's just in bed. In bed an' not living. We're making history, Martinelle. I got the Polaroids to prove it.

MARTINELLE: Who's gonna be around to look at 'em?

HOLLY: You 'an me. Your friend Charlie if he ever gets off the phone. Baby when the time's right. THE PEOPLE NEXT DOOR.

HOLLY *goes to stool. Sits. Holds her breath and rotates herself to look through the hole in the wall. Rotates back. Exhales.*

You gotta admire their determination even if you don't care much for their disease. Such endurance. Must be more men in there than's left on the entire Isle of Manhattan.

Looks back in.

Can't tell if they're breathing or not, though. What's the name of that place?

MARTINELLE: It's the Epstein Bar. It gets boys.

HOLLY: It GOT boys. Looks like the waxworks in there.

Sniffs.

Death and cologne.

MARTINELLE: It was always that way. Charlie kinda liked them. The way they looked at him.

HOLLY: What does Charlie look like?

MARTINELLE (*lighting cigarette, leaning back*): He's beautiful. He's the most beautiful man in New York. Even when there was more left, he was the most beautiful. When the Epstein closed at four all the boys who hadn't gotten lucky used to crowd out on the sidewalk an' stare in at him.

HOLLY (*shaking head, pouring another drink*): My Lord. Hold your breath.

MARTINELLE (*gradually losing herself in the memory*): Wasn't so much like they wanted him. Charlie wouldn'ta stood for it. Least I don't think. More like they all had some idea in their heads about what pretty was an' had to make sure it was still around someplace. Even if it wasn't available. Guy used to own this place'd sit right here until the last of the boys unglued his lips from the plate glass. Then he'd wipe it down with antiseptic.

HOLLY (*catching her mood*): I think I found a disease once floating in my drink. Rolled it on my tongue like a mareschino cherry. Didn't swallow it, though.

MARTINELLE: Charlie used to put his barstool right in the middle of the floor so's nobody'd have a bad view. Some nights the boys'd all hide their drinks in their coats an' it'd be like a block party out there, only everybody was depressed. When people started not feeling so hot it was pushing on Christmas an' too cold to hang out on the streets. That's when they carved the hole in the wall. With swizel sticks. Took two months. Still, you wouldn'ta noticed the hole unless you watched it constant. Like a clock. Just another crack in the plaster getting bigger all the time. Then one night I look over an' see there's twenty faces sipping outa fairy straws an' staring in at Charlie. Not saying a word. Charlie knew they was there but pretended not to notice. Just moved his stool to where everybody could see. He said his being beautiful was the closest thing most people in this city ever got to having a religion.

HOLLY: Charlie had an awful lotta girlfriends, huh?

MARTINELLE: Before. Now me. I'm Charlie's lump of pleasure.

MARTINELLE *coughs suddenly, violently. There is a tense silence as* HOLLY *studies her.*

HOLLY: Smoke went down the wrong tube, huh?

MARTINELLE (*stubbing out cigarette*): I AM SICK TO DEATH OF DOING MY NAILS. I WANT TO DO MY FACE. I WANT A MIRROR.

HOLLY: I'll take a picture.

MARTINELLE: Don't you dare. I don't want a record of myself looking like this. Somebody might make copies an' post 'em. I'd never work again.

HOLLY: I'll do your makeup. It'd be a pleasure.

MARTINELLE (*knowingly*): I bet it would.

HOLLY: I hate to put a damper on your evening, Martinelle, but wake up an' smell the fucking roses. I am the only one here's looking at you. Anything you'd fix'd be for my benefit alone. An' I think you look just fine.

MARTINELLE (*glumly*): I don't feel like I'm in the room without a mirror. And there's Charlie . . .

HOLLY: Your Charlie's been on the payphone an awful long time.

MARTINELLE: So? He's trying to get me some business.

HOLLY: Don't you think you should bring him a club soda or something? It's been two days.

MARTINELLE: Ain't no reflection on my being popular. All the conventions have been rerouted to healthier climates.

HOLLY: I'm runnin' kinda low on hair spray. Two days more an' you'll be embarrassed to have him meet me.

MARTINELLE (*indicating* HOLLY'*s drink*): Two days more an' you're gonna have to get scraped up off the floor.

HOLLY (*primping hair*): No, no. I guess I'm fine. I'm enjoying my vacation.

To stomach.

HOW YOU DOING IN THERE LITTLE PRECIOUS?

MARTINELLE: He's fermenting.

HOLLY: He's fine. He just kicked twice an' that means he's fine.

To stomach.

STOP KICKING YOUR MOMMY. MY INNARDS ARE NOT AN ESCALATOR.

Laughs.

Yes, Lord, I am having fun.

MARTINELLE *glares at her.*

HOLLY: Well, sweethart, SOMEBODY'S got to.

MARTINELLE: Sure. You an' the nuns. They all escaped the convent. Last three months they been riding around the city in a yellow schoolbus drunk outa their habits an' firebombing the neighbourhood so it'll be sterile for the Last Judgement. Hook up with them.

HOLLY: Nuns don't have hair.

MARTINELLE: Charlie says they'll live forever. They don't touch nobody but themselves.

HOLLY: I don't think that holds true anymore, dear. Now they're saying it travels on the air. Like radio waves.

MARTINELLE: Change the subject.

HOLLY: An' there was that entire high school in Lincoln, Nebraska that came down with it during a pep rally. I read it in a magazine.

MARTINELLE: Talk about something else.

HOLLY (*insulted*): I thought I was being topical. I'll get Charlie off the phone for you.

MARTINELLE: He's busy.

HOLLY: Give you someone else to interrupt.

MARTINELLE: He's doing business. He don't like to be bothered when he's doing business.

HOLLY (*arrogant, rising*): Well, he doesn't know me from Eve. I'd be a pregnant stranger.

MARTINELLE (*seductively*): Stick around. We can have some fun.

HOLLY (*flouncing away*): I need a little stretch. Get the alcohol circulating.

MARTINELLE: I'll do Miss Liberty. If you give me a quarter. It's gotta be official.

HOLLY: And do I get to wear your shoes?

MARTINELLE: I guess. An' find some music. I can't do it without music.

HOLLY *ambles over to MARTINELLE's table. Holds quarter out.*

MARTINELLE: Put it on the table. I'm not an automat.

HOLLY *takes shoes. Sits on stool, puts them on. Holds radio on the shelf of her stomach searching for dance music. Gets dead air. MARTINELLE turns her back and begins to undress. Music plays. HOLLY stretches her feet out in front of her, pretending to examine shoes, in fact staring hungrily at MARTINELLE.*

HOLLY: Oh, I love these shoes. I want to be buried in these shoes.

MARTINELLE *has stripped to her bra and panties. She opens her suitcase and takes out large silver stars that she applies to strategic points of her anatomy. Takes out crown, roller skates, puts them on. Also a huge torch made of sparklers.*

HOLLY: Does one dare to walk in these shoes? I mean, they are so very attractive, but you could fall an' break your hair.

MARTINELLE (*adjusting crown*): When I do this for the shut-in Charlie spray paints me green. He leaves a patch clear on my back so the skin can ventilate. I look pretty authentic. I've been asked back forty-three times.

MARTINELLE *rises and rolls to the centre of the room. She holds the unlit torch in one hand, a butane lighter in the other.*

HOLLY (*gasping, then bellowing*): LOOK AT YOU.

MARTINELLE: It helps if you pretend like waves.

HOLLY *drunkenly slams down her drink, holds a hand to her heart.*

HOLLY (*holding back tears*): NOW WHO WOULDA THOUGHT? WHO WOULDA EVER? If it wasn't for all that looting shaking me up so much the other day that I needed to duck in here for a snoot, we never woulda met. Never. Never ever. Every plague must have a silver lining, Martinelle, and the silver lining here is that we got to meet.

MARTINELLE: WOULD YOU KNOCK IT OFF WITH THE DISEASE ALL THE TIME?

HOLLY (*awed, a hand in her mouth*): OOOOOHHH.

MARTINELLE: You are the most gruesome person I ever met in my LIFE.

HOLLY: THANK YOU LORD. SHE'S BEAUTIFUL.

MARTINELLE: An' I go through all the damn trouble of getting into my working gear for some GHOUL . . .

HOLLY: WHERE'S THE CAMERA? WHERE'S THE CAMERA?

HOLLY *takes a flash picture of MARTINELLE.*

MARTINELLE: I TOLD YOU NOT TO TAKE MY PICTURE. I DON'T

WANNA BE REMEMBERED LIKE THIS.

HOLLY: I'D TOUCH YOU. I'D TOUCH YOU BUT I KNOW I'D CRY.

MARTINELLE: GET WITHIN THREE FEET OF ME AN' I'LL THROW YOU AN' PRECIOUS OUT THE FUCKING WINDOW.

HOLLY *rises drunkenly from her stool, a finger outstretched.*

HOLLY: I'LL TAKE THE RISK. I'LL TAKE IT. ONE FINGER FOR ONE TEAR.

MARTINELLE (*skating away from her*): YOU DEMENTED? AIN'T YOU NEVER SEEN A WOMAN BEFORE? DIDN'T YOU NEVER TAKE A SHOWER AFTER PHYS. ED.? HOLLY. YOU'RE EXPECTING.

HOLLY *reaches for MARTINELLE. MARTINELLE swings the torch. HOLLY stumbles on the platform shoes and falls on her stomach. HOLLY's hands reach quickly for her belly. She lets out a quick gasp.*

MARTINELLE: Holly? You okay? Is it the baby?

HOLLY *rolls on her back, stares up at the ceiling in shock.*

HOLLY (*after a long silence*): SQUISH.

Roars with laughter.

Oh, squish squish squish. Wrap me in plastic an' take me away.

Rubs stomach.

Hey there inside, little precious. Mommy loves you.

MARTINELLE *stares in disbelief. Skates around the room like a roller derby queen.*

MARTINELLE: BIIITCH. GET OUTA MY SHOES. GET YOUR IDIOT FEET OUTA MY GOOD SHOES. THAT BABY'S GONNA POP OUTA YOU ANY SECOND LIKE A TOMATO BOIL AN' BAG DINNER AN' THOSE SHOES COST ME FIFTY BUCKS.

MARTINELLE *rolls to the bar and pours herself a drink. Downs it. DWAYNE appears at the hole in the wall. He is dressed as before, but dirty and dishevelled. He wears a name sticker which reads, 'REMEMBER ME . . . DWAYNE . . . EPSTEIN BAR'.*

DWAYNE (*smiling, revealing a mouthful of braces*): PEOPLE.

MARTINELLE *gapes.* HOLLY *is oblivious.*

You don't have to stare at me. I know what I look like.

MARTINELLE: Who are you?

DWAYNE: Possible the ugliest boy left in New York. And what state are YOU representing?

MARTINELLE: I was just getting ready for the talent competition. The lush on the floor was gonna get Miss Congeniality, but the judges figured out at the last minute that she wasn't a virgin.

HOLLY *giggles from floor.*

Shut up, you. She got disqualified.

DWAYNE: What's your talent?

MARTINELLE *goes to her 'working' barstool, seductive.*

MARTINELLE: I'm famous for my fingernails. They etch glass. I'm Martinelle. That's French for something. When I was younger people used to call me Marty. I've developed since. I got a friend Charlie tells me I sound like something you'd order after dinner in a fancy restaurant. You look like a tongue sitting there.

DWAYNE (*climbing through hole, going to bar*): Is there any food?

MARTINELLE: Garnishes. Cherries. I'll let you buy me a drink.

DWAYNE: Isn't it free?

MARTINELLE: Everything's on the house tonight. But it's the thought that counts.

DWAYNE: Anything special?

MARTINELLE: I'm extremely easy. You're a school kid, ain't you? I should make you show me your . . . identification. How old are you, anyways?

DWAYNE: I hope to be eighteen on my next birthday.

MARTINELLE: I won't tell a soul. Times like these you get the urge to rush things. This your first bar?

DWAYNE: Actually, I've been living in the men's room next door.

MARTINELLE (*disappointed*): Figures.

DWAYNE: I heard you screaming from in there. I thought, LIFE.

MARTINELLE: How come you live in the can?

DWAYNE: The bulb's been out for ages and people keep telling me I look better in the dark. It's the only way I can make contact.

MARTINELLE (*to herself*): Everybody's a deal.

DWAYNE: I guess we always go back to the places we were most happy.

MARTINELLE: There a mirror in there?

DWAYNE: Somebody broke it while I was sleeping. I thought it was this one guy I'd been cruising for a while, but he turned out to be dead.

MARTINELLE: Bet you was never big on mirrors anyway.

HOLLY (*rising from floor*): HOLD YOUR BREATH, MARTINELLE.

DWAYNE: OH. SHE'S TERRIFIC.

MARTINELLE: No she's not.

HOLLY: It's all your fault. All this pain. You an' your kind. YOU started this.

DWAYNE: Don't you read the magazines? We're just trendy.

HOLLY: HOLD YOUR BREATH.

DWAYNE: With my luck I'll live forever. Nobody wants me.

HOLLY *sits on barstool, puffing her cheeks and holding her breath. Sticks out her feet to examine shoes.*

I KNOW THOSE SHOES.

MARTINELLE: They're mine.

DWAYNE: You used to work the corner of thirty-fourth and eighth.

MARTINELLE (*pleased, but nonchalant*): And sometimes the highway, depending on the weather.

DWAYNE: I had a friend who was ready to kill for those shoes.

MARTINELLE: They're one of a kind.

DWAYNE: Iris Schoenberger. She was ready to cut your feet off.

MARTINELLE: Do I know this person?

DWAYNE: Iris was my best friend from Saint Hilda's. She was Jewish, but her parents sent her there so she'd have to wear a uniform. She had the wildest taste in clothes. All the girls used to have their heads covered for chapel in the morning and Iris used to wear this four foot tall thing made of real fruit. She'd wear it every day, till it got mouldy or the insects started to bother her. We'd hang out at the Epstein together. Used to see you when we were coming out of the subway.

MARTINELLE: You two musta made quite a couple. She working the men's room too?

DWAYNE: She's institutionalized. Her mom was a shrink and had her pierce her ears at the age of seven so she could express her individuality. By the time I met her she was wearing phone receivers off her earlobes. She caught them on the rings once in gym. Bounced on the cords for half an hour screaming how she wasn't in right now while the nuns tried to pull her down. Her dad had her committed and her mom published an article on it.

MARTINELLE: Shame how things happen.

DWAYNE: I went to visit her once. She'd lost eighty pounds and was wearing a dozen hypo-allergenic pearls out of the one ear that wasn't ripped through. It was right after the first cases were reported. What the papers called 'The Winter That No One Had Sex.' Iris kept clippings. 'What FUN,' she said. 'What FUN to die and be an event. If dying's on your dance card at least die of something mysterious. Get lots of attention.'

MARTINELLE: They musta had her on something.

DWAYNE: Who knows? Maybe they let

her out. It doesn't matter. Pretty soon people are gonna be floating out on the ocean. Living on barges. Not many places left.

HOLLY *holds the radio in her lap. Dance music plays. Gentle, futuristic.*

HOLLY (*dreamy, to herself*): Music . . .

DWAYNE: How come you stayed?

MARTINELLE: Lotsa reasons. I know who I am here.

DWAYNE: It used to be this city was the one place you could live in your head twenty-four hours a day and have it condoned by everybody. It's the only city in the world's got steam coming up from the streets. It's not that way anymore.

MARTINELLE: Who says? Things ain't different. Just deal with what you want to. Same as before. Like, I don't want to 'deal' with you. I wanna dance.

Leans over to read his nametag.

Come on, Dwayne. Dance with the national monument.

DWAYNE (*rising, spining her on skates*): MISS LIBERTINE.

MARTINELLE (*laughing*): Yeah. If you was the only boy in the world and I was the only girl . . .

MARTINELLE *skates to the middle of the floor.* DWAYNE *follows. She stands behind him, steadying herself, her hands around his waist. They dance.*

MARTINELLE (*dreamily*): This is what I needed. This is like real people

HOLLY *ambles over. She cautiously places her hands on* MARTINELLE'*s bare midriff.*

MARTINELLE: You back?

HOLLY (*with great longing*): Please. It's my first New York party.

They dance in their line. MARTINELLE *dreamily running her hands over* DWAYNE'*s chest,* HOLLY *over* MARTINELLE'*s stomach,* DWAYNE *with his arms in the air. The lighting should be quite dim at this point. Dreamlike.*

MARTINELLE: This is good.

HOLLY (*trying to catch the mood*): Maybe Charlie'll get off the phone and join us. We could have a squaredance.

DWAYNE: There's a man here?

HOLLY: Maybe shut-in's from all over New York will hear our music and join us. People'll keep adding on an' we'll stretch clear out the bar, across the bridge to Jersey . . .

DWAYNE: You didn't tell me there was a man here.

HOLLY: . . . all the way to Pennsylvania where the air's still good.

DWAYNE: Who is the man?

HOLLY (*romantically*): The most beautiful man in New York city.

DWAYNE: Really?

HOLLY: Even when there was more left, he was the most beautiful. He's Martinelle's beau. Ain't I right, Martinelle?

MARTINELLE (*eyes closed, to herself*): As long as Charlie's hanging out, there's still beauty.

DWAYNE (*breaking from line*): Opposites attract. Maybe I should meet him.

MARTINELLE (*waking up*): He's busy.

DWAYNE: I just want a peek.

HOLLY (*clinging to* MARTINELLE): They's gonna roll off together into the night an' leave poor old Holly alone. Leave her to limp away into these wicked streets an' drop her baby the natural way.

MARTINELLE (*interrupting* HOLLY'*s speech*): Dwayne!

HOLLY: Sure hope it learns to talk quick. I'm runnin' low on things to say to myself

MARTINELLE (*breaking from* HOLLY): DON'T GO.

DWAYNE (*straightening tie*): Pickings are slim.

MARTINELLE *skates to bar, retrieving torch and lighter.*

MARTINELLE (*reciting desperately, badly*): GIVE ME YOUR TIRED, YOUR POOR

YOUR HUDDLED MASSES
  YEARNING TO BREATHE
  FREE,
THE WRETCHED REFUSE OF
  YOUR TEEMING SHORE,
SEND THESE, THE HOMELESS,
  TEMPEST TOSSED TO ME.

Lights sparkler torch, holding it up.

I LIFT MY LAMP BESIDE THE
  GOLDEN DOOR.

DWAYNE (*exiting off to payphone*):
Wish me luck.

MARTINELLE (*terrified, holding back
tears*): WELL IT HELPS IF YOU
ROCK BACK AN' FORTH. SOME
PEOPLE LIKE THAT. CHARLIE
ALWAYS SAID I HAD A LOT OF
TALENT. DWAYNE?? YOU
HOMELY TEMPEST TOSSED
FUCK!

HOLLY (*waving American flag*): Oh,
that was wonderful. That was worth all
the misery you put me through tonight.
Better'n the real thing, I'll bet. Her
stars don't twinkle when she moves.

*The music ends. A news report comes
on the radio. It is barely audible,
occasional phrases picked up through
the static.*

RADIO ANNOUNCER: Transmitted
sexually, through bodily fluids . . .

MARTINELLE (*crying, holding torch*):
Please, turn that off.

HOLLY: Radio's got moveable parts.

RADIO ANNOUNCER: . . . expected
mortality rate one hundred per cent
. . .

HOLLY: I don't think it's true what they
say. I think it's carried on the air. Like
snow.

MARTINELLE *watches helplessly as
her sparklers fizzle out. Turns off the
radio. Sits at the table with her head
in her hands.*

HOLLY (*drunk, child-like*): Never
snowed once back in Aurora. Did once
before I was born but everybody called
that a freak of nature. Used to have to
decorate the tree with soap flakes.
Spray the window an' carve out
pictures with a razor blade.

DWAYNE *enters.*

DWAYNE: I used to watch him through
the window.

MARTINELLE: Don't tell me how bad
he looks. I don't want to cope.

HOLLY: He's the most beautiful man
. . .

DWAYNE: He's decomposing.

HOLLY (*accusingly*): You said . . .

MARTINELLE: I said he was on the
payphone. I didn't say if he was
breathing. Christ. Hell of a time to
start taking me literal.

DWAYNE (*gently*): I'm real sorry.

MARTINELLE (*holding back tears,
ashamed*): Yeah? Well THANKS.
THANKS A LOT. I mean, you wanna
remember people when they look their
best, right? Take baby pictures but not
funeral shots, 'less you're real strange,
right? Like, not going out anymore
'cause it doesn't feel the same. You
know? You know what I'm talking
about? First day I go in an' do his hair
with the pick way he liked it. Second
day I go in an' there's a FLY sittin' on
one of his eyeballs. I screamed an' it
flew away. I ain't been back. Holly
shows up the next day with morning
sickness. What a deal she is.

HOLLY (*self-righteous*): You must have
loved him very much to deceive me in
such a manner.

MARTINELLE: I WAS ONE GIRL
OUT OF THIRTY. HE DIDN'T
KNOW MY *NAME* HALF THE
TIME. Hadda carve it on the fucking
barstool. I was Girlie, the one with the
shoes.

HOLLY: Deceitful, terrible thing to do.

MARTINELLE: Gets a lesion on his
cheek an' runs around breaking all the
mirrors. My compact even. I told him,
I told him 'Charlie, I gotta face too. I
gotta face too needs inspecting once in
a while.' He told me I didn't need no
mirror. He's the best mirror a girl
could ever have. I'm the only one who
stayed. Don't matter none if he gives it
to me too. I'm the only one left an' get
to sleep on the mattress with him down
in the beer room. I don't care. We

could wake up in the middle of the
night sweating an' coughing in
harmony an' that'd be fine, 'cause it's
Charlie an' pretty counts. FINE that
he keeps me working to get his mind
off his health. FINE that he calls me
Girlie when we're making love. FINE.
FINE.

HOLLY: Just who is it you think you're
fooling, Miss Martinelle? I can just
imagine where your thing has been to.
You coulda picked up disease
anywhere. Off the table like a half
dollar.

MARTINELLE: After five drinks from a
clean glass they all looked like Charlie.
Charlie on a shitty day.

HOLLY: Oh, don't you just wish you'd
DIED FIRST?

MARTINELLE (*after a pause*): No.

HOLLY (*drinking from bottle*): I'd cry,
but I'd run my liner.

DWAYNE (*to MARTINELLE,
comforting*): I was really in love once
with this guy who used to hang out at
the Epstein. I'd send him beers and
he'd nod and once I even smiled back.
Figured we'd built up some kind of
relationship and he wouldn't care that
I had braces. I didn't know what
colour eyes he had.

HOLLY (*dryly*): You both just break my
heart. My heart's just breaking.

HOLLY *removes a sheet of cleaner's
plastic from her suitcase. Holds it over
her mouth as if to protect herself from
germs.*

DWAYNE: Dumb stuff like eye colour
gets important at night. When you're
alone. One night when we were all
crowded out on the street here I sent
Iris over to find out. She stood next to
him for ten minutes. Finally she just
yelled, 'Shit if I can tell', then she
handed him a banana off her hat, and
he walked away. I left Iris glued to the
window and I followed him. I followed
him for miles and it was snowing. And
when it snows I always feel my age. I
can date my life by snowstorms. He
went into this place where there was
this little blonde transvestite sitting in a
booth, who directed me to a dark
room full of stalls. He was standing in

one. With the door closed. I waited for
him to notice me . . . wishing he would
come out or tell me to go away or
invite me for coffee, so I could tell him
that Iris was only looking at his eyes.
Finally, I just went into the stall next
to his where he couldn't see me and I
could think. I put my hands out to
brace myself, because it was dark and
I was drunk, and I felt his penis
coming through a hole in the wall. I
knelt on the floor and he shot all over
my braces and I stayed there, for what
seemed like hours hoping for
something. A kiss maybe. But he was
long gone. And I never saw him again.
Never. I went back to the holes a few
times after that and got friendly with
the transvestite, whose name was
Bunny, who said to me, 'Don't you
just HATE it when people disappear
like that? Don't you always think
they're DEAD?' Which was sort of
funny, because Bunny lived his life
through the personal ads. Bunny came
down with it and I went to visit him in
St. Vincents. Day before he died he
said to me, 'ENOUGH ALREADY. I
RENOUNCE MY LIFESTYLE. MY
NAME IS *SHERMAN*.' And he ripped
the wig off his head and pulled out a
black leather motorcycle cap from
under his bed that he'd been saving for
just such an emergency.

HOLLY: Sick, unnatural, and unhealthy.

DWAYNE: There's lots of ways to
embrace death.

HOLLY: If I had a son like you I'd bury
my head in the dirt. You'd embrace
anything.

DWAYNE (*grinning*): Anything that'd
embrace me back.

HOLLY (*abandoning plastic*): You
know I ain't sure I feel like being in
the room with either one of you at this
point. I have to thank God that when
MY life passes before my eyes I'll be
able to recognize all the faces pressin'
down on top of ME. Martinelle, you
may be the last woman left in New
York, but I've got by long enough
without you an' I'll find in me the
strength to do it again.

MARTINELLE: So go.

HOLLY (*losing conviction*): Cut the germs with a knife in here.

MARTINELLE: I ain't stopping you. I got company.

HOLLY: Maybe I'll just hold my breath.

HOLLY *sits on barstool holding hairspray. She defiantly puffs her cheeks. Her stomach has shifted noticeably.*

MARTINELLE (*confused*): Holly?

DWAYNE *advances on her, grinning.* HOLLY *tries to press her stomach back into form.*

HOLLY: Stay away from me now. You hear? Stay away.

DWAYNE *reaches up her dress.* HOLLY *screams.* DWAYNE *spins her on her stool.* HOLLY *sprays him with hairspray.*

OZONE. OZONE. STAY AWAY FROM ME. OZONE. STAY AWAY. I'M ENJOYING MY VACATION.

DWAYNE *removes a pillow in a Happy Face pillow case from beneath HOLLY's dress. It is leaking large amounts of feathers.*

DWAYNE (*shaking out feathers, laughing*): I hope you weren't expecting twins.

DWAYNE *and* MARTINELLE *howl with laughter.* HOLLY *grabs the pillow and attempts to stuff it back up her dress.*

HOLLY: DON'T YOU LOOK AT ME THAT WAY. BOTH OF YOU. BOTH OF YOU. I AM NOT WELL. I AM NOT A WELL LADY. DON'T YOU LAUGH AT ME, MARTINELLE. LIFE'S PRECIOUS. LIFE'S PRECIOUS.

HOLLY *reaches into her hair and effortlessly pulls out handfulls, holding it out to them, helpless.* MARTINELLE *and* DWAYNE *stop laughing for a moment, then begin again. Their laughter continues throughout the remainder of the play.*

DWAYNE: So what do we do now?

MARTINELLE: Paint my nails, I guess.

DWAYNE: Did you know your nails keep growing after you die? And your hair?

MARTINELLE (*her laughter mixed with coughing*): Say, Holly. You think your husband could exhume me once a month for a manicure and a perm? I'm going quick.

DWAYNE: We could turn on the lights and have Last Call. See what we really look like.

MARTINELLE: No. No, I never liked that part of the night. Not even in real time.

DWAYNE: I never saw a face once at the Glory Holes. Just cocks. Some nights they seemed to sprout from the walls. Like poison mushrooms.

MARTINELLE: Except you're too hungry to care. Too damn lonely.

DWAYNE: We could write our names on the bathroom wall. And the date.

MARTINELLE (*howling with laughter*): Somebody's in there. I think it's your friend Iris.

DWAYNE: We could save it for tomorrow.

HOLLY (*panicked*): ARE YOU ALL GOING SOMEWHERE?

MARTINELLE: Hey there, Little Mother.

HOLLY: ARE YOU LEAVING ME?

MARTINELLE *chuckles. Goes to* HOLLY. *Kneels on the floor and hugs her tightly.*

MARTINELLE: No, honey. I think Martinelle's staying in tonight. She's already at the party.

HOLLY: I never will forget you, Martinelle. Even if you go first, I still got your picture. I'll put it under my pillow like wedding cake.

MARTINELLE *laughs.* DWAYNE *turns on the radio.*

RADIO ANNOUNCER: . . . several months ahead of schedule, estimating the population of New York City, to this date the most severely ravaged of this country's urban centres, at somewhere in the vicinity of zero.

HOLLY (*admonishing radio*): THREE

AT LEAST. AT LEAST THREE.

RADIO: Evacuation procedures are
currently in effect in:
Montgomery, Alabama;
Little Rock, Arkansas;
Phoenix, Arizona;
San Francisco and Los Angeles,
California;
Boulder, Colorado;
Bridgeport, Connecticut;
Tallahassee, Florida;
Atlanta, Georgia;
Chicago, Illinois;
South Bend, Indiana;
Des Moines, Iowa;
New Orleans, Louisiana;
Boston, Massachusetts;
Bangor, Maine;
Jefferson City, Missouri;
Jackson, Mississippi;
Billings, Montana;
Lincoln, Nebraska;
Concord, New Hampshire;
Newark, New Jersey;
Santa Fe, New Mexico;
Raleigh, North Carolina;
Salem, Oregon;
Providence, Rhode Island . . .

MARTINELLE (*her ear to* HOLLY's
stomach): I HEARD A KICK. I DID.
DWAYNE.

HOLLY (*contentedly*): He kicked twice.
that means he's happy.

DWAYNE: I fell asleep once in the
Glory Holes and missed school. A
porter woke me up in the morning and
I thought he was God.

Laughs wistfully

Oh, it's too amazing. It was.
Everything and all of it. Too amazing.
Too much . . .

Smiles, hugs himself.

Freedom.

MARTINELLE *smiles warmly at*
DWAYNE. *Goes back to embracing*
HOLLY. *Prologue music begins to
filter in.* DWAYNE *rises. He picks up
handfuls of Holly's stray feathers.*
DWAYNE *blows the feathers around
the room, keeping them aloft on the
gentle wind of his breath. The effect is
that of snow.* HOLLY *watches in
wonder. She reaches out a hand to the
vision of the blizzard surrounding her*

*as the lights slowly dim to black.
Music, the constant drone of
evacuating cities, and*
MARTINELLE's *laughter mixed with
coughing continue in the darkness.*

LEVITATION

For John and Mertrice

TIMOTHY MASON has spent most of his life working in theatre, first as an actor in his native Minneapolis, and then as a playwright. He has won the National Society of Arts and Letters Award, a playwriting fellowship from the National Endowment for the Arts, the Twin Cities Drama Critics Circle Award, the Hollywood Drama-logue Critics Award for Outstanding Achievement in Theatre (for *Levitation*) and was nominated for *Newsday*'s Oppenheimer Award (*Levitation*). His plays include *In a Northern Landscape*, first produced by the Actors Theatre of Louisville in 1983; *Levitation*, which premièred in New York at the Circle Repertory Company in 1984; *Bearclaw*, initially presented in 1984 by Lucille Lortell and Circle Repertory at the White Barn Theatre in Westport, Connecticut; *Before I Got My Eye Put Out*, produced in 1985 by the South Coast Repertory in Costa Mesa, California and *Only You*, presented by New York's Circle Repertory in 1987.

Levitation

Several years ago, as the members of my family were sitting down to their Christmas Eve supper, my mother turned to one of my brothers and said, sotto voce, 'Whatever you do, don't get your father going on levitation.' I have the story second-hand from my brother, but I choose to believe it; in the context of my family, it has plausibility.

I began with this, and the fragmented collection of a lifetime of memories – swatches of remembered or half-remembered or invented plausibilities – and tried to make of them a patchwork which would clothe me when I was cold and comfort me when I was fearful.

The fact is, I had been feeling frightened and chilled for a couple of years. At some point in my twenties, I recognized the inevitability of my parents' mortality, and it nearly paralysed me. That recognition led to an awareness of my own mortality and that of others around me.

We all have parents. We all lose them. We all lose a great deal.

If it's true that you can't go home again, it's also true that you can't write about going home again without committing cliché. Since that was exactly what I intended to do when I began *Levitation*, I chose for my setting one of the most blatant clichés of the American stage: the old front porch. I thought the sight of a porch swing at rise might lull an audience into believing they were in for a naturalistic sort of evening, which would only intensify their sense of mild mystery as the naturalism began to unravel. I even hoped that by the close of play, these strangers in the dark might recognize that although the author's intent was wholly serious, regarding the setting his tongue was in the vicinity of his cheek. Some didn't; some did.

For those producing this play, I feel quite certain that there should be no directorial nods toward otherworldliness, nor should there be such hints in décor or costume. One should play it as it lays, and if the characters speak in language which might seem poetic to some, it should be remembered that there are regions of the American midwest (and elsewhere, I'm sure), where people are raised on the speech of the Bible (King James' Version), and the way they talk does not sound poetic, or lyrical, or sentimental, to them or anyone else.

I know that the night when my mother and father and I sat together in New York's Circle Repertory Theatre and watched this play marked one of the high points of my life. I was given the all too rare and, I think, enviable opportunity to speak to my parents about our shared mortality. (My father's only criticism of the piece was that I had not done justice to his scientific thinking and the book he had written, not on time-travel and levitation, but a serious work on the origins of the universe. And, indeed, I hadn't.)

Since that production, and others I've seen here and there around the United States, I have heard from a good number of strangers (and friends) who have written me about the comfort which the play provided them. I even played the part of Joe at the Portland Stage Company in Maine and there, for the sake of the role, temporarily reassumed the paralysis of fear from which the writing of *Levitation* freed me.

More than anything else I have written, I think of this play as a gift – to my friends and family, to a large body of strangers, and to my parents.

Timothy Mason
New York City, 1987

Levitation was first presented by the Circle Repertory Company, in New York City, on 12 February 1984. It was directed by B. Rodney Marriott; the setting was by David Potts; costumes were by Laura Crow; the lighting was by Dennis Parichy; the sound was by Chuck London Media/Stewart Werner; original music was by Norman L. Berman; and the production stage manager was Jody Boese. The cast, in order of appearance, was as follows:

JOE	Ben Siegler
ARTHUR	Michael Higgins
ADA	Lenka Peterson
MICHAEL	Eric Schiff
IRA	Bruce McCarty
JEAN	Trish Hawkins
INGA	Helen Stenborg
WRIGHT	Matthew Lewis
TOM	Adam Davidson

A residential section of Minneapolis. August.

*The early morning hours of an August
night. The front porch and façade of a
middle-class midwestern urban home,
dimly lit by a yellowed porch lamp; wood
siding, a porch swing and chairs, empty
clay flower-pots stacked one inside the
other. Crickets.*

*Headlights swing across the face of the
house and come to rest. A car door
slams.*

Enter JOE, *29, wearing jeans and
sneakers and a sweat-drenched tee-shirt.
He crosses the yard carrying a six-pack
of beer, sees the headlights shining on
the house, turns and exits. The car door
opens, the headlights are extinguished,
and the door slams.*

JOE *enters again, and climbs the steps
to the porch, searching his pockets for
the house keys. He opens the screen
door and drops the keys.*

JOE: Damn!

*He picks up the keys. He looks at the
locked door. He looks at the darkened
windows. Suddenly, his entire body
sags with a weary reluctance to enter
the house. He gives up for the
moment, slowly takes off his tee-shirt,
and collapses into the porch swing.*

ARTHUR (*from the darkness of the
lawn*): That brings me back. (JOE
leaps up, startled by the voice.)

JOE: Geez!

ARTHUR (*approaching*): Reminds me
of your senior class play.

JOE: Dad!

ARTHUR *is about 70, and dressed in
pyjamas.*

ARTHUR: Did I frighten you?

JOE: Good God! Dad! You nearly killed
me, that's all. What . . . (*Catching his
breath.*) What on earth are you doing
out here. Now. In your pyjamas.

ARTHUR: It reminded me of that play
you were in. In high school, that scene
where you came home drunk and
couldn't get the keys into the door. Is
that the story now? You drunk?

JOE: For goodness' sake, Dad, what are
you doing out here at . . . (*He checks
his watch.*) . . . at two fifteen in the

morning. On the *lawn.*

ARTHUR: Nothing. Sitting.

JOE: What do you mean, nothing?

ARTHUR: Are you all right?

JOE: No. Yes. I mean, you nearly
scared me to death, Dad.

ARTHUR: I *am* sorry.

JOE: Killer Pop Causes Kid's Cardiac.

ARTHUR: Shhh.

JOE: More on page three.

ARTHUR: We don't want to wake
Mother.

JOE (*forced undertone*): I mean you
were waiting *up* for me? On the *lawn*?
In your *pyjamas*?

ARTHUR: For you? Oh, no. For the
stars, the shooting stars. Meteor
showers predicted for tonight. It's that
time of year. No, I wouldn't be waiting
up for you. When you come to visit,
we want you to know that you're free
to come and go whenever you wish.
No, I set up a lawn-chair earlier, just
over there, a couple of them. And a
little folding-table, and a pitcher of
orange juice. You want some?

JOE: No.

ARTHUR (*looking up at the sky*):
Nothing so far, though. You were
awfully good in that play.

JOE: Preacher Praises Prize
Performance.

ARTHUR: Who writes the headlines
when you're not in New York?

JOE: Gnomes. And fairies. I guess I am
a little drunk.

ARTHUR: Then you shouldn't drive.
And you shouldn't be drunk in the first
place.

JOE: Wow. You. Here. Middle of the
night. Dressed in pyjamas and waiting
for the stars to fall. I mean it. This is
exactly how I want to remember you.

ARTHUR: Well. That's what I'm here
for, isn't it?

Small pause, ARTHUR *looking into
the sky.*

JOE: I guess so. (*Small pause.*) You do this often?

ARTHUR: Well, in August I do. When I can.

JOE: How long are you going to wait?

ARTHUR: Until we hit some. It's not as though *they* hit *us*, you see. *We* run into *them*. There are swarms of meteors that cross the path of the earth's orbit, and every year, on the same day every year, we run smack into them.

JOE: And today's the day?

ARTHUR: Well, different swarms, different days.

JOE: I see.

ARTHUR: What we'll be seeing tonight are known as the 'Tears of St. Lawrence.'

JOE: Sit down, Dad. Tell me about it.

ARTHUR: 65,000 miles per hour when they enter the atmosphere, some of them. They're fragments from a comet. The Perseid Shower, it's called. Where were you?

JOE: Out.

ARTHUR: Oh, I wasn't trying to pry. Your mother and I want you to know that when you come to town, we're not going to try to *pry*, for goodness' sake.

JOE: I appreciate that.

ARTHUR (*after a small pause*): It's just that you're so sweaty, I was wondering where you were. (*Small pause.*) Not that it matters. (*Small pause.*) Warm August night, it's natural you should sweat.

JOE: I was out dancing, Dad. (*Pause.*)

ARTHUR: Good exercise.

JOE: Yup.

ARTHUR: You're in pretty good shape.

JOE: Pretty good.

ARTHUR: Made you sweat something awful.

JOE: Uh-huh.

ARTHUR: You see Paul?

JOE: Yes, as a matter of fact.

ARTHUR: Yes, as a matter of fact. How was he?

JOE: Ambulatory. I don't know, Dad. I saw him, I didn't speak with him.

ARTHUR: Mother and I had him out here to dinner not long ago. He was fine then.

JOE: Good.

ARTHUR: After dinner he washed the dishes.

JOE: That's nice.

ARTHUR: Does this bother you?

JOE: No.

ARTHUR: Good. (*Small pause.*) Before dinner he mowed the lawn.

JOE: Geez!

ARTHUR: You two don't talk anymore?

JOE: Sometimes. Not much.

ARTHUR: You know, I've got a theory that the speed of light is *not* the speed limit of the universe.

JOE: No kidding.

ARTHUR: No, sir, I am not kidding. No, this is a theory that will take Einstein one step further. I've been working on it for the past couple of months, and now I am convinced: there is definitely something in the universe which travels faster than light.

JOE: What?

ARTHUR (*deliberately*): I'm . . . not . . . sure. (JOE *laughs.*) I *mean*: I'm not sure I want to *say* just yet. Not until I've had a chance to develop my theory a little more.

JOE (*pulling a can of beer from his six-pack*): You want a beer, Reverend?

ARTHUR: The thing to remember is that things here are not what they seem.

JOE: Tonight especially.

ARTHUR: Especially tonight.

JOE: A beer? (*Beat.*) Go ahead, Mom's asleep.

ARTHUR: Are you sure you should have another?

JOE: Positive.

ARTHUR: Well, in that case I'll join you. (JOE *opens a can and gives it to ARTHUR.*) Just one, now.

JOE: That's all you're getting. (JOE *opens a beer for himself. The two of them sit back on the swing and watch the night sky.*) Parson Poses Speedy Theory. (*Small pause.*) Fire from Heaven: Miracle or Menace? (*Longer pause.*) Pop to Einstein: Drop Dead.

ARTHUR: That could get a little tiring.

JOE: Gosh, Pa, don't I know it.

ARTHUR: But you're pretty good at it, aren't you?

JOE: When it comes to alliteration, nobody can touch me.

ARTHUR: Then you should be proud of what you do.

JOE: Ruined Writer Holds Head High. Finds Meaning in Macramé.

ARTHUR: I'm serious.

JOE: So'm I.

ARTHUR: Maybe if you didn't always write plays about death . . .

JOE: What?!

ARTHUR: People might warm to your work a little more.

JOE: I do *not* always write about death.

ARTHUR: Or, you know, crippling diseases . . . patricide . . . fratricide . . .

JOE: Dad . . .

ARTHUR: . . . ulcers. What was the title of that last play?

JOE (*sullenly, after a pause*): Her Final Summer.

ARTHUR: There, you see? I don't mean to criticize, but something's always dying.

JOE: Dammit, Dad, something always *is*. And I *do* mean to criticize.

ARTHUR: For that matter, of course, I'm dying.

JOE: Don't say that.

ARTHUR: So's your mother. So're you. You intend to attack the entire system?

JOE: Maybe. Come on, Dad, it's too late to talk about this.

ARTHUR: I'll say. It's been going on for quite some time.

JOE: As far as I'm concerned, it's been going on for exactly twenty-nine years, and I will *not* be reconciled to it, and I'm too tired to talk about it tonight. Besides, it doesn't matter anyway. I'm through with all that.

ARTHUR: All what?

JOE: The writing, the rejection, New York, all of it. I'm not going back.

ARTHUR: You're not going back.

JOE: Nope.

ARTHUR: Fine. Where *are* you going?

JOE: Nowhere.

ARTHUR: There. You see?

JOE: Dad! I'm staying *here*, that's all! And I don't want to talk about it tonight, O.K.?

ARTHUR: All right, all right. Case closed.

JOE: Good.

ARTHUR: Subject dropped.

JOE: Fine.

ARTHUR: Finis. (*Beat.*) Of course, all of us are hit by several meteorites a week, but they're the kind that weigh a billionth of a gram and fall at the speed of two feet per minute. Now that's slow. Can you picture it? Tiny fragments of the cosmos, utterly ancient, descending on our bodies with . . . such deliberation.

JOE: Carry Moonbeams Home in a Jar? It's No Joke, Says Potty Padre.

ARTHUR: But the odds have it that a more sizeable meteorite will strike one human being once every 9,300 years.

JOE: So stick around . . . (*Leans back and lights a cigarette.*)

ARTHUR: All I'm saying is, people are in need. They need miracles. They're tired of cynicism, they're looking for salvation, and you offer them death. Although I hope you don't think I'm criticizing.

JOE: Never.

ARTHUR: You have real gifts.

JOE: Thank you.

ARTHUR: And a real kindness.

JOE: Uh-huh.

ARTHUR: And we were thrilled when you called from the airport this afternoon.

JOE: I'm glad.

ARTHUR: Thrilled.

JOE: Good.

ARTHUR: Say: you *do* know where all the papers are, don't you? The deed to the house, the will . . .

JOE: You gave me the complete briefing.

ARTHUR: The key to the safe deposit box? Not that you're going to find much in there, of course. A copy of that thing I've been writing about time and travel . . . Jean's engagement announcement from the papers, that sort of thing . . .

JOE (*not wanting to hear this*): Please, Pop . . .

ARTHUR (*with a laugh*): An autograph I got when I was ten years old! (*Pause. Then* JOE *leaps to his feet and points.*)

JOE: There!

ARTHUR (*standing*): Where?

JOE: Gosh. That was lovely.

ARTHUR: Shoot.

JOE: You didn't see it?

ARTHUR: I must have missed it.

JOE: How could you miss it? It went clear across the sky.

ARTHUR (*disappointed and puzzled*): I'm an observing person.

JOE: It was beautiful.

ARTHUR: Well, I'm glad *you* spotted it, anyway.

ADA DAHL, *about 70, enters wearing a nightgown.*

JOE: There'll be others.

ARTHUR: Oh, I know.

JOE: One meteor does not a shower make.

ARTHUR: No indeed. (*Pause.*) I had a wonderful teacher when I was a boy. Oh, maybe seven years old. An old maid, they called her, but she was anything but. Of course she *was* old. Retirement age when she taught me, I suppose. And I have no doubt she was a maiden. But she was alive, completely. Miss Thorvaldson.

JOE: Miss . . .?

ARTHUR: Thorvaldson. And I remember one afternoon in late winter she asked if there was anyone in class who knew when the buds appear on the trees in spring. It was a trick question, of course, so I raised my hand and said, 'They don't. The buds appear in the fall, as soon as the old leaves drop.' And Miss Thorvaldson said, 'Now *here* is an observing boy.' (*Small pause.*) Now *here* is an observing boy.

ADA: Put your shirt on, Joe. You're all sweaty.

The two men turn.

ARTHUR: Ada! Did we wake you?

ADA (*resigned tone*): You might have. I don't know. I couldn't sleep. Put your shirt on, Joe.

JOE: Hi, Mom.

ADA: Well, what is all this?

JOE: Shooting stars.

ADA: Put your shirt on, don't be stubborn.

JOE: My shirt's as sweaty as me.

ADA: As sweaty as I.

JOE: As sweaty as I.

ADA: You always were stubborn.

ARTHUR: We were watching for meteors.

ADA (*to* JOE): Your favourite word was 'no,' always. You were 16 months old when you learned it, and it was the happiest day of your life. Have you seen Paul?

JOE (*suddenly irritated*): No.

ADA (*pleased*): There you see? All the time, 'no.'

ARTHUR: But you did see him. You told me.

JOE: Will you let me alone about Paul? What is this fascination with him?

ADA: We love him.

JOE: Right, right. (*Small pause.*) I'm sorry.

ARTHUR: No . . .

ADA: (*Going behind the swing, putting her hands on* JOE's *shoulders.*) I'm sorry. (*After a moment, taking her hands off his shoulders and wiping them on her robe.*) I'll go get you a dry shirt.

JOE: No, no – I've got one, Mom. Don't bother.

ARTHUR (*to* ADA): He was out dancing.

ADA: How'd you pry that out of him?

ARTHUR: It wasn't easy.

ADA (*to* JOE): Do you do much dancing in New York?

JOE: Not really. I was never a big dancer.

ADA: No, neither was I. But that's how you met your friend, isn't it?

JOE: What friend?

ARTHUR (*warning*): Ada . . .

ADA (*covering*): I mean, if you wanted to meet nice people your own age, you'd go out dancing or some such thing, isn't that it?

ARTHUR (*scolding*): For goodness' sake, Ada . . .

ADA (*to* ARTHUR, *embarrassed*): I know, I know . . .

JOE: What are you two up to here?

ARTHUR: Oh, you know your mother . . .

ADA (*overlapping*): Nothing, absolutely nothing . . .

ARTHUR (*overlapping*): She gets going and she doesn't know when to stop.

ADA (*overlapping*): Try to make a little conversation and people jump all over you. (*Pause.*)

JOE: *What?*

ADA (*startled, looking up*): Oh – my!

JOE (*same*): Geez.

ARTHUR: What?

ADA: Beautiful.

JOE: Wasn't it?

ARTHUR: Shoot.

ADA: Didn't you see it, Arthur?

JOE: Not *again*, Dad . . .

ARTHUR: Well, maybe . . . just out of the corner of my eye.

ADA (*pointing*): Oh! Another . . .

JOE: What a night! (ADA *and* JOE *look at* ARTHUR *expectantly.*)

ARTHUR (*grimly, after a pause*): I'll go get you a shirt.

ADA: Oh, it's so late – why don't we all go in.

JOE: Come on, Ma. Dad's been waiting here for hours and he hasn't seen *one* yet.

ARTHUR (*to himself*): I don't understand it. I am an observing . . . person. (*He exits into the house.*)

ADA: He doesn't need to see any shooting *stars*, for goodness' sake. At something o'clock in the *morning*.

JOE: Can't you just let things happen for once? It's important to him.

ADA (*irritated*): Just let things happen? For once?

JOE: Just . . . let it happen.

ADA: What is that, some *phrase*? I don't know why you're picking on me . . .

JOE: I'm *not*. I mean, it's not going to kill any of us to sit on the porch at . . . (*Checks watch.*) . . . two-thirty and look at the sky, is it?

ADA: Just let it happen, *man*.

JOE: All right, all right, I'm sorry, I give up . . .

ADA: No, no, I'm going to sit here and be spontaneous. (ADA *sits on the swing. Long pause.*) Well. Do you notice anything different?

JOE: Uh . . . Your hair?

ADA: Oh, no, it just gets more and more grey in it, no surprises there. Something here *is* different, though . . .

JOE: I give up.

ADA: Go ahead – guess.

JOE: No . . .

ADA: Do you want me to tell you if you're getting warmer?

JOE: No!

ADA: Do you mean you give up?

JOE: Yes, yes!

ADA: Dad lowered the porch swing.

JOE: Wow. (JOE *looks at her blankly.*)

ADA: My feet can finally touch the floor! (JOE *laughs and puts his arm around* ADA's *shoulder.*) For *years* I have hated this swing. My entire life I've been sitting in chairs that made me feel . . . insignificant. Go on, you're all sweaty.

JOE: Keep Feet on Floor Says Midwestern Matron. (JOE *withdraws his arm and kisses* ADA's *cheek; she is delighted.*)

ADA: Whew! You smell like potatoes.

JOE: Thanks, my aftershave. You feel more significant now?

ADA: Not really. When I was a child my teachers would say, 'We'll let the littlest girl in the class answer that one.' Can you imagine how that made me feel? No, your father is really very thoughtful, even when he has to be reminded to be. After twenty-six years living in this house, my feet dangling in the air every summer, one day he just up and lowers the swing. A remarkably *kind* man. You're thin. Do you know how thin you are?

JOE: Dad says I look good.

ADA: He would, he's not an observant person.

JOE: I'm not thin.

ADA: You're *terribly* thin.

JOE: Mom! I'm gross!

ADA: You're *gaunt*. You can see the bones in your face. You look like your Great Uncle Bredahl looked just before he started eating wood.

JOE: Well, maybe it runs in the family: a long line of unrequited *hunger*.

ADA: You look like a skeleton. Is that a beer? Is that a can of beer?

JOE: No. It's a medieval wind instrument.

ADA: No it's not, it's a can of beer you're drinking!

JOE: I thought it would fatten me up.

ADA: A steady diet of cigarettes and beer, oh, *yes*! Did he have one, too? Boy, oh, boy!

JOE: Would you like one?

ADA: No, I would *not* like one. (*Small pause.*) Out here where everyone can see me.

JOE: Everyone! Mom, it's two-thirty, there's nobody going to see you.

ADA: (*Significantly.*) They're out there. (*They both look out into the night.*) Perhaps just a little of yours, I'm so dry. (JOE *hands her his beer.* ADA *demurely takes a sip and grimaces.*) Augh! Awful. Tastes like potatoes. What on earth is keeping Dad?

JOE: How is he? I mean, how's his health?

ADA: Oh, he's fine.

JOE: No, I mean it: how are *you*?

ADA: Old.

JOE: Aw, Mom, don't say that.

ADA: Why not?

JOE: I don't know, I just can't stand to hear you say it, that's all.

ADA: All right, I'll say something else. (*Pause.*) Except I don't quite know how else to put it. Oh, I don't mean that I feel different than I ever did, except for in my body, of course. It's funny, the voice in my head is the same as when I was 18, or 12, or 60. I'm the same person, I keep waiting for that to change, but it doesn't, I keep waiting for some of that wisdom that's supposed to come with age, but I have a feeling it's just not coming. When I was a young woman, when I was having the first of the children, I remember pitying people who were forty. Poor things, I thought, 40 years old. Well, that's 40 years ago, now. Where did you eat supper?

JOE: That new French restaurant that opened up in St. Paul.

ADA: With whom?

JOE: A couple of friends from the *Dispatch*. I miss you, Mom. I miss Dad.

ADA: Well, we miss you, too. What did you have? You smell like garlic.

JOE (*opening another beer*): I woke up in New York this morning and realized how much I miss you.

ADA: Don't have another . . .

JOE: I . . . worry about you. (*Small pause.*)

ADA: What have you heard about me? Is Dad keeping something from me?

JOE: No! No, no, no . . . Dad's not *keeping* anything from you, you're fine.

ADA: Of course I'm not fine! My arthritis is a constant torment . . .

JOE (*exasperated*): Oh, geez. (*Snaps fingers.*) Like *that* it's out of control.

ADA (*quietly*): It's . . . out of control?

JOE: Oh, my God.

ADA: Don't take the name of the Lord in vain. Did Dad call secretly and tell you to come?

JOE: No! I'm as fearful for him as I am for you.

ADA: You mean . . . he has it, too?

JOE: Mom! Nobody has anything! I'm sorry I brought it up! Whatever it was! (*Pause.*)

ADA: I wish you wouldn't frighten me like that.

JOE: I guess I'm just . . . missing the two of you, that's all.

ADA: Well, if you miss us so much, don't you think you could have eaten with us your first night home?

JOE: Oh, maybe we *should* turn in.

ADA: I'll never get to sleep now. (*Pause.*) Last night Dad and I were sitting here and a family of ducks waddled out from that clump of pines, crossed the road and disappeared, down over the river bank. She reminded me of me.

JOE: Who?

ADA: The mother duck, she looked so ragged.

JOE: You're too much, mom.

ADA: She looked completely beat.

JOE: Domestic Abuse Among the Ducks! It Could Happen In Your Own Backyard.

ADA: Dad said he'd invited them.

JOE: The ducks?

ADA: He's forever inviting. I don't know, Joe. He's fine, but . . .

JOE: But what?

ADA: Just promise me one thing.

JOE: Sure.

ADA: Whatever you do, don't get your father going on levitation.

MICHAEL LUNDGREN, *16, enters from the house, wearing pyjama bottoms, slamming the screen door behind him.*

MICHAEL: Hi, Uncle Joe. Where are you going to sleep?

ADA: What are you doing up?

JOE: Mike!

MICHAEL: Wow!

JOE: Wow! Good to see you!

MICHAEL: Yeah!

JOE: Great! (*To ADA.*) What's he doing here?

ADA (*to MICHAEL*): What are you doing up at this hour? (ARTHUR *enters from the house, carrying a sweatshirt.*)

JOE (*to ARTHUR, indicating* MICHAEL): What's he doing here? (*To MICHAEL.*) Mike! Great! You're looking terrific. I'm just . . . trying to figure out why it's you that I'm seeing here.

MICHAEL (*pointing*): Wow! Was that a shooting star?

ARTHUR (*wheeling and looking up at the sky*): It's just not fair.

JOE (*to* ADA): I guess I didn't quite realize we had other guests.

ADA: You don't know the half of it, believe me. (*To* MICHAEL.) Now why are you out of bed?

MICHAEL: Grandpa came in Uncle Joe's old room and woke me up.

ARTHUR (*to* ADA): I didn't want to go through Joe's bags. I want Joe to know that whenever he visits I'm not going to go through his *bags*.

MICHAEL: He woke me up to ask if he could borrow one of my shirts.

ADA (*admonishing*): Arthur . . .

MICHAEL: It's okay. I don't think he woke Tom. So, what's everybody doing?

JOE: Who's Tom? At the risk of being indelicate.

MICHAEL: An old friend of mine.

JOE: Oh. Well. In that case.

MICHAEL: We're on our way to oboe camp.

JOE: You've got to be kidding.

MICHAEL: This year I'm going to make first chair, *and* my lifesaving certificate.

JOE: Oboe camp?

ADA (*to* MICHAEL): Your mother won't be happy if she finds you up.

JOE: His *mother*? Is Jean here, too? What's she doing in town? (*Immediately, to* MICHAEL.) Bringing you to oboe camp. (*To his parents.*) Well, why don't you *tell* me these things?

ARTHUR: Actually, Joe, you're the surprise guest here. All the others were expected, more or less.

JOE: I see.

ADA: Not that we're not thrilled to see you – we *are*, very. We were just wondering what prompted . . . If there was anything . . .

ARTHUR: He told me he's not going back.

ADA: Well, where's he going?

ARTHUR: Nowhere.

JOE: Geez.

ADA: He told *me* he's afraid of death.

JOE: I did not!

ADA: Well, not in so many words, perhaps . . .

ARTHUR: Whose death?

ADA: Ours.

JOE: *Geez*!

ARTHUR: What do you mean? Did he come out here to prevent it, or to witness it?

ADA: Don't ask me.

ARTHUR (*to* JOE): Well. Here's that shirt for you.

JOE (*taking the sweatshirt*): Dad, this is a sweatshirt. It's over eighty *degrees*, Dad.

MICHAEL (*taking the sweatshirt from* JOE): Did you come all the way from New York to see Paul?

JOE: No.

MICHAEL: Have you met the guy he's living with now? I have.

ARTHUR: Michael . . .

MICHAEL: Do you miss him?

JOE: Not any more.

MICHAEL (*during the following, he ties the sweatshirt around his head like a turban*): I do. I mean, I was 8 when he moved in with you, and 15 when he moved out, so that makes him, like, a part of *my* life, too, and even though we didn't get here to the cities all that often, I had a really good time with you guys when we did, and so I miss him, don't you? (*Beat.*) I mean, I know we're not supposed to talk about it. (*Beat.*) So? I'm the Sheik of Araby. (*Beat.*) What are you, thirty?

JOE: Twenty-nine.

MICHAEL: Same difference. What's New York like?

JOE: An incubator.

ARTHUR: I think I'm safe in saying that neither of us *wants* to die just yet. There's so much more that we want to do and see and *know*.

JOE: I *know* . . .

ARTHUR: But have you ever considered the alternative? Just . . . *being* here, eternally? No, I don't suppose you have, you're too young.

MICHAEL: Young? He's nearly thirty.

ADA: Be careful, Michael.

ARTHUR: You remember that camping trip we took up north, Joe, to Itasca State Park?

JOE: I was seven.

ARTHUR: And we saw that little rivulet come bubbling up out of a rock? Just a tiny little stream that you stepped over.

JOE: I remember.

ARTHUR: Well, that's the same Mississippi River that's across the road. Picture it if it didn't go on out to the Gulf eventually. If it just . . . accumulated. In some unspeakably massive lake. Like the Dead Sea.

ADA: Dad, it's awfully late . . .

ARTHUR: How stagnant. How repellent.

JOE (*an edge*): I don't buy it, Dad.

ARTHUR (*same*): You don't have to. By no means.

JOE: I mean, you don't tell somebody who's about to die about the Mississippi River, for God's sake. Or some man whose wife or son or father has just kicked off from emphysema or a mugging in the park: you don't tell him about *streams* and the natural *order* of things.

ADA: Michael, you go on back to bed, now.

ARTHUR: What *do* you tell them about?

JOE: I don't *know*.

ARTHUR: Futility?

JOE: I don't know.

ARTHUR (*turning and looking up at the sky*): Futility?

ADA (*to* MICHAEL): We're all going to bed, there's nothing happening out here.

ARTHUR (*looking at the sky*): You can say that again.

MICHAEL: So what are you doing out here, Grandpa?

ARTHUR (*with a sigh*): Looking for meteors.

MICHAEL: You mean there's gonna be more?

ARTHUR (*as sardonic as he gets*): More? More of what?

MICHAEL: Wow, I'm gonna go wake Tom.

He turns and runs into the house, slamming the screen door behind him.

ADA (*calling after him*): Don't you dare!

JOE: I'm beginning to get a distinct sense of unreality here.

ADA *and* ARTHUR *exchange glances.*

ADA (*looking at the sky again*): It's about time.

ARTHUR: Many very early men ate juicy steaks, using no plates. (JOE *does an astonished take, first to* ARTHUR, *then to* ADA.) It's a mnemonic device for remembering the order of the planets out from the sun. Many very early men – Mercury, Venus, Earth, Mars – ate – that stands for the asteroid belt – juicy steaks – Jupiter and Saturn – using no plates. Uranus, Neptune . . .

JOE (*overlapping*): Uranus, Neptune, Pluto. (*Small pause.*)

ARTHUR: Comes in handy.

JOE: I'm sure. Might make a page three headline for the Post. 'No Plates for Early Steaks!'

The screen door opens and IRA SHERMAN, 24, enters, tying his dressing gown around him. JOE looks at him in utter disbelief.

IRA: So this is what people do in the Midwest? Pretend to go to bed at 10:30 so they can sneak back out at 3?

ADA: Ira . . .

IRA: It's fun, I like it. Good morning, Mrs. Dahl. Reverend Dahl. Top of the morning to you, Joe.

JOE *slowly rises from the swing, as though looking at a ghost.*

ADA: Oh, Ira, I can't tell you how sorry I am we woke you . . .

ARTHUR (*overlapping*): Waiting up for meteor showers, you see . . .

ADA (*overlapping*): Normally we don't . . .

ARTHUR (*overlapping*): I'm afraid my grandson has been slamming doors and . . .

ADA (*overlapping*): I'm so embarrassed . . .

ARTHUR (*overlapping*): It all got a little out of hand . . .

IRA: Listen: I'm very flexible.

JOE (*to* IRA): What on earth are you . . . (*To his parents.*) You *know* him?

IRA: Do they know? Please. We have had supper together. And very delicious it was, Mrs. Dahl. (*To* JOE.) Swedish meatballs.

ADA: Do call me Ada. Or Mrs. Dahl, if you prefer. Or anything.

IRA: Phoebe? Dolores?

ADA: Would you like some hot milk?

IRA (*after a beat*): I think you'll have to give me a little time to get used to your traditions. But thanks, Ada, believe me.

JOE: Ira . . . How . . .

ADA (*pointing to* IRA's *dressing gown*): Is that what you're wearing?

IRA (*he looks down at his gown for a moment*): I think so.

ADA: You'll catch your death of cold in that.

IRA: Well, given the temperature, I doubt it, but if I do, I hope I leave you with fond memories.

ADA (*laughs coquettishly*): Does your friend always talk like that, Joe?

IRA: Ceaselessly.

ADA: He kept me laughing all evening.

IRA: Well, lady, you got off some pretty decent one-liners yourself. (*To* JOE.) Right in the middle of supper, your mother suggested we all take naps. Between the meatballs and the mince pie.

JOE: I don't believe this. Ira. Why are you *here*?

ADA (*admonishing*): Joe . . .

ARTHUR (*to* JOE): Ira arrived late this afternoon, soon after you went out.

IRA: Surprise!

ADA: We put you both in the basement bedroom, I'm afraid. I hope it's not too damp . . .

IRA: Fine with me.

JOE *propels* IRA *by the arm down the porch steps.*

JOE: Ira . . .

IRA (*undertone, briefly parting his robe*): Quick, Joe. Tell me if I'm sprouting mushrooms.

JOE (*undertone*): Shut up, Ira.

ADA: I think I *will* make some hot milk.

IRA: Hot milk!

ARTHUR: I'll take a cup, Ada.

ADA: I hear one cup. Do I hear two?

IRA: I pass.

ADA: Joe?

JOE (*strained*): No thanks, Mom.

ADA: Going, going, gone!

She exits into the house.

JOE (*undertone to* IRA): What the hell are you *doing* here? When did you leave New York? How did you find my parents?

IRA: I found them utterly unbelievable. And I begin to understand you. I mean, you come from completely queer stock.

ARTHUR: How long'd you say you two have known each other?

JOE (*primarily to himself*): A couple of *weeks* for goodness' sake.

IRA (*to* ARTHUR): It'll be three

months tomorrow.

JOE (*undertone to* IRA): Well I hope you didn't think things were at a point where I wanted to take you home to meet the *folks*.

ARTHUR: Just think of it, Joe. Mr. Sherman has incorporated himself, and he's only . . . How old did you say, Ira?

IRA: Twenty-four.

ARTHUR: Twenty-four years old and already he's running his own private catering service!

JOE (*to* IRA, *incredulous*): You told them about the Naked Cake?

IRA: And why not? (IRA *joins* ARTHUR *on the porch steps*): We do wedding parties, birthdays and shivas.

ARTHUR: Shivas?

IRA: I think you people call them wakes. Sitting shiva: you cover up the mirrors, remember the dead, and eat.

JOE: What is going on here?

ARTHUR: Say, Joe. Why don't you write about your friend, here? There must be interesting stories in private catering.

IRA: There are seven million stories in the Naked Cake.

ARTHUR: Come on, Joe. Sit down. Join us.

IRA: Your father was telling us all about the universe at supper, you should have been there. What was that passage you quoted, Mr. Dahl?

ARTHUR (*after a brief silence, he raises his 'preacher's voice' and recites in Hebrew*):

KĒ Ā-LĬF SHÄ-NĒM
BĔ-Ā-NĔ-KŬ,
KĔ-YŬM ĔT-MŎL
KĒ YÄ-VÔR,
VĔ-ÄSH-MÔ-RÄ
VÄ-LĪ-LĔ

Brief pause.

IRA: For four years I went to Hebrew school, and did I get anywhere? Don't ask.

ARTHUR: Psalm 90. 'For a thousand years in thy sight are but as yesterday when it is past, or as a watch in the night.'

After a moment, IRA *suddenly stands and points to the sky.*

IRA: There's one! Do you see it?

ARTHUR: Yes, I see it.

JOE (*after a beat*): It's an *airplane*, Ira.

IRA (*deflated*): Oh, yeah . . .

MICHAEL (*from within the house*): But Mom, please? Tom'll *kill* me if I don't get him up for this . . .

MICHAEL *and his mother,* JEAN LUNDGREN, *enter from the house.*

JEAN: That's nothing to what I'll do to you if you do. Hi, Joe.

JOE: Jean.

JEAN: How are you?

JOE (*embracing her somewhat awkwardly*): It's good to see you. A real surprise.

MICHAEL: Ma . . .

JEAN: You look good. Where's your shirt?

JOE: Mom says I look like a skeleton.

JEAN: Of course. At death's door, no doubt.

JOE: Exactly.

MICHAEL (*a whine*): Ma . . .

JEAN: Forget it, Mike.

IRA (*musical*): Hello, again!

JEAN (*lukewarm*): Hello. (*Turning to* ARTHUR, *admonishing.*) Dad . . .

ARTHUR: I know, I'm afraid I woke him.

MICHAEL (*sitting and sulking*): Yeah, but why did *she* have to get up.

IRA: Come on, kid, don't be a pain in the ass.

JEAN: Please don't . . . use that language with my son.

IRA (*innocently*): Language? You mean English? All right, I'll put it another way. Mike, you're a nice kid, you played a dynamite oboe after supper, but please just try not to make everybody's *seat* hurt, will you? (*To* JEAN.) Is besser?

JEAN: You go on to bed now, Michael.

ARTHUR: We were just speaking of aeroplanes. You know I can remember the first aeroplane I ever saw? Quite an event. And to think what has transpired in the heavens just in my lifetime. A miracle. Levitation. It just dropped out of the sky. I don't suppose you know what knee-pants are, do you, Mike?

MICHAEL: What?

ARTHUR: Knee-pants. Oh, well, it doesn't matter. But all of us boys were wearing them which means that I must have been less than . . . 10 years old at the time, and that it was a day in summer when the first airplane dropped out of the sky. Michael: never forget the advantages you and I have over these city boys, here, having known the unutterable pleasures of growing up in a small town.

MICHAEL: I don't think it's so hot.

ADA *enters from the house, carrying a tray with four cups of hot milk.*

ARTHUR: You will. Anyway. I don't know what we were doing that we all happened to be in that field south of town . . . or perhaps we all just came running when we saw that creature in the sky, dipping its wings and descending. It bounced, twice – very high – then rolled to a stop in the long grass. And a god stepped out. He was tall and laughing and buttoned up in a stiff white collar and a dark suit, although it was a summer's day, and he was . . . undeniably . . . from another world. (*Small pause.*) By that time, of course, some of the grownups had run out to the field, and to our profound dismay they took the fellow off, to feed him and fawn over him. We stood guard over his chariot, half protective, half fearful of it. I know now that he was making a coast to coast flight, some record or other, but to us . . . he was spreading the gospel of levitation.

ADA: All right, who got him started? (*To* JOE.) Did you get him started?

JOE (*a finger to his lips*): Shhh, Ma, please!

ARTHUR: When it came time for him to fly away . . . my goodness, what a thought that was then . . . still laughing, all teeth and mustache and bright eyes . . . he threw out long ropes from the cockpit and the strongest of the men held them until the tiny engine had worked up enough power. And then he was gone from us, trailing little ribbons of rope, and dipping his wings, and disappearing. (*Small pause.*)

ADA: I knew I was right to make more than two cups. You'll have some hot milk, won't you, Jean?

JEAN (*taking a cup*): Thanks, Mom.

ADA: And there's more coming, so don't be shy. Michael?

MICHAEL: No thanks, Grandma.

JEAN: Michael . . .

MICHAEL: I don't *care* for any, all right?

ADA (*offering the tray to* IRA): I think you'll be pleasantly surprised, Mr. Sherman.

IRA (*taking a cup*): Are you sure you have enough?

ADA: Oh, there are so many comings and goings in this house, especially as we get older, it seems . . . I never know who Dad is going to invite, or when, or how many . . . So I always make plenty of everything.

INGA, *an elderly woman in a nightgown and robe, enters with another tray of cups.*

Oh, there you are. Thank you *so* much.

INGA (*offering her tray to* ARTHUR). Arthur?

ARTHUR (*offering her tray to* JOE): Please, Joe, it will let you sleep. So much better for that than all those cigarettes and beers.

JOE *takes a cup, staring without recognition at* INGA.

ARTHUR (*to* INGA, *taking a cup*): Not much sleep tonight, I'm afraid.

INGA: Sleeping or waking, it's all pretty much the same to me.

JOE (*undertone to* ADA): Mom. Who *is* that?

ADA (*relishing her opportunity*): Oh, for goodness' sake, Joe. Can't you just let things happen for once?

JEAN: Mike, take some hot milk.

MICHAEL: In case you didn't happen to know, too much milk causes *excess mucus*.

JEAN: If you're angling for one of Joe's beers, you're gonna have to do a lot better than excess mucus.

ADA: Dad? Do you know what I would like?

ARTHUR (*looking up at the sky*): I'm afraid I do. You want me to make popcorn.

ADA: Well, we do seem to be up . . .

INGA: Now that *would* be a treat.

JEAN: Popcorn!

ARTHUR: All right, all right, I submit to the will of the majority.

INGA: So. What is it, exactly, that we're doing?

IRA: I'm not sure you could pin it down, exactly.

INGA (*suddenly pointing to the sky*): Oh! What was that?

ARTHUR (*wheeling around*): Where?

MICHAEL (*looking up*): Wow.

ARTHUR: Shoot! Shoot!

JEAN (*to* INGA): Dad's waiting for a meteorite shower.

INGA: Oh, star-gazing, are we?

ARTHUR: Hardly.

INGA: (*noticing* JOE): Here's a newcomer. Jean – could this be your brother? (*To* JOE.) How do you do?

JOE (*stupified*): How do you do?

INGA: Well, there's not a *great* deal of family resemblance, is there. I don't know that I would have taken you for brother and sister.

JEAN: Maybe not, but we both have identical birthmarks in exactly the same place, so there must be *some* connection.

IRA (*to* JOE): You mean that thing that looks like a map of Italy on the inside of your left thigh? (*Silence. Then, to* JEAN.) You have it, too? (*Silence.*)

INGA: I, myself, have never travelled in Europe.

ADA: What about that popcorn, Papa?

ARTHUR (*looking at the sky*): As soon as I turn my back it'll all start, I just know it.

INGA: What a vast expanse of lawn you have here, Ada. You could hold a cotillion on the green.

ADA: Joe used to hang lights from the trees and stage Hollywood spectaculars out there.

JEAN: He recruited me to lead a chorus line of neighbourhood girls one summer, all of us in swimsuits and capes.

ADA: Which he recruited me to make.

IRA: If you only knew then where it was all going to lead, huh?

ADA: Why don't you write plays like that anymore, Joe? With dancing and singing?

JOE: I'll get right on it, Mom.

INGA: I don't know why I should be so hungry, but I feel like something more substantial than popcorn . . .

ADA: It's no wonder. The meatballs were so dry, people hardly touched them.

INGA: Not at *all*, Ada.

ARTHUR: Mike, you want to go get that popcorn started?

MICHAEL (*looking at his mother*): If I can wake Tom up . . .

JEAN: Not a chance.

MICHAEL: O.K. but Tom's gonna be pretty mad about this, that's all I have to say. (MICHAEL *exits into the house*.)

INGA (*to* ADA): What about muffins? I don't suppose they really *go* with popcorn, but I have such a craving . . .

ADA (*doubtfully*): Well . . .

INGA: I won't make much more than a couple dozen . . . cracked wheat?

JOE (*beyond comprehending anything*): Cracked wheat? Why not? Why not *muffins*. And then we can all dance around on the lawn.

INGA (*to JOE*): *Now* you've gone and done it. (*Wistfully, as she exits into the house.*) I was raised in a strict Lutheran parsonage, Joe. As were you. I don't even know how to *waltz*.

ADA (*over her shoulder, going into the house*): Arthur . . .

ARTHUR (*still looking at the sky*): Coming, Ada. Coming.

ARTHUR *exits into the house. The remaining three sit and stand in silence for a few moments. Then, a mustached older man dressed in a bathrobe comes walking from the darkness of the lawn into view.*

WRIGHT: Afraid I dozed off in that lawnchair over there. Did Arthur call it a night? Oh, you must be Arthur's son, Joseph. (*He distractedly shakes JOE's hand and passes on to the door of the house. Then he turns back.*) You know, your father is a remarkable man. Now *Einstein*, whom I met once, by the way, at some sort of awards banquet in New Jersey, Einstein said that as an object approaches the speed of light, time slows down. At least, for that object it does. And that if anything *were* capable of travelling faster than light, time itself would be reversed: it would go *backwards*. Well, says Arthur, with not a shred of scientific jargon but with total assurance, nonetheless, well, he says, what do we know that travels *backwards* in time? What, indeed, he says, but memory? Well, I didn't think I could let him get away with that sort of mystical double-talk, but he goes on to insist that we make our mistake when we think of memory as an *abstract concept*. He maintains that it's *quantifiable*, the old coot. And that we've lost sight of that, but that vestiges of an ancient understanding of memory can still be found *in language*. Do we not, he asks, do we not say 'I *have so many* memories,' or that so-and-so has '*lost*' his memory?

Quantifiable. Imagine that. (*Beat.*) Anyway, I seem to have polished off Arthur's orange juice and I was wondering if there were any more. (*Gesturing toward the night sky.*) Just yell if anything starts happening.

He exits into the house. JOE stands perfectly still for a moment, then throws back his head and yells, inarticulately.

JOE: Ahhhhhh! (*Immediately after, very fast.*) I'm terribly sorry, everything's all right, I'm fine, I'm sorry, just a whim, *nice night.* (JOE *opens the screen door and shouts into the house.*) Sorry! False alarm! Nothing doing! Thought we spotted the Hindenburg! Never mind! (*Shuts the door, empties his cup of hot milk over the porch rail, pops open a can of beer, and flings himself down on the swing.*) So. (*Small pause. He jerks a thumb toward the house.*) Was he at dinner, too?

IRA: Sure.

JOE: Of course.

JEAN: So. Joe. What's all this about death?

JOE: What?

JEAN: Out in the kitchen, Mike announced that Uncle Joe was freaking out about Grandma and Grandpa dying.

JOE: He said what? I'll kill him.

JEAN: It's not true?

JOE (*uncomfortable*): Well. Freaking out? No. You let him use cheap phrases like that?

JEAN: Actually, that was my phrase. What Mike said was that you were having problems coming to grips.

IRA: That kid's got a future. On the West Coast.

JEAN: What about it, Joe? Mom and Dad's death.

JOE: Well . . . I mean, doesn't the thought nearly kill you? Am I alone in this? Completely odd, or clinging, or dependent or something?

IRA: What do you mean?

JOE: What I mean is that I live twelve hundred miles away from them, and I have a life of my own, such as it is, and yet whenever I feel time slipping away from me, and it does, oh God, it does, it is their time I'm feeling, it's those two slipping away from me and I nearly die of it. (*Beat.*) And what I want to know is am I alone in this?

JEAN: No.

IRA: Uh-uh. (*Small pause.*)

JOE: Oh. (*Beat.*) Well, that settles that. (*Beat.*) I picture coming back to this house and not finding them in it and I can't . . . picture that. (*Beat.*) That's what death is for me: looking for someone and you can't find them. Throughout the empty house, from one room to another, no matter how many times you search and search again, you can't find them. You won't ever find them. (*Beat.*) Who was that man?

JEAN: I guess all that started for me when the kids came along . . . Each one of them gave new meaning to the phrase 'hanging on for dear life,' because that's what I did to them, at least to begin with. I suppose that's what I did to you, too, Joe, when I was a kid.

JOE (*with a little edge*): 'Tie your shoes, wipe your nose, cut your hair, chew your food and don't slurp your soup!' And that's the sort of advice she was giving me while I was in college.

JEAN: Eventually, of course, you learn to let go. You learn you don't have any choice. Maybe you were the hardest to let go of, because you were the one who taught me how to cling.

IRA: My mother died two years ago. Irene. Of cancer.

JEAN: I'm sorry.

IRA: She was an accountant for the mob.

JEAN: Oh, for Pete's sake.

IRA: No – she was. If you ever need something to fall back on, Ira, she'd say, become a bookkeeper for the Mafia, they hire 'em by the gross.

JEAN: I thought you were being serious, for once.

IRA: I am serious. So was Irene, I mean, she kept the books for some piss-elegant hotel in midtown. Very olde English, with olde oak panelling and the sort of doorman who wouldn't look at you if you weren't a WASP, much less hail you a cab, and in the role of president, proprietor, whatever, was this cultivated white-haired ex-headmaster, but you know that the power behind the throne was some guy named Nuncio or Bugsy or something, and that he was only running the place for his great Uncle Scarface. Anyway, Irene got cancer, only nobody in the family, including her, was allowed to use that word. My aunts would gather together when Irene wasn't around and say that she had 'the real one.' The real one. It sounds like an ad for a cola.

JEAN: Can't you ever be anything but flippant?

IRA: Sure. But I try to live up to people's expectations of me. (*Moving into camp.*) Like this whole astronomy thing? You want flippant, you got it. (*Very camp.*) Like I was telling your father earlier, last summer there was this total eclipse of the sun? And all day long on the radio they kept saying, 'Don't look at it, don't look at it! It'll *ruin* your eyes!' So I said to my friend, Gay Morris, 'Gay Morris,' I said, 'If these eclipses are so bad for you, why do they *have* them?' (*Back to his 'straight voice.'*) There, you see? It's simple.

JEAN: That's *amazing*. I mean, how do you *do* that?

IRA: Amazing? It isn't even *interesting*. It's what you're taught to do. So anyway, Irene died, and my father, Eugene, who sold belts wholesale before he retired and who was always pretty much all right with me, as was Irene, by the way, suddenly turned into this sad old guy. There's only my sister, Ruth, and me left, and Ruth is married and lives in Bayshore so Daddy and I go for little bachelor dinners together in the city, once a week, and in one way he's cool because Ruth can and is handling the whole grandchildren thing, I mean, providing them for him, but in another sense it's a little depressing every Wednesday night because sometimes Eugene forgets to shave. (*Small pause.*) Which in him is a thing almost impossible to conceive.

JEAN (*sincerely*): I'm sorry about your mother, Ira.

IRA (*same*): Yeah. Thanks.

JOE (*To* IRA): Hear that? Patronizing. Condescending.

JEAN and IRA (*overlapping*): What?

JOE (*to* IRA): It's what she does. When Paul split, she sat me down to talk to me about historical inevitability.

JEAN (*to* IRA): It wasn't that way.

JOE: Patronizing? Wow. I'm bleeding for God's sake, and she's telling me it's for my own good. *Politically*, can you believe it? That it's time for me to move on . . . to get outside of myself . . .

JEAN (*to* IRA): All right, all right. My timing was . . .

JOE: She's a militant, my sister. Oh, yeah. Marx and Jesus.

JEAN: I see. We're going to start with the Christian Marxists again.

JOE: You gotta watch your step around her, believe me. Watch your politics, watch your language, your thoughts . . .

JEAN (*to* IRA): He attacks the things he doesn't understand. It's what he does. And that's what I'm here for, I guess.

IRA: The Christian Marxists?

JEAN (*to* IRA): You see, we're a couple of do-gooders, my husband and I. And me, I'm an aging earth mother.

JOE (*to* IRA): Earnest. God, is she *earnest.*

JEAN: And that's a big mistake, I know. Futile, right? Try to feed hungry people? Pointless. Take homeless people into your home? Forget it.

JOE: You see, Marx and Jesus have a lot in common, Ira. For one thing, neither one of them has much time for queers.

JEAN: Neither one of them says a damned thing about any of that, but both of them have a hell of a lot to say about cynics!

JOE (*to* IRA): Oh, yeah, she's the champion of all the right causes, but when it comes to perverts, well, let's just say she wouldn't want her son to marry one.

IRA: I see.

JEAN (*to* IRA): And that is precisely what he *wants* to believe.

IRA: I see.

JEAN (*to* IRA): I have a houseful of children who idolize their Uncle Joe, and my husband and I love him more than he'll ever admit and can you blame us if we didn't want to see him mired down in a basically dead-end lifestyle?

IRA: Not me.

JOE (*to* IRA): That 'lifestyle' was *Paul*, and he wasn't a lifestyle, he was my *life*, and her kids loved him, and so did Mom and Dad and *they're* not even *liberals*, and where does she get off with this 'basically dead-end' bullshit? She and Jerry showed Paul the last word in courteous contempt and *he felt it.*

JEAN (*to* IRA): We did *not!*

JOE (*to* IRA): For seven *years* they did!

JEAN (*to* IRA): Did *not.*

JOE (*to* IRA): *Did! Did!*

JEAN (*to* JOE): He *left* you!

JOE (*to* JEAN): I *know!*

ADA *enters, unnoticed by the others, and stands with a bowl of popcorn at the door.*

JEAN (*to* IRA): He left him.

JOE (*to* JEAN): He knows.

IRA (*to* JEAN): I know. It's all he ever talks about.

JEAN (*to* JOE): So you've decided that Jerry and I are the villains and you ridicule our work . . . (*To* IRA.) . . . which is not with the 'right causes' in the least, and he knows it, and he never answers our letters . . . (*To* JOE.) . . . and you never answer our letters and besides, what have *you* ever done for anybody . . . (*To* IRA.) . . .

what stand has *he* ever taken . . . (*To* JOE.) and how can you possibly be so smug and self-righteous when you've spent the past year shying away from any sort of commitment and trying your damnedest to pose as some sort of cold fish, for God's sake!

IRA: Touché.

JOE: Shut up, Ira!

JEAN: Don't talk to him like that!

JOE: Why not?

JEAN: I don't know!

ADA: Oh, my . . .

JEAN (*to* JOE): Maybe I don't understand completely yet, but I'm trying, I've been trying, and you make it impossible for me to open my mouth without first examining my entire structure of belief, and how can you dare do that when you don't demand the same of yourself?

JOE: I loved him. I miss him.

JEAN: I know that. (*To* ADA.) He acts like I don't know that. (*To* JOE.) I know that. And now because maybe I made some mistakes at one point, am I dead to you? Will you let me be dead to you? (*Pause.*)

JOE: Every Christmas it was Paul who picked out the presents for the kids. Every year. Sherlock Holmes and sheet music for Mike . . . oh, shit . . . Disappearing ink for Andy. Necklaces and pins for Tra, picture-books about horses for Vin. An erector set once, for George, that he got second-hand from the Salvation Army.

IRA (*quietly*): Jesus.

JOE: For Pilar, drawing paper and those pens with four different colours of ink in them . . .

JEAN: There was a dictionary for Kwami one year, and a doll-house for Rebecca . . .

IRA (*quietly*): My God.

JOE: And always puppets for . . . what's her name?

JEAN: I forget. (*Starting to giggle.*) I can't remember! (*To* ADA.) Which one always got the puppets?

ADA: The what?

JOE (*also starting to laugh*): Hand puppets! Marionettes! Dummies!

ADA (*also starting to laugh*): *I* don't know. Wasn't it the one with all those wires on her teeth?

IRA: How many of them *are* there?

ADA (*to* IRA): Oh, you don't know the half of it, believe me.

JEAN (*giggling, embarrassed*): Mother, *please.* Don't make me sound like a factory!

JOE (*to* IRA): Some of them *were* adopted. From all over.

IRA: Which?

JEAN: It's so hard to remember. Well. Michael, for one.

JOE: Judith! Hand puppets! Marionettes! Dummies!

JOE, JEAN *and* ADA *all burst into renewed laughter.*

JEAN (*to* IRA): We got Mike in Chicago.

IRA: Wow. Does this have anything to do with Christian Marxism?

JEAN: It's a long story.

JOE (*subsiding*): I was crazy about them all, but . . . *I* don't know what to get a kid for Christmas. So it was Paul . . . who took . . . such . . . care.

ADA (*giving the bowl of popcorn to* IRA *and putting her arm around* JOE): It's like he's dead, isn't it.

JOE: Uh-huh.

ADA: But he's not.

JOE: I know.

ADA: He mows our lawn.

JOE: I *know.*

ADA: Neither is your sister. Dead.

JOE: I know.

ADA: When you were born, I . . . was having a hard time. And you were so very sick. We both were. But we nearly lost *you.* One night we realized you could be gone before morning and so we baptized you right there in the parsonage . . . and your sister was your godmother and because I was so very sick it was Jean who stayed up with you all through the night, night after night, and she . . . *insisted* . . . that you live.

JOE: I know.

ADA: You still haven't got a shirt on.

JOE: I know. I'm cold.

ADA: I *know*.

JEAN: I'll go get you one.

JOE: No . . .

JEAN: Sure I will.

JOE: Wait . . . Wait . . . Listen.

They all listen. INGA *enters from the house.*

ADA (*finger to lips, to* INGA): Shh. We're listening.

INGA (*whispering*): What for?

ADA (*whispering*): We don't know.

A single bird is heard, chirping.

JOE: Hear that? It's the first bird. There's always *one*. The birds don't all just wake up together and burst into song, there's always one who takes the lead. Way before dawn. Sings alone for about half an hour. Before the other birds join in. All alone. I've been listening to him for years. When I'm writing all night . . . When I *used* to write all night . . . the moment *he* began, I felt *I* could finish. It's the same bird, *always*. Everywhere. (*They all listen in silence to the solo bird-song.*) Many's the time I've wanted to kill that bird.

INGA: Know what you mean.

IRA (*overlapping*): Uh-huh.

JEAN (*overlapping*): Yup.

ADA (*overlapping*): Me, too.

JEAN (*to* JOE): I'll go get you that shirt.

JOE: That's what they all say.

MICHAEL *enters, bearing a bowl of popcorn.*

MICHAEL (*to* JEAN): I mean it, Mom, there's four more bowls of this stuff in the kitchen, and if I don't wake Tom . . .

IRA (*cutting him off*): Michael, just . . . go help your grandfather.

MICHAEL (*appealing to the higher authority*): Ma . . .

JEAN (*surprising herself*): You heard . . . what Ira said.

MICHAEL: So who's Ira all of a sudden?

JEAN: Ira is . . . Ira.

MICHAEL: No kidding.

IRA (*primarily to himself*): Sometimes. Not often. Almost never. (*To* MICHAEL.) Hey, Mike. You want a hand in the kitchen?

MICHAEL: Aw, that's O.K., man. See, I mainly just wanted Tommy to meet Uncle Joe because Tommy's gay, too.

A moment of profound silence.

JEAN (*quietly*): Tommy is what?

MICHAEL: Well, he's not sure, but he thinks he might be, so he's decided just to give it some time, to find out.

JEAN, JOE, INGA, *and* ADA *all do a slow unselfconscious unison take to the upstairs window where, presumably,* TOM *is sleeping.*

IRA (*after a small pause*): You're expecting maybe he glows in the dark?

MICHAEL: Didn't you know about Tommy, Mom? You didn't guess?

JEAN: We'll talk about it later.

MICHAEL: I thought after that course you took, you'd be hip.

JOE: What course?

JEAN: Mike, that's enough.

MICHAEL (*to* JOE): After all that stuff went down between you and her, she enrolled in a class on human sexuality. (*He snickers a little.*) To understand you better. It must have been a good one: she wouldn't let me see the textbooks.

JEAN (*to* JOE): I'll go get you that shirt.

JEAN *exits into the house.*

MICHAEL (*to* INGA): You want some popcorn?

INGA: Thank you, Michael.

MICHAEL: Mr. Wright says your muffins are almost done.

INGA (*to* ADA): Would you mind checking on them for me, Ada? I think I need to sit for a while.

ADA: Not at all.

JOE (*to himself*): Mr. Right?

ADA (*to* INGA): You might try to talk him out of staying here, while you're at it.

INGA: Who? Joe?

IRA: Staying here?

ADA: He says he's not going back.

INGA: I don't talk anyone in or out of anything anymore, Ada. I am no longer a schoolteacher.

ADA: Well, whatever. Come on, Mike. (MICHAEL *gives the bowl of popcorn to* INGA, *and rises to go into the house.*) I mean, he's perfectly welcome to stay if he wants, but I just think there comes a time, don't you?

MICHAEL: I'll say.

MIKE *and* ADA *exit into the house.*

INGA (*offering the bowl of popcorn*): Want some, Joe? Ira?

IRA: Huh? Uh, not right now, thanks.

He joins JOE, *who stands at the porch rail.*

INGA: Well, it's here if you want it.

IRA (*to* JOE): You're, uh, not coming back?

JOE: I would have written you.

IRA: Terrific.

JOE: I had dinner with some friends from the local paper. I can get my old job back.

IRA: And what was that again? Paperboy? (*Pause.*) What about the plays?

JOE: Finished.

IRA: What about Paul?

JOE: Dead issue. That's not why I'm staying.

IRA: What about me?

JOE: What do you mean?

IRA: What about me? I'm not dead.

JOE: Who said you were?

IRA: Oh, I don't know. Every now and then I seem to get a little news bulletin, a little flash announcement, 'Ira Sherman, only son of Eugene and Irene nee Baumgartner Sherman, passed away on his knees today, begging for attention.'

JOE: I don't know what you're talking about.

IRA: You know, somehow that doesn't surprise me? Somehow that doesn't come as the shock of a lifetime, you know? What happens is, first your eyes glaze over, like when I'm laying bare the secrets of my soul or some such thing, and then you heave a little sigh or two, for God's sake, and then . . . I cease . . . to be. What's happened is you've climbed into your little time machine and gunned the engines back to the era of Paul the Great.

JOE: Ira, please, I don't need a scene right now.

IRA (*very angry*): From me you don't get scenes! For three months I've been waiting just to make an entrance!

INGA (*cheerfully*): Are you boys talking about relationships?

JOE (*to* IRA, *intensely*): You have no way of understanding me.

IRA: Oh, dear God, the presumption of the man!

JOE: You haven't been through the wringer, that's all I mean!

IRA: Sweetheart, you don't have to go through the wringer if you were born on the rack. The wringer! You with your mince pie Midwestern upbringing, with parents you could eat for dessert, who say to you, Oh, you're gay? Well, that's okay, and Oh, this is the boy you love? Well, we'll love him too, and Now you're blue? Well, we feel it with you, and you're talking about going through some wringer? You're a sissy, that's what you are! You're a fucking coward!

JOE: Yes! Yes! I am! I'm afraid!

IRA (*wheeling, to* INGA): Translation: he's afraid I'll do to him what the legendary Paul did to him, although just what that might be is a little hard to pin down. I mean, what was this poor guy guilty of?

INGA: I'm sure I don't know.

IRA: Well, lady, neither do I. Are you going to let me have some of that popcorn or not?

INGA: Why, certainly.

IRA (*sitting beside* INGA *on the swing and eating a mouthful of popcorn furiously*): He didn't live happily ever after with him, that's what he did. First love and it was supposed to last forever. Christ!

JOE: I just . . . didn't want to die alone.

IRA: God. Always thinking ahead.

INGA: Well, one of you would have had to. Don't you think?

IRA: At last! Some logic! Tell me, do you Midwesterners have a thing about first love?

INGA: I know I did.

IRA: Well, then you're both so naive I could choke. (*To* JOE.) All this pain, and you never once call on me. Even when we're together, you have never once called on me to be with you.

JOE (*to* IRA): It's not as though I didn't want to. Ira?

IRA (*weary, his anger spent*): Oh, shut up, Joe. Look, why don't you just sit down and have some popcorn?

INGA (*suddenly pointing*): Oh! (JOE *and* IRA *look up into the night sky.*) And your father said there weren't any shooting stars tonight!

JOE (*after a pause*): Midnight Madness in Mystery Lodge.

IRA: Joe: do not start.

JOE: Dateline: Anywhere, USA. In the wee hours of Saturday last, the members of an occult society gathered on the front porch steps of seemingly respectable retired parson, Rev. Arthur Dahl, a.k.a. Father John Doe, Fast Eddie, Faster-than-Light Eddie, Louie the Popcorn King. Professing a love of muffins and good cheer, these sinister soubrettes set about ensnaring yet another sad disciple. (*Pause.*)

INGA: Did they suceed?

JOE: It's too early to tell. (*To* IRA.) I did hear you ringing, you know. The phone and the buzzer.

IRA: I figured you just unplugged it. The phone.

JOE: Well. Eventually.

IRA: Why did you do it, Joe?

INGA: What's he done now?

IRA: He locked me out! All this past week. He locked everybody out, no one could get through.

JOE: It was . . . very hot.

IRA: Hot! (*To* INGA.) We were watching t.v. in his apartment, *I* was watching t.v., *he* was sitting in a chair watching the wall, as far as I could tell.

JOE: A fun couple.

IRA: I said I'd go out for some lo-mein, and when I got back he wouldn't buzz me in.

JOE: What did you do that night?

IRA: Do? I'm sitting on the stoop, it's 97 degrees, and I'm thinking lo-mein was a pretty stupid choice to begin with.

INGA (*to* IRA): You mean no one's seen him for a week?

JOE (*to* IRA): I wasn't watching the wall, I was watching your face and all I could see there was a death's head.

IRA: Thanks.

JOE: No, no. It's . . . a very nice face, really. I just mean that suddenly everyone I saw was so unmistakably doomed and everything I had I was going to lose, one way or the other, and the city was an incubator for the still-born, for God's sake, and after a week of that it was either get myself into a plane and fly out here or . . . I don't know . . . never buzz anyone in. (*Pause.*)

INGA: You write headlines for a newspaper in New York City?

JOE: Until recently.

INGA: Just the headlines?

JOE: Just . . . some of them.

INGA: Do you play sports?

JOE (*does a take*): No.

INGA: Well you should. You should play golf. Writers like golf. Myself, I never married, so I wouldn't know. *What* to advise you. And I don't pretend to understand a thing about you young men who seemingly marry each *other*, I come from a different generation, a different *world* it was, so you could hardly *expect* me to understand, although I've always held a hearty interest in anthropology.

IRA: What's to understand? Think of us as hunters and gatherers. He hunts, I gather, it's crazy but it works.

INGA: Oh, no, no, no – I've got a hold on all *that*. What I don't understand is this: Now here is this perfectly nice young man . . . (*Indicating* IRA.) . . . intelligent, very good looking, I know he's Jewish but anyway. (*To* IRA.) You won't believe this, Mr. Sherman, but you're the first Jewish person I've ever met to *talk* to.

IRA: I *believe*.

INGA: I'm afraid that out here, and during my years, we were very *limited* in our experience although I do have *one* East Coast friend from way back, an inventor, he . . . well, he just dropped out of the sky one summer afternoon and into my life, but *anyway*. We struck up acquaintance, and then many years of correspondence and occasional visits, but he's the son of a Methodist bishop and not Jewish at all and I suppose really not East Coast but Midwestern although once he became famous, which was a few years before I met him, he spent much of his time in the East, which is why I think of him like that. As East. (*After a beat, to* JOE.) Anyway. Here's this intelligent young man, and it's obvious he cares about you very much, he sang your praises all through supper and says he thinks you're a very good writer although he does allow that you are perhaps a bit morbid and anyway he loves you so what's the problem? That's what I don't understand.

Pause. IRA *waits intently for an answer, but when none comes he gets up abruptly, descends the steps of the porch and stands looking at the sky.*

What is it, that Paul thing? But that's history, isn't it? When I say I'm from another generation, Joe, I don't mean I stayed there, that would be such a waste, I live now, in people's memories, and so do you, isn't that a thought? It's what your father was talking about at dinner, that every moment you live you're planting seeds in people's minds, seeds of yourself, and they keep you alive, not in some fixed form but always changing because of course there's nothing so unreliable as the human mind but in a sense nothing so predictable at the same time, so that while you *are* there, always, you may end up becoming many different people, as many different people as the number of seeds you've planted. (*Immediately, to* IRA.) What do you mean, he hunts, you gather? He's unfaithful?

IRA: Only to himself, Miss Thorvaldson, only to himself.

INGA: Obviously. In that respect he's utterly fickle. (*To* JOE.) Well. I am disappointed, I must say.

JOE: Thorvaldson. My father had a grade school teacher named . . . Miss Thorvaldson.

INGA: Well, of course.

IRA: I'm going for a walk.

JOE (*to* IRA): Don't leave me. I mean, what's going on here?

IRA (*suddenly angry*): *I* am going . . . around the block. It's not often I get to be a tourist. (*Intensely.*) You disappoint *me*, too. (*Walking out into the darkness.*) Ladies.

JOE: Ira . . . (*Pause.*)

INGA: So I wasn't *allowed* to dance, or even to learn how, but I'll tell you what I once did. Twice a year some of the wealthier farm families would get together and give a ball in one of the large barns. None of this square-dancing, country stuff – a genuine ball with white tie and tails and gowns and an orchestra and *waltzing*.

JOE: Wait a minute. Excuse me. Please. Who are you?

INGA: Inga Thorvaldson.

JOE: My father's grade school teacher.

INGA: Well – not any more, of course.

JOE: Of course. And my father is seventy. And you were of retirement age when you taught him. So that makes you . . . about . . . one hundred and thirty years old.

INGA: Oh, for goodness' sake, who's counting? And more to the point, I suppose, *how* are you counting? Anyway, when I was thirteen I escaped my parents somehow one night and trekked across the fields to the old Benson place and climbed up into the rafters of the barn and *watched*.

JOE: I don't like this. I don't like miracles.

INGA: And nothing I've seen since has moved me as the sight of those waltzing couples that night.

JOE: My father . . . invited you?

INGA: Spinning, spinning. A blur in my eyes.

JOE: Faster than the speed of light.

INGA: Oh, at least. And the music! Can you imagine how it struck my ears? Thirteen years old and nothing in them until that night but hymn tunes on an old pump organ.

JOE: Are any of the others here? Is Ira really here? My sister? Anyone?

INGA: I had to pay for my night of sin, of course. Old Benson's nephew, Willie, found me crouching up there, spellbound. Oh, what a beautiful young man! *Raven* hair and dressed in black, and dark eyes and pink, pink skin. Of course, he may just have had too much cider to drink, but anyway. He lifted me up and led me down and asked me for the honour of a *dance*. (*She breaks off, lost in memory, and also pained by it.*)

JOE (*anguished*): Is this house *empty*?

INGA: I couldn't speak. Not a word. And then to my horror, I began to cry, all of them standing about me in a circle and Willie Benson at my arm and while a moment earlier they had all been laughing, now they began to clear their throats and cough quietly and all I wanted to tell them was how beautiful I thought I had been, spinning, and how I didn't want them to stop, ever. But I couldn't utter a word. Do you know the sensation? (*He nods.* WRIGHT *enters with a platter of muffins.*) Willie was very kind. He bundled me up in a blanket and perched me up beside him on his carriage and flicked his whip over the horses' heads and drove me home, telling me jokes and stories all the way, although I answered him not one word. (*Small pause.*) I had fallen in love. (*Looking up.*) Did I ever tell you that story, Mr. Wright?

WRIGHT: Yes, Inga.

INGA: I thought so. (*Beat.*) Two years later he took his own life. There was no connection, of course. He hadn't fallen in love with a child, or anything like that. I never knew what it was. (*Beat.*) He hanged himself from the rafters of his uncle's barn. (ARTHUR *enters, eating a muffin.*) Do I smell muffins?

WRIGHT: I should say you do.

ARTHUR: Drowning in butter.

JOE (*sincerely*): Miss Thorvaldson . . .

INGA: Do call me Inga.

JOE: Your story. Where's the lesson?

INGA (*sternly*): There are no lessons. Only stories. I am no longer a schoolteacher. (ADA *enters.*)

JOE (*gentle, almost pleading*): Miss Thorvaldson. Do you know what I really write for that paper in New York?

INGA: Not the headlines?

JOE: Oh, yes, but the ones I really have to write, for my living, every day, they're like . . . Father Slays Son and Self . . . Calcutta Kids Trampled, Twenty-Four Dead . . . Hurricane Havoc in Retirement Haven . . . Second Infant Found in Incinerator . . .

INGA: Please . . .

JOE: It just goes on and on . . . Pension Couple Starve in Westside Rooming House . . . *Third* Incinerator Baby Found . . . Terminal! It's all terminal!

INGA: I'm sorry, Joe. I just . . . have no more lessons in me.

ARTHUR: Father slays son, my dear God have mercy on us.

JOE: Son and self.

ARTHUR: Son and self. Son and self. As if all the natural loss with which we are encumbered weren't enough. (*To* ADA.) Remember that situation in Montana? (*To* WRIGHT.) We had a parish out there in the early years.

ADA (*to* ARTHUR): But that was the other way around.

ARTHUR: Son slays father and self. (*To* JOE.) Of course, you weren't born yet.

ADA (*to* ARTHUR): But you told him about it. I remember.

ARTHUR: An *unbending* man he was, toward his son. A *stiff-necked* man.

ADA: The poor boy's name was Roger.

ARTHUR: Son and self. Father and self. (*With a steadily rising anger.*) I *quit* the seminary, you know.

WRIGHT: I *didn't* know.

INGA: Oh, yes indeed, for nearly two years.

JOE: After your internship. You had doubts.

ARTHUR: Doubts? I had no doubts! For two years I did my work, I studied and read and wrote and thought, for two years, so conscientiously, because I was preparing myself to *serve*. And then, with a face like *milk*, I marched forth into the field.

INGA (*singing*):
Rise up, o men of God!
Have done with lesser things . . .

ARTHUR (*to* INGA, *annoyed at the interruption*): Yes. Thank you. (*Resuming his story.*) The field being a tiny parish outside of Fargo, North Dakota, two hundred and forty-one in the congregation. And by the end of six months, I knew more about those two hundred and forty-one men,

women and children, body and soul, than I ever wanted to know about anyone! I couldn't go on. *Serve* them! I couldn't even *face* them! They were so full of *want*. And what had *I* to give them?

JOE: Everything for me, you had everything to give, always.

ARTHUR: So I quit! Couldn't face my family, couldn't face myself . . . I was actually going to form a one-man Protestant monastery, emphasis on the *protest*, like Jacob I was going to spend my entire life alone, wrestling with the angel. Wrestling!

JOE: But you didn't.

ARTHUR (*a little embarrassed*): No, I . . . I met your mother.

ADA (*also a little embarrassed*): Oh, go on, Arthur . . .

ARTHUR: And coming to love her, and being loved by her, somehow I came to realize that anyone who is *awake* . . . must look at the universe in all its . . . (*A gesture fails to encompass the pain.*) . . . and must say either yes . . . or no. And to say no would be to take death into one's arms. And by that time I was . . . *already* . . . married. (*Beat.*)

ADA: Our first child died in Montana. She was four days old. (*Beat.*)

INGA: Rise up, o men of God!
Have done with lesser things
Give heart and soul and mind and strength
To serve the King of Kings!
(*Beat.*) Whew!

WRIGHT (*offering a platter of muffins to* INGA): Inga?

INGA: No more for me, thanks. Have you met my young friend, Joe?

WRIGHT: Only in an off-hand sort of way, I'm afraid.

INGA: Joseph, meet Mr. Orville Wright.

WRIGHT: Hello, Joe.

JOE (*spent*): Oh, hello, Orville. How are you?

WRIGHT: A little tired, but who's complaining. Want a muffin?

JOE: Sure. (*Taking a muffin.*) I'm a little tired, too.

WRIGHT: Of course you are.

JOE: Well. (*Beat.*) Congratulations . . .

WRIGHT: Why, thank you. Of course, equal credit goes to my big brother.

JOE: Of course.

INGA (*offering* WRIGHT's *platter of muffins to* ADA): Ada? Cracked wheat. (ADA *takes one.*) Here it was, my silly idea in the first place, and then you end up doing all the work.

ADA: Oh, listen to that . . . (*The song of a single bird.* WRIGHT *turns to* ARTHUR.)

WRIGHT: You don't have whip-poor-wills out this far west, do you, Arthur?

ARTHUR: Only by invitation, Orville.

WRIGHT: Their cousin, the nighthawk, *yes*, but . . . (*They all listen.*) Both of them we found extremely difficult to study, being birds of the night. And their flight, so rapid and erratic, this way and that. But you can be sure that many a moth is tumbling dimwitted into its beak at this very moment. (*They listen.*) There was a whip-poor-will that kept us company on Kill Devil Hill, all during the trials. For four years. Wilbur used to say the creature was mocking our clumsy efforts to fly, and he may have been correct. Even after we . . . succeeded. I mean, there is flight and there is flight, don't you agree, Joe?

JOE: Uh-huh. Dad?

ARTHUR (*putting his arm around* JOE's *shoulder*): I'm here, Joe.

WRIGHT: No, for study, we had much better luck with the vultures, actually.

They listen.

ADA (*to* WRIGHT): You say you boys picked up your mechanical flair from your mother?

WRIGHT (*with feeling*): Oh, Mother could fix anything. And she was a kindred spirit, for a time. Almost a conspirator with us boys. Once, when Father was away, out on the evangelistic circuit, I took a machine can and filled it with water and put it on the stove. I was about nine. After a little while, of course, the boiling water came squirting out the top, about a foot or two. It also went all over the kitchen floor, naturally, but Mother, when she came running into the room, had no word of remonstrance for me – none. And when I clapped with joy, she applauded that machine can, too. I remember, it was in that same week our old cat died. (*Small pause.*) Wilbur was the one who took care of Mother while *she* was trying to die, some years later . . . I was 17 and my brother 21, and in poor health *himself*, after a rather bad accident. Ice-skating. (*Small pause.*) And then we lost Mother, and then we learned how to fly, and then . . . in just a matter of years, the typhoid took Wilbur off, loss after loss. But he went away *much* too soon. (*Small pause.*) He used to say the whip-poor-will was mocking our attempts to fly, and the vultures mocked our desire for fame. (*They listen.*) The whip-poor-will is a voice in the dark.

ARTHUR (*suddenly pointing*): Look . . . (*Turning to the others, excitedly.*) Did you see it?

INGA: I always said you were an observing boy.

ARTHUR: Look! Another!

JOE: There you *go*, Dad.

ARTHUR (*pointing*): See, Joe? I think it's starting. Oh! Two at a time! Ada, I *knew* it: it was just the calm before the storm.

ADA: It was worth it, wasn't it? The waiting.

INGA: Isn't it exciting, Mr. Wright?

WRIGHT: Miraculous.

JOE: Jean! Get out here! Jean! Mike!

ARTHUR (*to* ADA): I've never *seen* such a storm!

JOE: Where's Ira? (*He walks down the first of the porch steps and hollers.*) Ira! I – *ra*!

ADA: Joe! Hush! You'll wake the dead!

MICHAEL *enters, carrying a pitcher of orange juice.*

JOE: (*Shouting.*) I – *ra*!

MICHAEL: Who wanted the orange juice?

ARTHUR: See, Ada? There's no stopping it now.

MICHAEL (*looking at the sky*): Wow. (*Turning to shout up at an upstairs window.*) Tom! Tommy! Wake up! (*Turning back down and pointing to the sky.*) Will you look at that, Uncle Joe? Tom! (JEAN *enters.*)

JEAN: What's going on?

ARTHUR: Jean, you're just in time!

JOE (*pointing up*): Look.

JEAN: Amazing.

JOE: Isn't it?

JEAN: Uh-huh. Oh! For Pete's sake! I forgot your shirt!

She turns to head back into the house.

JOE: No! Wait! Here. My t-shirt's dried out anyway.

JEAN: Yeah?

JOE: Well, sort of.

ARTHUR: There!

JEAN: O.K. Come on. Hands up! (*She puts the t-shirt over* JOE's *head.*) First one arm . . . You're shivering.

JOE: I've missed you.

JEAN: I've missed you, too.

JOE: And Jerry and the kids . . . I've missed . . . everybody.

IRA *enters from the lawn, carrying a large plastic flamingo.*

IRA: Hi, Joe. I heard you calling for me.

JOE: I was calling for you.

IRA: I know. I heard.

ARTHUR: Ira.

ADA: Mr. Sherman! You got that from the neighbours!

IRA: Isn't it wonderful? Wouldn't you love to give this as a wedding gift to someone you really didn't care for?

ADA: That's Mr. Albright's flamingo!

IRA (*setting the figurine down*): You must tell me about this Mr. Albright some time.

JOE: Ira. Look.

IRA (*looking up*): Oh, my God.

WRIGHT: My father, the bishop, used to quote a line from the New Testament about a God who calls into existence *things that are not.*

JOE (*putting his arm around* IRA): I'm glad you're here.

IRA: You called for me.

JOE: I know.

IRA: It's a first, I think.

JOE: Maybe . . . I don't know . . . Maybe with practice . . .

IRA: Maybe.

MICHAEL: I bet you could see it better from over there on the river bank.

JOE: Don't . . . you . . . dare! Nobody moves! Everyone, everyone, just hold it right where you are! No more muffins! No more coming and going! No orange juice, no river bank! Just stop! Stay! Please! (*Beat.*) I am grateful, I want you to know that, I'm grateful, but would you please just stay here and let me enjoy it, for God's sake! (*Accelerating.*) Hold onto it, together, the night, that damned bird out there, the waltzing in the barn, Orville, Orville: Dad, why didn't you ever tell me it was him who landed in that plane, or did you? You must have. You must have told me about the baby in Montana that died, Ma, but I just forgot, how could I do that? Ira, your face in the light of a tele . . . And the Christian Marxists of Minnesota, Jean, all those letters I tried to ignore, all that stuff I just threw away, all that ignoring! All that throwing away!

ARTHUR: Joey!

JOE: Pa?

Long pause, with some slightly embarrassed shiftings of feet among the others; some smiles.

ARTHUR: You don't have to throw away a thing. (*Beat.*) But you're gonna have to let go. (*Pause.*)

ADA: I haven't seen him so excited since one day when he was sixteen months old.

MICHAEL: It's a regular shower, isn't it, Grandpa.

ARTHUR: It's a downpour.

MICHAEL: Isn't it terrific, Mom?

MICHAEL, *his eyes fixed on the sky, walks down the steps and disappears into the darkness of the lawn, carrying the pitcher of orange juice.*

JEAN: Sure is.

IRA (*offering his arm to* JEAN, *who takes it*): Jean?

JOE: Ira.

IRA: Joe?

JOE: I'll call you.

IRA: Long distance?

JOE: No. I'll see you. Soon.

IRA: O.K. (JEAN *and* IRA *start down the steps*, IRA *carrying the flamingo under his other arm and* JEAN *carrying a platter of muffins.*) How do you like it?

JEAN: What do you call it?

IRA: Albright.

JEAN: Of course.

IRA *and* JEAN *walk across the lawn, out of sight.*

INGA: I feel as though I were thirteen years old again.

WRIGHT: Miss Thorvaldson. Let's just waltz on out to the lawn, shall we?

INGA: Orville, you know I don't . . .

WRIGHT: It's simple. One, two, three, and all of that. Come on . . . (*He takes her in his arms.*) Just a matter of mathematics, believe me. *One*, two, three, *one*, two, three, *good*, two, three, *one*, two, three . . .

They waltz haltingly across the lawn and into the darkness. Pause.

JOE (*to his parents*): There's no . . . getting over it, I suppose, is there? Your death. In a sense.

ADA: I don't suppose.

ARTHUR: In a sense, that will keep us with you, if you're careful.

JOE: I suppose. (*Small pause.*) The house feels as empty as me.

ADA: As empty as I.

JOE: As empty as I.

ADA: Paul. Drop him a note from time to time, he'd appreciate it, I know he would.

JOE: All right, Ma.

ADA: And don't forget Jean's birthday anymore. It falls so close to Christmas, she's always being neglected.

JOE: I promise.

ARTHUR: Michael looks up to you, Joe, he admires you. That's a responsibility.

JOE: Maybe I'll invite him out to New York, before school starts up. Ira could take him to Coney Island.

ADA: That sounds fine.

JOE: Thank you, Ma. Dad. For all of it.

ARTHUR: It was nothing. (*They each look up into the night sky.*)

JOE (*after a pause*): They won't be coming back, will they.

ARTHUR: Oh, I don't know. Sooner of later, they all come back. (*Pause.*)

ADA: Arthur? I'm here.

ARTHUR *offers her his arm, and* ADA *takes it. The two of them walk slowly down the porch steps and across the lawn into the darkness, looking at the sky. Pause.* JOE *slowly turns up and approaches the house. He opens the screen door and* TOM, *a sleep-tousled fifteen-year-old boy, walks out of it and exits onto the lawn.* JOE *looks after him. Pause.*

JOE: Good luck at oboe camp.

JOE *turns and opens the screen door. He finds the inner door locked. He takes keys from his pocket, opens the door, and goes into the empty house.*

THE PRISONERS OF WAR

To My Father

J.R. ACKERLEY (1897–1967) was the literary editor of *The Listener* from 1935 until 1959. He was a tireless traveller and a prolific correspondent. His books include: *My Father and Myself, Hindoo Holiday* (Chatto & Windus, 1932), *We Think the World of You* (The Bodley Head, 1960), *My Dog Tulip* (The Bodley Head, 1987), *Micheldever and Other Poems* (Ian McKelvie) and a biography of E.M. Forster (Ian McKelvie).

The Prisoners of War

'I was born in 1896 and my parents were married in 1919' wrote J.R. Ackerley at the beginning of his posthumously published autobiography *My Father and Myself* (The Bodley Head, 1968, reprinted Penguin 1971). He volunteered at the outbreak of the First World War (along with his brother Peter, killed in 1918), serving in the trenches of the Western Front until he was wounded at the battle of Cérisy and taken prisoner. He was sent to a hospital in Hanover, subsequently to prison camps at Karlsruhe and Augustbad and then invalided to Switzerland where he was interned until the end of the war. While an internee, he drafted his only play: *The Prisoners of War*. He went up to Cambridge in 1919, by which time he had published some poems. His other publications include *Hindoo Holiday: An Indian Journal* (Chatto & Windus 1932), *My Dog Tulip: Life with an Alsatian* (Secker & Warburg, 1956), *We Think the World of You* (The Bodley Head, 1960) and *My Father and Myself*. He was the Literary Editor of *The Listener* between 1935 and 1959 and died in 1967.

The Prisoners of War was published in 1925, to coincide with the first production of the play by the Three Hundred Club (founded in 1924 by Mrs Geoffrey Whitworth who intended it to present 'dramas of distinguished merit . . . likely to appeal in the first instance to a small public'). Staged for one performance only on Sunday, 5 July, that first cast included Raymond Massey and Robert Harris with Donald Wolfit as Assistant Stage Manager. Nigel Playfair transferred the production to The Playhouse on 31 August.

'The facts are dark, it may be, but the treatment is full of light – the light of which no audience can fail to be continuously aware when a man, who is deeply and sincerely moved by his subject, writes with a superb naturalness and a real control of the stage,' commented the anonymous critic of *The Times*, reviewing the Three Hundred Club production. Not all responses were so favourable – as the reviewer in the *Sunday Times* made clear when he covered the transfer: 'I have been surprised and grieved by the reception given by some of my colleagues to this really beautiful and moving piece . . .'

Yet the play had distinguished supporters. 'It seemed to me that Joe Ackerley's *The Prisoners of War* led to unanswerable conclusions against modern war,' reflected John Lehmann in the first volume of his autobiography, *The Whispering Gallery* (Longman, 1955). 'I was deeply moved, even without seeing it on the stage.'

And that most famous of veterans and protestants against the First World War – Siegfried Sassoon – confided to his diary (21 April 1925) that in his view the published text of the play was 'painful but interesting'. After seeing the play in performance, Sassoon wrote (15 September 1925) that it was 'painful but impressive', adding 'It was strange, to watch, on the stage, the sort of behaviour which I've mildly indulged in myself, when "attracted by an incompatible object".' Arnold Bennett, Sassoon notes in the same entry, 'condemned *The Prisoners of War* as "no good at all, and quite untrue to life". E.M. Forster disagreed, and called it "a fine thing".'

It is worth noting that Ackerley's play had important consequences for E.M. Forster. When Ackerley was living at 6 Hammersmith Terrace, Hammersmith in West London, he struck up a friendship with a young (and gay) policeman called Harry Daley, who recognised him as the author of *The Prisoners of War*. The two men became friends, Ackerley introduced Daley to Forster and Daley introduced Forster to another policeman, Bob Buckingham, who was to become central to Forster's life.

Of course, *The Prisoners of War* is highly autobiographical. In Chapter 12 of *My Father and Myself*, Ackerley admits that the central character, Captain Conrad, is 'myself of course' and makes abundantly clear that Conrad's obsession with Second-Lieutenant Grayle parallels two 'attractions' he felt whilst interned in Switzerland ('One was a captain of my own age named Carlyon . . . the other, a consumptive boy who died of his complaints soon after the Armistice . . .'). Like Conrad in the play, Ackerley was a virgin – and remained so until he reached Cambridge (after which he became caught up with the lifetime pursuit of the Ideal Friend from the working-classes).

The Prisoners of War is a play about confinement and repression and about the way in which enforced proximity to others can heighten and distort emotion. Clearly – at least to modern sensibilities – Conrad is homosexual and in love with the uncomprehending and, on the whole, rather worthless Grayle. There are two passages in the play which make Conrad's inclinations quite evident. In Act One, when fellow internee Adelby is talking to Conrad about the Theban band, he is gently indicating his understanding of Conrad's feelings for Grayle. In Act Two, in an exchange between Mme. Louis and Conrad, the Jewish adventuress makes reference to 'the fair sex'. 'The fair sex?' Conrad asks. 'Which sex is that?'

Yet – even though Ackerley considered his other characters 'entirely normal' – there is at least one further instance in the play of a relationship which – to our eyes today – is emotionally homosexual and *because of this* the cause of much of the internal tension of the piece. 'And although Tetford regards Rickman as *his* pal, the notion of their going to bed together ought to be as unthinkable to the audience as I meant it to be to them,' Ackerley wrote in a letter to Stephen Spender (132 in *The Ackerley Letters*, 1975). Surely the dramatist was deluding himself?

Surely the friendship between Lieutenant Tetford and Captain Rickman is subliminally homosexual? Surely their friendship – because of their confinement, their proximity – *has* turned into love? How else to explain Tetford's jealousy when Rickman drops him and takes up with Grayle? How else to explain Tetford's glee when he holds Rickman to a previous arrangement – thereby separating him from and abandoning Grayle to tea alone with Mme. Louis. And the conversation in Act Three, in which Tetford and Rickman discuss setting up together in Canada after the war doesn't include any reference to marriage, or to women. Going to bed together might be 'unthinkable' within the confines of the play but once they've set themselves up in Canada it becomes an altogether different proposition.

It is worth noting that *The Prisoners of War* was designed by James Whale (himself gay), now best remembered as director of *Frankenstein* (1931) and *The Bride of Frankenstein* (1935) – but who directed the London and Broadway productions of *Journey's End* and made his full directorial debut in Hollywood with the screen version of that play.

As with any play of the period, *The Prisoners of War* contains attitudes which are unacceptable today – casual racism (Mme. Louis is dismissed and derided as much for being Jewish as for being a woman); classism (this is very much a world of masters and servants – though preference for working-class youths may have inclined Ackerley away from making *his* servants into the comic caricatures which so mar R.C. Sherriff's *Journey's End*) and snobbery. Yet it remains an effective and affecting piece – and has been heard on radio (3 May 1953, repeated 8 May and 20 June) and revived on stage (1955).

In the letter to Stephen Spender already cited, Ackerley explains why critics of the first stage production 'voiced an understandable surprise to find not barbed wire and bayonets, but comparative luxury . . .' He felt the play had been misnamed. 'It should never have been called *The Prisoners of War*,' he wrote, 'but *The Interns*'. And it was under this title the play was broadcast. Though to modern audiences even the concept of internment of the 1914–1918 war might seem incomprehensible. Yet during the First World War injured officers could find themselves internees in comparative luxury in non-combatant countries and repatriated to their homelands so long as they were likely to remain unfit to serve. It was a very different kind of war.

I should like to thank Joe Mitchenson of the Raymond Mander & Joe Mitchenson Theatre Collection for supplying details of The Playhouse production of *The Prisoners of War*.

Peter Burton
Brighton, 1988

The Prisoners of War was first presented at the Three Hundred Club, London on 5 July 1925, transferring to The Playhouse, London on 31 August 1925, with the following cast:

SECOND-LIEUTENANT GRAYLE	Robert Harris
LIEUTENANT TETFORD	Carleton Hobbs
CAPTAIN RICKMAN	Raymond Massey
MARIE	Antonia Brough
LIEUTENANT ADELBY	Ivor Barnard
CAPTAIN CONRAD	George Hayes
JELLERTON	Gordon Harker
MRS PRENDERGAST	Marie Ault
MME. LOUIS	Leah Bateman
DR. CROZ	Hector Abbas

Produced by Nigel Playfair
By arrangement with Ida Molesworth and Templer Powell
Designed by James Whale

The action of the play throughout takes place in Captain Conrad's sitting-room in a hotel in Mürren, Switzerland during the summer of 1918.

ACT ONE

CAPTAIN CONRAD's *sitting-room in an hotel in Mürren, Switzerland at midday on 20 July 1918. The door which gives access to the room from the passage is, from the spectators' point of view, about one-third of the way up the right-hand wall. Beyond the door, against the wall, is a table, and above it a bookshelf. The door opens inwards against this table. Beyond the table again and in the corner is a tall white cupboard let into the wall. Two large, glass-pannelled verandah doors occupy the middle of the middle wall. To the right of them is a chair, with a map of the Berner Oberlands pinned to the wall above it. In the top left-hand corner are a pair of skis and some ski-sticks. Against the left wall, in the centre of it, is a big table with a chair at each of the three sides. A picture hangs on either side of the table. Low right, centre, stands a smallish round table, with a long sofa (stage left) and an easy wicker-chair (stage right) behind it.*

The room is in a mild state of confusion. The tables, except the centre one, are piled with a mixed assortment of books, papers and articles of clothing, such as hats and gloves. In addition to these things, the left-hand table has some tennis balls, a racket and two packs of cards scattered upon it. There is a book on the centre table.

The windows at the back are open, and through them can be seen a broad-railed grass-covered verandah, ending upon the edge of a slope, and beyond, across the Lauterbrunnen valley, but apparently so near that one feels one can touch them, the Grosshorn, Mittaghorn, and Ebnefluh, snow-capped and impressive, with their light blue glaciers, white avalanche paths, and murmuring, cascading streams. The sunshine strikes a burning, eye-wearying brilliance from their hardened snows and ice, and the faint tinkling of cow-bells mingled with the murmuring of restless water floats in through the open windows.

SECOND-LIEUTENANT ALLAN GRAYLE, *an observer in the RAF, comes in by the door on the right, followed by* LIEUTENANT TETFORD, *a pilot in the RAF, and* CAPTAIN RICKMAN, *of the 2nd CMR's. They are all dressed in tunics and slacks, except* TETFORD, *who is wearing khaki shorts and stockings.* RICKMAN *is rather like a wild horse. Of the other two,* GRAYLE (19) *is the better-looking, but* TETFORD (22) *has the better face.*

GRAYLE: Come in and make your yourselves at home.

He throws his cap negligently on the centre table, and strolling over to the verandah windows, opens them wider.

RICKMAN (*dropping into the wicker chair and opening his cigarette case*): Where's Conrad?

TETFORD (*to* RICKMAN): Don't put your case away.

RICKMAN (*proferring cigarettes*): Sorry, Bo'!

TETFORD (*taking one*): Thanks.

GRAYLE (*sprawling on the sofa*): Conrad? I don't know.

TETFORD: He's probably out with Adelby.

He sits in the chair by CONRAD's *table, left, and puts his feet on it.*

GRAYLE: Probably.

There is a pause. They came into the room hurriedly as though there was some objective in view. But their only object apparently was to get into the room, and this they have achieved. Presently, one can't help thinking, they will all get up and hurry out of the room, just in order not to be in the room any longer. RICKMAN *shifts restlessly and gets up.*

RICKMAN: Well? What's doin' this morning?

TETFORD (*laughing*): That's the fourth time. (*To* GRAYLE.) Make a note of it, old bean; he's asked that question four times in the last half-hour.

RICKMAN: Then why don't you answer it instead of sitting there like a half-bake?

GRAYLE: You know yourself there's nothing doing unless you want to go and play tennis, so why ask silly questions?

TETFORD: Seconded.

GRAYLE: And personally I'm sick of tennis.

Pause.

RICKMAN: Christ! This is the life! What about a drink?

TETFORD (*lazily*): Thanks very much, I will.

RICKMAN (*producing dice from his pocket*): I'll roll you for it.

TETFORD: It's your turn. I bought the last one.

RICKMAN: I just forget who bought the last one, but you're a goddamn liar, so I guess I did!

TETFORD (*with a laugh, taking the proffered dice*): QED. Who goes first?

RICKMAN: You're in this, Grayle.

GRAYLE: No, thanks.

RICKMAN: Eh?

GRAYLE: Isn't it rather early . . .?

RICKMAN: Shoot that! You roll after Harry. I'll go last. What's it to be? One roll or three?

TETFORD: One. I'm thirsty.

RICKMAN: Right. Watch him, Grayle; he's as crooked as a dog's hind leg!

TETFORD (*bending forward and rolling the two dice on the carpet*): Tut! Tut! A three and a one. Four! My luck's out. (*He hands dice to* GRAYLE *and falls lazily back in his chair.*)

GRAYLE: Who pays? The one who makes most or least?

RICKMAN: Least, you silly stiff!

GRAYLE (*rolling*): A five and a three. Eight. I'm out of it.

RICKMAN (*taking dice*): I guess I can beat Harry, anway. (*He rattles dice in his hand.*) Come on, little bones! Fever in the South! (*He rolls.*) Well, I'll be bitten by rattlesnakes! A two and a one! Three!

TETFORD (*dreamily*): Mine's a vermouth.

GRAYLE (*laughing*): So's mine. (*He has only lately enjoyed the confidence of Rickman and Tetford. But he is not shy.*)

RICKMAN: We'll roll three each and then add 'em up. It's fairer. (*He has a delightfully naif way of making preposterous remarks like this, as though he does not for a moment expect that anyone will gainsay him.*)

TETFORD: Optimist!

RICKMAN: Come on! Be a sport, Grayle.

GRAYLE: What a hope you've got!

RICKMAN (*injured*): Oh, all right. Ruddy sharks! (*He rings bell, right.*) Jesus! This is the life . . . this is the life! Do you think I'm failing with it? Look how my hand shakes! (*He holds out a rigid arm.*)

TETFORD: Horrible! Drink's killed many a better man.

RICKMAN: Drink be blistered! It's running around this joint like a goddamn fool with nothing to do but hang my hat up.

GRAYLE *laughs.* RICKMAN *strides about jangling money and keys in his trouser pockets.*

I've just about reached my limit. Breakfast. Sit around or go and worry the men. Same after lunch; same after tea. It's no life for a man. Its hell! That's what it is.

GRAYLE: I wish the snow would come. Then we should be able to ski and bob, and so forth.

TETFORD (*singing to himself*): 'But when that summer time is over, Oh! Oh! That is the time . . .'

There is a knock at the door.

RICKMAN: Come in! (MARIE, *a Swiss maid, opens it.*), Three vermuths, Marie. (*He pronounces vermuth as it is spelt.*)

MARIE: Yes, sir. (*She drawls slightly on the 'sir.'*)

RICKMAN: Put them down to Mr Tetford.

TETFORD (*jumping up*): Don't you,

Marie! Put them down to Captain Rickman!

RICKMAN: They were your drinks.

TETFORD: Well, of all the . . .

MARIE *withdraws, wreathed in smiles.*

GRAYLE: Steady on, you chaps! Conrad doesn't like horseplay in his room.

RICKMAN (*laughing*): Poor old Harry! Did y'see his face? He nearly keeled over! Jesus! It was funny!

TETFORD: You're a low swine, Eric. That's my opinion. But I daresay the jury will let you off, since you were born in Canada.

RICKMAN (*throwing himself into his chair again*): Never mind, Harry. (*Pause.*) What d'you say we all get tight?

TETFORD: What you mean is who'll put up the gelt for *you* to get tight on.

GRAYLE: There isn't enough drink in the village for that.

RICKMAN: Well, what the hell else is there to do? Come and put in for leave to Montreux (*he pronounces it 'Montro'*) with me, Harry?

TETFORD: What's the good? We've just had ten days' leave, so they won't give us more than three days this time, and it takes a day to go and a day to come back.

GRAYLE: Let's all go down to Interlaken for the night. Anything's better than staying up on this rotten precipice. We might have rather a rag. (*His face is quite eager.*)

TETFORD: Conrad would have to come too, then.

GRAYLE: Jim? Why?

TETFORD (*mischievously*): Well, he's your great pal, after all, isn't he? I didn't think you'd want to go down to Interlaken without him. (*Indicating* RICKMAN.) Eric and I always hunt together.

GRAYLE (*disconcerted*): Ye-es . . . but it's rather different. Besides, he wouldn't want to come. He hates

Interlaken and . . . women and . . . so forth.

TETFORD (*winking at* RICKMAN): He'd want to go if you're going, though, wouldn't he? We'd better ask him for appearance sake, anyway.

GRAYLE: Oh, no! Don't let's ask him. He'd only be in the way.

TETFORD (*as if surprised*): In the way?

GRAYLE: Well – you know what I mean. He's not a sport like you and Rickman. He'd only cast a damper on everything. He'd advise me not to go, or something.

TETFORD: But you needn't take his advice.

GRAYLE: Of course, not. (*Lamely.*) But I'd sooner go as we are. Just us three.

RICKMAN: Conrad's a virgin, isn't he?

GRAYLE: So he says.

TETFORD (*to* GRAYLE): So are you.

GRAYLE (*blushing with shame*): Yes, but I'm only nineteen. Conrad's twenty-four.

TETFORD (*cynically*): Scandalous, isn't it?

RICKMAN (*to* GRAYLE): Is that what's preying on Conrad's mind? He's always gettin' out of bed the wrong side, and grumblin' at someone.

GRAYLE: No, I don't think so. He seems to take a great pride in it. I think it's rather priggish of him not to do what other fellows do.

TETFORD: I rather like old Conrad, even though he does carry things to extremes. Do you remember when Chilvers was up here and Crawley got him on to talk about his lurid past?

GRAYLE: I don't think I was here then.

TETFORD: Funniest thing out! Conrad told Chilvers that his mind was like a dung heap, and he wasn't going to have it exposed in his room! Chilvers turned a sort of pale mauve.

GRAYLE (*laughing*): Of course, that's Jim all over.

RICKMAN: There was hell a-poppin' then, I bet!

GRAYLE: I don't think virginity is

anything to be ashamed of. But Conrad oughtn't to let it become an obsession with him.

TETFORD: So you want to tear yours, do you? You want to come and look for romance with us in Interlaken?

GRAYLE (*blushing*): Well . . . it would be a change from this place, anyway. It's so dull up here.

TETFORD: And we won't say a word to your nurse about it.

GRAYLE (*indignantly*): Shut up! Of course I'd go with Jim if he wasn't such a spoil sport. He seemed quite different when I first came up here. He's always nagging now.

TETFORD: It's very decent of him letting you use this room of his, anyway.

GRAYLE (*without warmth*): Oh yes, it is.

RICKMAN: What's bitten Conrad lately? He used to be a civil sort of fellow once, and now he's changed so's you wouldn't know him. He makes me mad as hell sometimes with his soft sarcasms.

He rubs his forehead, half apologetically – for he's a decent fellow at heart – and jumps up.

I dunno. How d'you stick him, Grayle? Sharing this room with him as you do, I'd be licking hell out of him inside of a week! Where's those drinks? (*He rings again.*) The Kitchen Mechanic's taking her time.

GRAYLE: We used to get on all right together. I don't know what's been biting him lately. I suppose it's just . . . (*He pauses, searching for a word.*)

TETFORD: Just what?

GRAYLE: Oh, being a prisoner of war and so forth. Of course you two don't know him as well as I do. He bores me stiff with his nagging and preaching and . . . I'm sick to death of him. That's why I leave him to himself so much now.

TETFORD: I should have thought if you disliked him as much as all that you wouldn't accept favours from him.

GRAYLE: What do you mean?

TETFORD: Well, this room, for instance.

GRAYLE: But I like this room. It's the warmest in the hotel, and no one else has got a private sitting-room – except the Major. You wouldn't chuck it up if you were in my place. After all, he picks the quarrels always; it's nothing to do with me. The only reason I humour him at all is because I want to use the room, not for the pleasure of his temper. Fat lot of pleasure!

TETFORD: Hardly friendly, is it? I wonder he *lets* you use it and bring your pals here, since you've given him the cold shoulder. However, it's not my business – except that I rather like the old bird!

GRAYLE: Pooh! I can do what I like with him.

Upon which amicable observation there is a knock at the door.

RICKMAN: Come right inside!

MARIE comes in with three vermuths on a tray, which she sets down on the centre table.

We'd better have another round. What d'you say?

GRAYLE (*anxious to do the right thing*): It's my turn this time.

RICKMAN: Bring three more, will you, Marie? And put them down to Mr Grayle.

MARIE: Yes, sir.

She retires.

RICKMAN (*taking his*): Help yourselves.

TETFORD: Pass mine along, Grayle. Thanks.

RICKMAN: Well – here's over the river! (*He tosses his off.*)

GRAYLE: Cheer oh! (*He sips his.*)

TETFORD: Here's to the Repatriation Board on the thirtieth! May it take pity on us!

GRAYLE: Hear! Hear!

RICKMAN: Yes, by God! If I don't pass that goddamn Board this time, I'll eat my hat!

GRAYLE (*laughing*): You! You're the strongest, healthiest fellow in Switzerland!

RICKMAN (*angrily*): Who says? What the hell do you know about it, anyway? (*He glares at him, for it was an ill jest.*) That's the sort of damn-fool remark that don't do no one any good.

He shoots his cuffs fiercely and shrugs his tunic up on to his neck, where it never seems to fit.

I've got about an ounce of shrapnel in my lungs for one thing, and my nerves are all gone to hell. I went to see the doctor this morning.

TETFORD: What did he say?

RICKMAN: He didn't say nothin'. He's so damn clever he hates himself! I told him I was ill and wanted to be recommended for this Board. I told him I was going potty, cracky, bughouse, nuts.

GRAYLE: I should think he understood a lot of that! What did he say?

RICKMAN: Oh, he gave me some pills or something – goddamn fool! I pitched 'em in the gutter.

TETFORD (*lazily*): Dirty Schweizer!

RICKMAN: It's true, too. It's getting me crazed, this life. It's waste; that's what it is, waste! Day and night . . . day and night, and nothing to it. Not a ruddy skirt in the whole shootin' match! It's got me beat! Conrad's beat! You watch him! And we'll all be the same in a bit; sarcastic, grousing, hangdog – oh, hell! (*He pauses.*) Let me out from this and I'll be off to Canada like a cut cat, and if you see me back here again you can borrow a fiver off me.

TETFORD: You let things worry you too much, old bean. Look at me! I never worry.

RICKMAN (*sitting*): You've not got anything to worry you.

TETFORD (*smiling*): I wouldn't let it worry me if I had.

RICKMAN: What's the good of us now? We're has-beens. I've forgotten every ruddy thing I ever knew about timber, and now the Army's got no goddamn use for me.

TETFORD (*murmuring*): Chevaliers de la crosse en l'air.

RICKMAN (*complainingly*): I'm soft now . . . soft as a fool; but I used to be strong as an ox and hard as hard.

Little ADELBY comes in. Nobody thinks very much about ADELBY. He is such a silent little man that his existence is forgotten except when he is in the room, and often even then. He is rather grey and ugly too, and seems to be interested only in the large pipes he smokes and tends like babies, for he rarely speaks unless he has something worth saying. What goes on behind that placid mask, what moods, what ambitions, what passions are unknown to us; but we imagine him to be a simple little man of simple ways, unsuspicious of God and man alike.

GRAYLE (*to whom ADELBY's entrance means a welcome break in the conversation*): Hullo! Here's old Adelby! Just too late for a drink.

RICKMAN: No, he's not. Have a drink, Adelby?

RICKMAN is always generous in collecting people to another's party.

ADELBY: No, thank you.

A declination from ADELBY is usually sincere, so they do not press him; also, they do not much care whether he drinks or not.

GRAYLE: Hot milk's his speciality.

TETFORD: Where's Conrad?

ADELBY: He's just coming up. He's speaking to Mother Prendergast and the Major down below.

TETFORD: Anything exciting?

ADELBY: It's about a dance, I believe. They're going to get one up here soon.

RICKMAN: Dance! There ain't any skirts.

GRAYLE (*eagerly*): Yes, there are – if you look carefully. We can rake in all those Swiss girls – the two daughters of old Kammermann of the Hotel Alpenstock, for instance – and the officers' wives and Mrs Prendergast and Mrs Olly, and so forth. . . . You could easily find enough for a dance. Oh – and there's a Swiss lady coming up from Basel, Mrs Hauser says. Madame Louis, I think the name was. After all, there are only nine officers.

There is a knock at the door.

GRAYLE: Come in!

Enter MARIE with three more vermuths, which she places on the centre table.

RICKMAN: Well . . . what's doin' to-day, Adelby?

TETFORD (*with a shriek of joy*): Five! Poor old Eric! Tell him the worst, Adders.

ADELBY (*bringing a chair from the back towards the table and filling his pipe*): I don't think there's anything unusual. The courts aren't dry enough for tennis, I hear.

GRAYLE (*to MARIE*): Thank you. (*He studies her thoughtfully.*)

MARIE: Thank you, sir. (*She retires with the first lot of glasses.*)

RICKMAN (*taking his drink*): Help yourselves.

GRAYLE (*handing drink*): Harry.

RICKMAN: Here's over the river. (*He tosses it off.*)

TETFORD: Thanks. Chin-chin.

GRAYLE: Cheer oh. (*He sips his.*)

TETFORD (*to ADELBY*): And how's the fire-eater this morning?

ADELBY: Who's that?

TETFORD (*smiling*): Conrad.

ADELBY: Oh, Conrad. I really don't know. He seems all right. Why?

TETFORD: I only wondered.

ADELBY: Is he supposed to be ill?

RICKMAN (*heavily*): Ill? No. Damned unsociable! (ADELBY *closes like an oyster.*) Surly as the devil he was yesterday.

GRAYLE: He may be in love.

TETFORD (*glancing at him*): Don't you know?

RICKMAN: Swinging the lead for the Repatriation Board more likely.

ADELBY (*quietly*): He's not going up for it.

TETFORD (*surprised*): Why not?

RICKMAN: Of course he is.

ADELBY: The doctor said he'd recommend him if he liked, but he hadn't the smallest chance of being passed, so he isn't going to try.

RICKMAN: So *that's* what's soured him.

TETFORD: Damn it, Eric. He's been up here in Mürren longer than any of us and he never takes any leave, and I *know* he's been hoping to get home for a long time, so you can't expect him to howl with joy!

RICKMAN: Then why don't he go on leave or put in for a transfer if he don't like the place, instead of runnin' around with a bee in his bonnet?

ADELBY (*quietly from behind his pipe*): I suppose he's like most of us; he wants to go home. But if he's *got* to stay in this country he doesn't care very much what part he's in. He's ambitious, and it hits that sort hardest – being prisoners of war.

RICKMAN (*after a pause*): Well, he'll go bughouse if he stays here much longer – as mad as a dog that's sat in turpentine.

GRAYLE (*laughing*): You have got some wonderful expressions.

RICKMAN: He seems to like this joint, what's more. Christ! He must be fond of England!

ADELBY: It's not a bad little place. Why do *you* stay here if you don't like it?

RICKMAN: 'Cos I've got to, that's why. You don't suppose I'd be kicking my heels here if I could go down to Montro? They didn't cotton to me down there, so they sent me up to this strafe-camp as a punishment.

ADELBY: Well – since you're here, it wouldn't be a bad thing if you made the best of it.

RICKMAN: You and Conrad make a pair. You'd better stay up here together and (*with a wave of the hand towards the mountains*) admire the beautiful scenery at your leisure (*which he pronounces 'leesure'*).

The door is swung violently open and CONRAD (*24*) *bursts in. He stops dead on seeing* RICKMAN *and a slight frown crosses his face.*

CONRAD: Hullo! What's all this? Temperance meeting?

RICKMAN: Just a pow-wow. Any objection?

CONRAD: Oh, no. I rather want to write a letter, if *you* don't object.

RICKMAN: That's funny, I s'pose. Why don't you try getting out of bed the other side every now and then?

CONRAD (*ignoring* RICKMAN, *to* TETFORD): D'you mind, Harry? There's room on the sofa.

TETFORD (*getting up and strolling to the sofa*): Sorry, old bean.

CONRAD *sits down at his table, and taking a writing pad opens it.* GRAYLE *is whispering to* RICKMAN, *telling him to humour* CONRAD.

CONRAD (*looking round*): By the way, I want some stamps. Who can lend me a couple? Allan?

GRAYLE: Sorry, I haven't got any.

ADELBY: I think I have.

He pulls a little black case from his pocket and opens it. Something drops near RICKMAN. *It is a photo.*

RICKMAN (*picking it up*): You've dropped something. Hullo! Who's the girl, Adelby? You're a sly old fox! I'll tell your wife!

ADELBY (*quietly, holding out his hand*): It happens to be my wife.

RICKMAN (*astonished*): Your . . .! Well, I'll be . . .!

ADELBY (*quietly, interrupting, his hand outstretched*): If you don't mind.

RICKMAN (*handing it back*): Sorry, Bo'!

ADELBY (*taking it*): Thank you. Here you are, Conrad. (*He gives him two stamps.*)

CONRAD: Thanks. Remind me, will you?

ADELBY *takes his chair out on to the verandah with him and sits out of sight in the sun.*

RICKMAN (*to* TETFORD): Well . . . can you beat that?

TETFORD: No. I think it was damned rude of you.

RICKMAN: I wasn't thinking. It knocked me sideways. (*Pause.*) Did you see it, though? Damned pretty girl!

GRAYLE: No? I wish I'd seen it.

RICKMAN: Old Adelby, too! (*He laughs.*) That's rich!

CONRAD (*who has been searching for something on his table*): I wish you wouldn't use my table as a lumber room, Allan. (*He pushes the tennis racket and balls to one side.*)

GRAYLE: You never use it yourself.

RICKMAN: They're my things, anyway. (*He cannot keep the challenge out of his voice.*)

CONRAD: Then they wouldn't be out of place in *your* room. Besides, it's bad policy to make *my* sitting-room uncomfortable, since you regard it as yours.

RICKMAN: Shoot . . .! (GRAYLE *silences him by dragging at his sleeve.*)

CONRAD: Where's the ink? This thing's dry. I know I bought some.

TETFORD (*yawning and getting up*): O dear! Where's Adelby? I believe the old bird's sunning himself. Come on to the verandah, Eric.

He strolls out, taking a book from CONRAD's *shelf on the way, and is seen to lie down on the grass near the only part of* ADELBY *visible – his feet.*

CONRAD: Do you know where the ink is, Allan?

GRAYLE: No, I don't.

CONRAD: Look on that other table, will you? (*But somehow or other it is not quite the right tone, and*

RICKMAN *laughs shortly*.)

GRAYLE: Why don't you look yourself? I'm not your orderly.

This is pure 'swank' on GRAYLE'*s part and for the benefit of* RICKMAN. *If* RICKMAN *were not here he would have looked for the ink without a murmur.*

CONRAD (*quietly*): Because I asked you to.

RICKMAN (*mockingly*): Get a move on, Grayle!

GRAYLE: I don't see why I should look for your ink. If you want it you'd better look for it yourself. (CONRAD *scrutinises him, but says nothing.*) You get your own way too much; that's why you're always so bad-tempered. Perhaps you like picking quarrels?

CONRAD (*getting up*): Never mind. (*He finds the ink on the right-hand table and fills his inkpot.*) I'm a bit irritable this morning, I expect. (*He puts the ink back on the table. (R.) on a heap of books and papers.*) What do *you* think, Rickman?

RICKMAN (*bluntly*): I guess so.

CONRAD: So do I. (*He sits down and begins to write.*)

RICKMAN: Have a drink with me? It'll make you feel a noo man.

CONRAD: No, thanks.

RICKMAN: Just to show there's no ill-feeling?

CONRAD: No, thanks. I never drink in the middle of the day.

RICKMAN: Shoot that! Just a vermuth.

CONRAD (*irritably*): No, no, really, thank you. I don't want one.

RICKMAN: I shall feel kind of insulted if you don't.

CONRAD: Can't help that.

RICKMAN: You're a goddamned unsociable swine!

GRAYLE: You'd better have a drink with him, Jim, if he wants you to.

CONRAD (*irately*): Good Lord! Haven't I told you I don't want a drink! Why on earth can't you leave me alone?

GRAYLE: Oh, all right.

CONRAD: I told you I didn't want a drink about three times. Isn't that enough? I don't want a drink so I won't have a drink. Is that definite?

RICKMAN (*going over to him and putting his hands on his shoulders*): God! Conrad; I have a kind o' feeling sometimes that a goddamn licking wouldn't do you no harm!

CONRAD: And you might be improved by an English lesson.

RICKMAN (*dragging CONRAD from his chair*): What the hell d'you mean by that? You . . .!

GRAYLE (*simultaneously*): Oh, don't quarrel, you two; for heaven's sake!

GRAYLE (*intervening*): Shut up! What the devil's the matter with you, Jim? I'll leave your room if you don't shut up! (CONRAD *seems to subside at once and stares at* GRAYLE.)

RICKMAN: He's so goddamn clever he bores himself to death.

CONRAD (*to* GRAYLE): I'm sorry. (*Explosively to* RICKMAN.) But why don't you leave me alone? Can't you see I'm ill? (*He passes his hand over his forehead.*)

RICKMAN: I guess I will, before I lam you. You make yourself about as popular as a skunk at a garden party! (*With which he leaves the room, banging the door.*)

CONRAD (*irritably*): Why do you keep on bringing that fellow into my room, Allan?

GRAYLE (*rebelliously*): He's a jolly decent fellow. I get on with him, anyway. It only wants a little tact. Besides, I don't bring him; he comes.

CONRAD: You can't possibly like him. He's not your sort.

GRAYLE: That's no reason why I should be rude to him, like you. (CONRAD *does not reply.* GRAYLE *stands in the middle of the room, talking.*) It's dull enough up here as it is, without going out of the way to make enemies. I hate all this bickering and back-biting and so forth.

CONRAD (*sitting down*): Well, I've asked you two or three times not to bring him into my room, and I think you might take some notice of me.

GRAYLE: I tell you I don't bring him. What's wrong with him, anyway?

CONRAD: I don't like to see you knocking about with him.

GRAYLE: Oh, rot! I'm not a baby.

CONRAD (*after a pause*): Why are you so restless these days, anyway?

GRAYLE: What d'you mean?

CONRAD: Well . . . you're always knocking about with Tom, Dick, and Harry. I hardly ever see you at all now, (*Bitterly.*) and when I do you seem to have come up simply for the pleasure of annoying me.

GRAYLE: That's rot, and you know it. I'm often in here, every day in fact.

CONRAD: Yes, but always with Tom, Dick, and Harry at your heels. Never alone, and for the pleasure of seeing me as before.

GRAYLE (*his mind reverting to their former theme*): Well, I can't help you not liking Rickman. You used to be friendly enough with him once. When I disliked him, too, that was! *I* didn't make a fuss.

CONRAD: Great, hulking lout; he was sent away from Montreux for misbehaviour, and now he grouses because he can't find a chance of doing the same thing up here.

GRAYLE: I know he's got faults. Everybody's got faults of some kind. But he means well.

CONRAD (*sneering*): Does he? I'm glad of that.

GRAYLE: I think he's rather amusing, personally, and if you weren't so jolly touchy you'd think so too.

He throws himself onto the sofa, knocking the book off the table (C.) as he does so.

CONRAD (*looking round*): What's that?

GRAYLE (*making no attempt to retrieve it*): Only a book.

CONRAD: *Only* a book! Pick it up, man! You're getting devilish clumsy these days.

GRAYLE (*picking it up and slinging it on to the chair*): Sorry.

CONRAD (*getting up*): Steady on, for God's sake. That's not the way to treat a book. (*He examines it.*) I hate to see books spoilt.

GRAYLE: I haven't spoilt it.

CONRAD: You might have. (*He puts the book back on the shelf (R.) and returns to the table.*)

GRAYLE: I suppose you're trying to pick another quarrel with me now?

CONRAD (*licking his envelope*): Not at all. You know I look upon my books as children, so you might take more care of them (*Smiling.*) instead of slinging them about the room.

GRAYLE (*yawning*): What's the good of them, anyway? They're no use to you when you've once read them.

CONRAD: Now you're talking nonsense, and . . .

GRAYLE: All right! All right! I've heard that argument before.

CONRAD *sinks his face in his hands for a moment.* GRAYLE *notes this, his brows contract unsympathetically, and he turns his head away from this tiresome claim upon his compassion.*

CONRAD (*rising and sitting on the end of the sofa near* GRAYLE*'s head*): You're not much of a pal nowadays, are you, Allan? (*He looks lonely and dispirited.*)

GRAYLE (*uneasily*): What do you mean?

CONRAD: You always stood up for me once, and now you take everyone's side against me. What have I done?

GRAYLE: I dunno. You're a bit of a bear.

CONRAD: I can't help it. I've always been the same. I haven't got much tolerance. I wish I had.

GRAYLE: It's only a question of trying. You don't even try. *I* manage to pull along all right without fighting.

CONRAD (*gloomily*): I suppose it's all my fault. When you're always rubbing up against the same people you get to know too much about them. I remember hitting a fellow in one of the camps in Germany because he always whistled the same tune.

GRAYLE: I think it's a jolly good thing to be always cheerful – to pretend to be. I mean – like Adelby and Tetford, for instance.

CONRAD: I can't. I don't know why. I *do* try, really; but somehow it doesn't work.

GRAYLE: I've never seen you trying, as you call it.

CONRAD (*earnestly*): But I do – honestly. To please you, really, because – I don't know. What do you think I ought to do?

GRAYLE: I think you ought to try a change and go to some other place.

CONRAD (*astonished*): And leave you? And leave – this?

GRAYLE: Why not?

CONRAD: Good God! It would kill me. Leave you and this room and the mountains, and go down to a sweltering, dago-ridden town?

GRAYLE: I think this is an awful hole.

CONRAD (*sadly*): Do you?

GRAYLE: And you won't have a friend left in the place if you stay here much longer. That's certain.

CONRAD: Except you. You'll stick by me, won't you? You know I don't mean it, and it's only the life. You could help me no end, you know, if you were decent to me. It's the sort of thing I'm always wanting to talk to you about – only you're never alone. I'm not well either; I haven't been at all well lately. This is a decent room too, and we shall be quite comfortable together. It's when I'm like this that I want you most. You'll stick by me, eh? (*He strokes the curly head affectionately.*)

GRAYLE (*who has been educated at a good public school*): Look out!

Someone might come in! (*He sits upright.*) You ought to apologise to Rickman, anyway.

CONRAD (*surprised*): What for?

GRAYLE: Because you were damned rude to him, of course.

CONRAD: I wasn't.

GRAYLE: Yes, you were. He asked you – quite politely – to have a drink.

CONRAD: Well, I refused – quite politely. I didn't want one.

GRAYLE: Well, you oughtn't to have refused. He only asked you because he wanted to patch up the quarrel and be friends.

CONRAD: Oh! (*Pause.*) So you think I ought to apologise?

GRAYLE: Of course.

CONRAD (*anxious to propitiate*): All right. (*Suspiciously.*) You're a jolly sight more anxious not to hurt Rickman's feelings than mine. I believe you like him better.

GRAYLE (*who hates sentiment above all things*): Oh, shut up!

CONRAD (*smiling and getting up*): You might clean your nails, anyway.

He puts his cap on and, bending over his writing table, addresses and stamps his envelopes.

GRAYLE: Where are you off to?

CONRAD: Only to post these letters. (*Pause. GRAYLE gets up.*)

GRAYLE: Have you seen a letter of mine lying about anywhere? I know I wrote one the other day. (*He goes over to table (R.).*)

CONRAD: It wouldn't have been a bad idea if you'd posted it.

GRAYLE (*rummaging among the papers on the table*): I never post my letters until they've been lying about two or three days. You know whether you want to send them or not by that time.

Through the window TETFORD can be seen lying stretched upon his back, apparently asleep.

CONRAD (*crossing to the door*): Mind

that ink, anyway.

GRAYLE: It's all right.

CONRAD (*at the door for a moment*): You'll have it over if you're not careful!

GRAYLE: No, I won't.

CONRAD *goes out;* GRAYLE *goes on rummaging until the ink-bottle topples over and falls on to the carpet, the ink spreading in a black stain over it.*

GRAYLE: Blast! (*He seizes some blotting-paper from* CONRAD's *table and tries to mop it up. He calls for assistance.*) Tetford!

TETFORD (*raising himself*): Hullo?

GRAYLE: Just a second.

TETFORD (*coming in*): What's up? I say, you *are* in a mess.

GRAYLE (*impersonally*): It fell over.

TETFORD: Conrad *will* be pleased!

GRAYLE: Well, you might help, instead of standing there gassing.

TETFORD: I believe salt's a good thing.

GRAYLE: I'll get some. Chuck some more blotting-paper on it.

He dashes out. TETFORD *languidly secures another piece of blotting-paper from* CONRAD's *table and, dropping it on the stain, dabs at it with his toe.* GRAYLE *returns with some salt.*

GRAYLE: How's it going? Let's jam this on. (*He pours quantities of salt on it and rubs it in.*) That ought to do the trick; it looks better already.

TETFORD (*pessimistically*): Do you think so?

GRAYLE: What *will* Conrad say? What about some hot water?

TETFORD: I should leave it alone if I were you. You couldn't make it look any worse if you tried.

GRAYLE (*dismally surveying it*): It's just my luck. He *will* be wild! We've had about eight rows this morning already. How about shoving a chair over it?

TETFORD: Better take your licking like a man.

GRAYLE (*suddenly – turning away*): I don't care! It wasn't my fault. He ought to have put the stopper in.

TETFORD (*crossing to door*): Well, I should lock up those ski-sticks if I were you.

GRAYLE (*surprised*): Why?

TETFORD: And any other weapon of castigation which happens to be lying about. (*He drifts out laughing.*)

GRAYLE (*annoyed*): Ass!

He stands looking at the ink as though he hopes to eradicate it by the mere mesmerism of his eye, when suddenly he hears steps outside and turns hurriedly to scrutinise the books in the bookshelves. CONRAD *comes in. In a single glance he takes in the scene, makes as though to speak, thinks better of it, and crosses to his table.*

CONRAD (*sitting down and taking some papers from his pocket*): More returns to be in at the Orderly Room by this afternoon. (*But he speaks rather elaborately.*)

GRAYLE (*in the tone of a man who will not countenance hedging*): I crashed that ink, after all.

CONRAD: So I saw. (*He is writing.*) I spent enough of my time in France signing my name.

GRAYLE (*tenaciously*): I cleared up as much as I could with blotting-paper and Mother Hauser's salt.

CONRAD: Oh, yes. Thanks.

GRAYLE: I meant to try some hot water, but I don't think it will improve it, do you?

CONRAD (*as though he isn't attending*): Er . . . no; I shouldn't think it would.

GRAYLE: I'll get some if you like. (CONRAD *shifts restlessly.*)

CONRAD: It doesn't matter.

GRAYLE: Well, it doesn't improve the look of the carpet.

CONRAD: Never mind.

GRAYLE: However, it's your carpet. (*Silence falls on this stupendous statement of fact.*) I'll buy some more ink for you if you like.

CONRAD: You're very generous, but don't worry yourself; I'll get it.

GRAYLE: Oh, no. I'll buy it. But you might put it in a safe place, old chap, next time.

CONRAD (at breaking point): Good God! Is there a single place in this room where a bottle of ink would be safe from your clumsiness?

GRAYLE: Now, don't get ratty.

CONRAD: Ratty! That's the sort of ruddy word you would use! What else have you been trying to do since you came in here but make me ratty?

GRAYLE: Not at all. I always like to have these matters out.

CONRAD: What d'you mean? Are you trying to put the blame on me now?

GRAYLE: Well, I think you're a little to blame. You must see that.

CONRAD: Go on!

GRAYLE: Of course I knocked it over, and all that, but you left it lying about without a cork. Anyone might have knocked it over, and it happened to be me, but if it had been corked it wouldn't have spilt.

CONRAD: Are you really trying to argue about it?

GRAYLE: Of course, You see my point, don't you?

CONRAD: Your point! Good God, man, when I saw what you'd done I determined to be nice about it and not throw the abominable 'I told you so' in your face, and then you go on like this. You haven't even said you're sorry.

GRAYLE: Oh, that goes without saying.

CONRAD: It doesn't. If you understood the amount of self-control a man needs to choke back the phrase 'I told you so' you'd realize that it doesn't go without saying. You ought to be jolly pleased that I let you off like that.

GRAYLE: Oh, rot! Who wants to be let off? You never could argue without losing your wool.

CONRAD: Argue! Argue! I don't want

to argue. There's nothing to argue about. You made a fool of yourself and a mess of my room and I was willing not to notice it – and then you must needs go shoving it under my nose and insisting on talking about it.

Little ADELBY *strolls up to the window to see what the noise is about, but no one minds him, so he turns his back on it.*

GRAYLE: Well, you've got to argue. I don't want your high-and-mighty forgiveness. (He is getting angry.) You looked as smug and self-satisfied as though God Himself was making a note of it. Who put the ink there, I'd like to know?

CONRAD: Who knocked it over after he'd been warned? That's all you need occupy your puny little mind with.

GRAYLE: I did. I'm quite willing to admit my share, only you won't admit yours. I was careless to knock it over, but you were just as careless not to have corked it up. You might have knocked it over yourself and there wouldn't have been any fuss then.

CONRAD (white with rage): Are you sure I didn't? Can't you argue that I did that too, since you're so good at arguing?

GRAYLE: That's not funny.

CONRAD: As if anything would ever be safe from your shambling, Newfoundland-puppy movements. If it had been your room it would all have been different, but it's mine, that's it, it's mine; and who cares if the carpet is stained with ink, or the books spoilt, or the place choked up with flotsam and jetsam from the whole of Mürren. (He pants, hardly recognisable, beside himself.) You call yourself my friend, and you fill the room with people I don't like, and drink and gamble in it, and probably jeer at me behind my back! God! Grayle! I'll kill you one of these days!

GRAYLE (rather frightened): All right . . . all right. . . . Keep calm. I'll pay for your carpet for you!

CONRAD: That's it! That's it! That's just like you, you puppy to talk of payment when I only want the word 'sorry.'

ADELBY (*mildly – from the door*): I think it is going to rain. (*The effect of this is almost electrical. There is silence, then . . .*)

CONRAD: Well?

GRAYLE: Well, what?

CONRAD: Haven't you anything to say? (*His wrath has evaporated as suddenly as it rose.*)

GRAYLE: If you think you're going to bully me into saying I'm sorry, you're not.

CONRAD: You're not sorry, then?

GRAYLE: No, I'm not! I *was* sorry, but you've been so damned rude that I'm not sorry any longer. I'm jolly glad!

CONRAD (*looking at his carpet and then back at* GRAYLE): Why? I lost my temper, but so did you.

GRAYLE: I'm not going to argue any more. I'm going to Rickman, who knows how to behave like a man, and doesn't sulk like a kid. You were quite right. I like him better. I'm tired of you and your rotten temper. I don't want to speak to you again.

He goes out, leaving CONRAD *standing silently in the middle of the room. He shrugs his shoulders, moves towards his writing table, halts indecisively, then sits down to write.* ADELBY, *blinking from the effect of the sun, comes in carrying his chair and stands looking at* CONRAD'*s bookshelf. He takes down a book.* CONRAD'*s thoughts wander and he drops his pen.*

ADELBY: May I borrow this?

CONRAD (*preoccupied*): What is it?

ADELBY: Plutarch's 'Lives.'

CONRAD: If you like. I'd sooner you took some other book.

ADELBY: What can you spare?

CONRAD: O take it; take it. It doesn't matter.

He gets up, walks up the room, returns, and sits down again in the same seat.

ADELBY: I've read bits of it before. When I was a boy I used to be so stirred, I remember, by some of the tales of the heroes. The Theban band! I used to cry, too – I suppose because they were such fine heroic figures, and I (*he smiles*) – wasn't. It's a pity we've lost all that, that great hero-worship. Each man used to take his intimate friend to war with him, didn't he? And they'd protect each other. It gave a man something *real* to fight for. (*There is a pause.*)

CONRAD: Er . . . yes.

He gets up again and crosses to the door, stepping nervously on the patterns of the carpet.

Adelby – what's the matter with me?

He returns to his chair, stepping carefully on the patterns, but does not sit down.

ADELBY (*his chair held grotesquely under one arm*): I believe it's what clever people call your ego. (*He blinks at him amiably.*)

CONRAD (*returning to the door, spelling out the syllables on the carpet as he goes*): My e-go. I suppose that means I'm too selfish?

ADELBY (*putting his chair down and sitting on it*): Er, no, it doesn't.

CONRAD: *Am* I too selfish?

ADELBY: Well – introspective, repressed.

CONRAD (*on the march again*): Yes, I am. (*Pause.*) I suppose. (ADELBY *puffing at his pipe, contemplates him gravely.*) But that's relative. There's no one who shares me, frees me, takes me out of myself. There never has been.

ADELBY (*complacently*): Perhaps there never will be. Anyone *really* satisfactory, I mean. One can't tell, of course. But usually there is; though some of us have to wait rather longer than others. So it's bad, don't you think, to treat all this so seriously? Makeshift and fever. Isn't it better to go calmly? Lightly? It's difficult, of course. One needs a sense of humour, and you haven't got much sense of humour, you know.

CONRAD: Oh, yes, I have. I think you're wrong there.

ADELBY: If you had you wouldn't be walking up and down on those patterns.

CONRAD (*sitting on the edge of the table and staring at him perplexedly*): I don't quite see what that's got to do with it. (ADELBY *blinks at him.* CONRAD *laughs.*) Well, what else do you diagnose?

ADELBY: Isn't it rather better to wait on life instead of expecting it to wait on you? Can't you, I mean, look at things from a more detached – philosophic – point of view, instead of getting so desperately involved in . . . side-issues? You'll only get hurt – over and over again; and I think that's so distressing.

CONRAD: But you see . . . that's all very well . . . but how can you tell – I mean, how can one help . . .? After all, it's so personal.

ADELBY: But we have to keep a balance. It's proportion, Jim, isn't it? You get everything out of proportion, so that all your values are false, and all your weights misplaced.

CONRAD: But isn't that the point? *My* values. . . . (*Pause. Rather lower.*) *Are* they? (*Turning away.*) Oh, what's the good? (*Pause.*) Anything else?

ADELBY: You've got an awful temper.

CONRAD: I know. I can't help it. It's got worse, too, recently. I've been having headaches and things which don't improve it.

ADELBY: I know, Jim. But the controls will never work if you let them rust.

CONRAD: You mean I *can* help it? That I don't try? That it's all my fault? That's what he said. I suppose it's true . . . really.

ADELBY: I don't think you do much to help yourself, Jim – in that or any other way. Don't you rather tend to encourage a certain . . . unhealthiness of mind? And one has to help oneself, you know – such a lot. Nothing else is of any use otherwise.

CONRAD: Is all this of any use – in *any*

case? You see – you don't quite understand. I'm – I think I'm – different.

ADELBY: Like everyone else, Jim. That's what I meant by your ego. But don't be unhappy about it. It's such waste – to be unhappy.

CONRAD (*abruptly*): How old are you?

ADELBY: Thirty-eight.

CONRAD: Yes. (*He continues his march.*) Then I'm a hundred. (*Silence.*) Do *you* look upon yourself as being a very complicated piece of mechanism?

ADELBY: I used to.

CONRAD: I suppose you're more or less settled down? You understand yourself now?

ADELBY: I don't think I shall ever astonish myself again.

CONRAD: Are you very happy?

ADELBY: Underneath all this fret – yes.

CONRAD: You haven't always been?

ADELBY (*disturbed*): No. No, I haven't. But that's – over. I shall never be unhappy again. I'd – I'd throw my life away rather than be unhappy again.

CONRAD: Would you? I get very tired of life sometimes. (*Pause.*) Are we, any of us, as complicated as we think we are, I wonder. Do you think religion helps a man?

ADELBY (*trying to follow*): Religion, Jim?

CONRAD: Abstract beliefs, or – idols, you know. Mere symbols?

ADELBY: I don't know, Jim. A man's own religion helps him sometimes, I suppose; but no one else's – unless it happens to fit.

CONRAD: Yes, that's it – 'unless it happens to fit.' When I was interned in Germany I met an officer who loved a rabbit. He'd bought it for twelve marks. There was nothing else in his life. (*Whimsically.*) He used to read short stories to it out of a magazine. (*Abruptly.*) Poor devil! He was mad, of course. (*Pause. Very low.*) But he was happy. (*Getting lost.*) I was happy then, too. In a way. I almost wish I was back.

ADELBY: It's only a transitory mood.

CONRAD: No. It's more than that. It was a more satisfactory life. I knew where I was. I was a prisoner – and lame. There was no hope for me, I never thought of Repatriation Boards. Switzerland seemed unattainable – like England. I got used to the idea in time and ceased to brood. Soon I forgot. But this is different. We get a little freedom, and so we want more. It's like being allowed to stretch out a hand to England, but not touch it.

ADELBY (*after a pause*): Isn't this rather a digression?

CONRAD: Is it?

ADELBY: You want to talk about Grayle, don't you?

CONRAD (*nervously*): Yes . . . Grayle. (*Pause.*) Did you hear us?

ADELBY: Most of it, I'm afraid. I couldn't help it.

CONRAD: I know. I suppose I was wrong?

ADELBY: Why do you like him, Jim?

CONRAD: I don't know. He's clean. Fills gaps. Does it matter?

ADELBY (*quietly*): Yes, of course. Surely it's the root of the matter? Isn't he terribly heartless?

CONRAD: He was very decent to me once when I was ill. I like people who like me. He's sincere, anyway, and . . . and clean. I value that. His life's like an open book.

ADELBY (*uncontrollably*): But hardly worth reading.

He is astonished and grieved after he has said this, but it is too late.
CONRAD *halts suddenly in his elimination of patterns, and then turns again to his table.*

CONRAD: You may be right. Let's talk of something else.

He signs the rest of his papers while ADELBY *puffs at his pipe for inspiration.*

CONRAD (*crossing to the window*): How funny the glaciers look! Rather like Turkish Delight. (*A gong sounds.*)

ADELBY (*getting up*): I think I shall go for a walk.

CONRAD: That's lunch. Don't you want any?

ADELBY: No. I often go without meals.

CONRAD: Where do you walk to?

ADELBY: Grütsch Alp. (CONRAD *closes the windows.*) I'm sorry I said that about Grayle, Jim.

CONRAD (*touching him on the shoulder as he repasses*): You're a funny old thing; forget it.

He gathers up his papers and puts them together. ADELBY *goes out with his book.*

ACT TWO

The same scene two days later, 22 July. It is about half-past three in the afternoon. The verandah windows are open and rain can be seen falling. The summits across the valley are wreathed in a thin, vapour-like mist. A bush of azaleas in a flower-pot stands on CONRAD's *table (L.) in a saucer.* CONRAD, *wearing khaki shorts and an old green blazer, is writing at the centre table. He is sitting with his back to the door. He does not appear to be progressing very fast, but leans back for the most part, wrapped in thought, muttering to himself. A file lies open on the table beside him. There is a rap at the door and* TETFORD *comes in, looking a little tired but still retaining his superficial gaiety.*

CONRAD *does not move, but his eyes slide round in momentary hope.*

TETFORD (*closing the door*): Thought I'd just drop in for a chat.

CONRAD (*immediately discouraged and without enthusiasm*): Oh, yes. (*He closes up his file.*)

TETFORD: Who gave you the flowers?

CONRAD: I bought them. Two francs. Rather nice, aren't they?

TETFORD (*smelling them*): No scent. (*Yawning.*) Nice colour, though.

CONRAD: I thought they'd brighten the room.

TETFORD (*dropping on to the sofa*): Good idea.

CONRAD: What's the latest communiqué?

TETFORD (*yawning*): I dunno. Ruddy day, isn't it?

CONRAD: Nothing unusual. They say it's an exceptionally bad summer.

TETFORD: Who do?

CONRAD: The Swiss peasants. They said last winter was exceptionally bad, too.

TETFORD: Fat lot they know about it. The post-office man told me it was going to be a topping day today. Said he knew by the look of the mountains. You'd think they might know a little more about their own weather by now – considering how exceptional it always is. (*He yawns again.*) I hate the Swiss. They're so jolly conceited because their weather's always exceptional and they've got more mountains than they know what to do with. (CONRAD *is not listening. He is staring at his writing.*) Silly little country. How's the novel going?

CONRAD: It isn't. I can't concentrate. I shall have to give it up.

TETFORD (*settling himself more comfortably*): Hard cheddar!

CONRAD: I suppose they've postponed the hockey match?

TETFORD: Yes.

CONRAD: Were you playing?

TETFORD: No. They asked me to, but I told them it was too near the Repatriation Board. No good trying to persuade a doctor you're dying and want to breathe your last in England when he's seen you playing hockey two days before. Besides, I'm tired of hockey.

CONRAD: I don't know why you worry yourself about these Boards. You only lay up trouble for yourself, for you're not likely to pass.

TETFORD: I stand as much chance as anyone else. Crawley's the only one with a good chance, and all the rest of us are about equal.

CONRAD: What's the matter with Crawley? Lungs, isn't it?

TETFORD: Yes. He had a bullet through one. Lucky devil!

CONRAD: Hasn't Rickman got shrapnel in his lungs or something?

TETFORD: So he says. I don't believe it any more than he did before he heard that the Board was coming. He's been talking about it so much since that he honestly believes it's true now.

CONRAD: I suppose he's quite convinced he's going to get through?

TETFORD: Oh, yes; he always is. He's as happy as a dog with two tails at present, borrowing money off everybody and forgiving all his enemies. He'll be as sick as mud for a week after he's failed. He always is.

CONRAD: I hope he's passed.

TETFORD: Do you? Why?

CONRAD (*carefully*): Because I think I should be happier up here without him. God knows I want to get home myself, but as I stand no chance I hope he does.

TETFORD: Hum. I like old Eric. He gets on my nerves a bit at times.

CONRAD: I didn't know you had any nerves.

TETFORD: Eric does. He seems to have taken a great fancy to young Grayle lately.

CONRAD: Oh, yes? I haven't seen much of Grayle these last two days.

TETFORD: Haven't you made it up yet?

CONRAD: Made what up?

TETFORD (*undaunted*): You quarrelled, didn't you?

CONRAD: How did you know?

TETFORD (*yawning*): Oh, everybody knows everybody else's affairs in this place; there's nothing else to talk about.

CONRAD: I suppose Grayle told you?

TETFORD: I suppose so. But I daresay he'll be up here again soon, so you'll be able to ask him yourself. He must be missing this room no end! (*Pause.*) Don't like Grayle. However, far be it from me to speak unkindly of your little friend.

CONRAD: Why don't you like him?

TETFORD: He makes me feel I want to sit very near a big fire. (*Laughing.*) And also probably for the same reason that you don't like Rickman – because they seem to prefer each other's company to ours. Lord! How quaint!

CONRAD (*contemplating him with interest*): I admit . . . I miss Grayle . . . a lot.

TETFORD: Yes, and you'll go on missing him. You're made that way.

(*He yawns.*) But if your pal Grayle thinks he's going to relieve me of Eric, he's mistaken. You ought to look after him. He's drinking too much.

CONRAD: It's his affair.

TETFORD: There you go again! He must have lost a few hundred francs at vingt-et-un lately, too. They're playing down below now.

CONRAD: Who are?

TETFORD: Grayle, Eric, and the Black Peril.

CONRAD: The Black Peril?

TETFORD: Madame Louis. I called her that. It's rather a good name for her, I think.

CONRAD: Is she the woman Rickman tried to introduce me to yesterday?

TETFORD: I suppose so. Did he?

CONRAD: She only came the day before yesterday, didn't she? She seems to have made herself pretty thoroughly at home in a short space of time. What's she doing up here?

TETFORD: Can't you guess? If you asked her, of course she'd say she only wanted to comfort the poor British soldier in his distress. Pooh! They all say that. All her type. She's out for what she can get.

CONRAD: Does she speak English?

TETFORD: Oh, rather. Lived in England, I believe. She's a widow, you know.

CONRAD: I suppose your friend Rickman's on the usual stunt?

TETFORD: He is. But only for the moment. I've got a word to say yet. I've learnt quite a lot about her from Sergeant Jefferies, who's just come back from Basel, and nothing to her credit.

CONRAD: Does she come from Basel then?

TETFORD: Yes. She lived there until she was practically driven out by the people that matter there. They say her husband shot himself six months after they'd been married. Pleasant woman, from all accounts. Grayle doesn't get a look in, of course. He simply hangs on to Rickman like grim death. (*Pause.*) She tried to get off with me, but I wasn't having any. Not my type.

CONRAD (*getting up*): Rickman! (*He seems to grind out the word.*) I wish you'd keep a hold on your friends, Harry.

TETFORD: I might return the compliment. (*He takes out a cigarette.*)

CONRAD (*looking out of window*): We're both in the same boat. (*He turns and contemplates* TETFORD.)

TETFORD (*thumping his cigarette on his case*): Are we? I wonder! (*He gives his cigarette an extra thump.*)

CONRAD (*irritably*): Does that improve your cigarette?

TETFORD: What? This? (*He thumps again.*)

CONRAD: Yes. (*His brows contract slightly.*)

TETFORD: I don't know. Why?

CONRAD: I only wondered why you did it. It looks unnecessary – and it's rather irritating.

TETFORD (*laughing*): Poor old Jim!

CONRAD (*pettishly*): What's the joke?

TETFORD: You are, sometimes, old bean.

CONRAD (*turning away*): Am I? (*He laughs suddenly.*) I suppose I am. (*There is a knock at the door.*) Come in! (JELLERTON, CONRAD'S *servant, a middle-aged soldier with a drooping moustache, appears.*) What is it, Jellerton?

JELLERTON: Beg pardon, sir. Mrs Prendergast wants to know if she can speak to you, sir.

CONRAD: Where is she?

JELLERTON: Downstairs in the 'all, sir.

CONRAD: Yes, of course. Ask her to come up, will you? (JELLERTON *goes out, leaving the door open.*) I wonder what brings her through all this rain.

TETFORD: Ought I to go?

CONRAD: I don't know. I don't suppose it's anything.

MRS PRENDERGAST *appears in the doorway. She is a large, motherly woman of about fifty, and is wearing a mackintosh and a pair of big, black snow-boots, both of which are glistening with rain.*

CONRAD (*going to meet her*): Come in, Mrs Prendergast.

MRS PRENDERGAST: Good afternoon, Captain Conrad. Good afternoon, Mr Tetford. (TETFORD *rises.*) Please don't get up. (*To* CONRAD.) I met your servant downstairs, and was so relieved to hear you were in. I hope I'm not disturbing you at all?

CONRAD: No, of course not. Won't you take off your things? You look horribly damp.

MRS PRENDERGAST: No, I must be going in a minute. Isn't this weather simply shocking?

CONRAD: Come and sit down. *Do* let me help you off with that. (*She submits.*)

MRS PRENDERGAST: Well, only for a minute. I've got to go round and serve in the YMCA. Thank you. (*She sits in the chair vacated by* CONRAD.) How snug you are here!

TETFORD (*pointing to* MRS PRENDERGAST'*s feet*): Wouldn't you like to take off your dreadnoughts and have some tea?

MRS PRENDERGAST: No, thank you. I really haven't time. And do you know I was really terrified I wasn't going to find you, Captain Conrad. It's wonderful how people get lost, in a tiny little village like this, even on wet days. I wanted to see you about this dance.

CONRAD (*sitting on the arm of the sofa*): What about it?

MRS PRENDERGAST: I don't know *what* to do. I declare you have to have the patience of Job to try and organise anything in this place. People simply *make* difficulties.

CONRAD: Who is it now?

MRS PRENDERGAST: The Band-Sergeant; Sergeant Drummond. He says the band's refused to play unless Private Allen, the 'cello man, is let out of prison. The Swiss put him there for being drunk, you know.

TETFORD: That band's more trouble than it's worth.

CONRAD: Where's Drummond likely to be found now?

MRS PRENDERGAST: In the YMCA. He said he'd meet me there in ten minutes' time from now, and I rather hoped you'd come, too – but I didn't like to ask you because it's raining so hard.

CONRAD (getting up and changing his blazer for a tunic): We'll go over there together.

MRS PRENDERGAST: Isn't he obliging, Mr Tetford? What an example to you! I declare the whole wretched business has made me positively angry.

TETFORD: When's the dance coming off?

MRS PRENDERGAST: Nobody seems to know. Major Anstruther wants it given in honour of the Swiss officers of the Repatriation Board, on the thirtieth; but all this trouble will have to be settled first. I do so hope you are all passed by this Board, for your own sakes.

CONRAD: Why? Why entertain such a vain hope?

MRS PRENDERGAST: Oh, yes; I know. You aren't even going up for it, are you? But let's both hope for the best – for the others.

CONRAD: It's much better not to think about it at all, as I was just saying to Tetford. Blessed are they that expect nothing.

MRS PRENDERGAST: Oh, by the way, I meant to ask you; what's been the matter with Mr Adelby lately? He looks as if he's seen a ghost.

CONRAD: His wife's ill.

MRS PRENDERGAST: His wife? Oh dear! What's the matter with her?

CONRAD: This new disease – grippe – so I gathered.

TETFORD: I didn't know that.

CONRAD: He doesn't talk about it much. (To TETFORD chiefly.) You'd better not say anything about it.

MRS PRENDERGAST: Poor man! And I suppose they won't allow him home. Oh, I do hope the Board will pass him. You know Switzerland's simply swamped with grippe, and they've had so many deaths among the interned in Chateau d'Oex. Isn't it terrible? And after all they've been through!

CONRAD: What does it matter? Prisoners of war aren't of any account. They must be a great expense and nuisance.

MRS PRENDERGAST: What nonsense! I do think it's so sad. To go out like that with home in sight! I want to go down and nurse them, but they won't let me, because I haven't had the disease. (Getting up.) As if I should catch things at my age! The Swiss aren't fit to have authority, I declare; I could manage matters better myself.

TETFORD: No one doubts that, Mrs Prendergast. You're a marvellous woman.

MRS PRENDERGAST: Thank you, Mr Tetford. Come along, Captain Conrad, or we shall be late.

TETFORD (helping her on with her mackintosh): I wish I had an appointment to be late for.

MRS PRENDERGAST: Then come along with us. Thank you.

TETFORD (looking at his hands, wet from the touch of her mackintosh, and then at the pouring rain outside): Oddly enough, I've just remembered one. I'm tremendously sorry!

MRS PRENDERGAST: Now, Mr Tetford, I simply don't believe it. With whom?

TETFORD: Er . . . fellow named Tetford. Nice chap. D'you know him?

MRS PRENDERGAST (severely): Yes – he's quite the laziest man I know.

TETFORD: And the best looking.

MRS PRENDERGAST: I didn't say so. Be good.

She goes out, followed by CONRAD. TETFORD *strolls over to the table* (R.) *and turns over some of the paraphernalia lying on it. The door opens against him, inwards, momentarily hiding him, and* GRAYLE *enters hurriedly. He crosses to* CONRAD's *table, halting incidentally at the table in the centre to take a handful of cigarettes, which he drops loosely into his jacket pocket.* GRAYLE *does not look as healthy as usual.*

TETFORD (*pleasantly, closing the door*): Can I be of any assistance?

GRAYLE (*starting and flushing*): Hullo, Tet; didn't know you were here. I want Conrad's cards.

TETFORD: Conrad's gone out with Mrs Prendergast.

GRAYLE: I know. (*Trapped, he flushes again.*)

TETFORD (*genially*): And you're making the most of it, eh?

GRAYLE (*loftily*): I don't know what you mean.

TETFORD: Of course I'm no judge, but it strikes me as being rather a dirty trick to come into a fellow's room and pinch his cigarettes when you know he's out.

GRAYLE: Nobody asked your opinion.

TETFORD: Of course I'm no judge, but it seems to me to be almost like stealing to take the cigarettes of a man you don't like when you know he's out.

GRAYLE: You don't know what you're talking about. The cigarettes are as much mine as his.

TETFORD: Of course I'm no judge . . .

GRAYLE: Oh, shut up!

TETFORD: . . . but I don't think Conrad would be very pleased if he knew.

GRAYLE (*making for the door*): Tell him if you like.

TETFORD (*his back to the door*): Of course I'm no judge, but I think it would come better from you, old bean.

GRAYLE (*trying to get at the handle*): Don't be an ass. Let me out, there's a good fellow. They're waiting for me downstairs.

TETFORD: Do tell me, just before you go, if you think you're behaving like a little gentleman?

GRAYLE: What on earth are you talking about? Let me out at once. I'm not a schoolboy.

TETFORD (*pleasantly*): What else can you be? (GRAYLE *barges into him.* TETFORD *quickly seizes* GRAYLE's *right wrist and twists it behind his back.*) You mustn't do that, you know.

GRAYLE (*bent backwards*): Ow! Let go, you fool! What the hell d'you think you're doing?

TETFORD (*full of unnatural excitement at having this boy, whom he does not like, discomfited*): Suppose we sit down and talk it over quietly.

He guides the helpless GRAYLE *to a chair, centre.*

GRAYLE: Let go my wrist, you ruddy swine.

TETFORD: Asseyez-vous.

He gives his wrist an extra twist, which puts GRAYLE *on his back in the easy chair.*

GRAYLE (*with a cry*): Steady on! You're hurting me.

TETFORD (*easing the wrist a bit*): More comfortable now? (*He sits on the left arm of the chair.*)

GRAYLE: Look here, if you think you're funny, you're not.

TETFORD (*happily*): And if you think you're going, *you're* not. I thought I had an appointment this afternoon, but now I find I'm quite free; so we'll just hold a court of inquiry into this.

GRAYLE: Don't be a damn fool. I'm not free this afternoon.

TETFORD: The more you talk the longer we shall be. The case is like this. You were once a friend of Conrad's and he gave you the use of this room. You quarrelled with him and said you weren't going to use his room again. . . .

GRAYLE: I didn't, so that's where you're wrong, you see. You're not so ruddy clever as you thought.

TETFORD: You gave him to understand it, anyway.

GRAYLE: I didn't. I said I didn't want to speak to him again. That's very different. Let go my arm!

TETFORD: But you intended to use his room all the same, did you?

GRAYLE: I don't see why I should be uncomfortable just because he was rude to me. He called me a 'puppy.'

TETFORD: Whereas you're almost a full-grown dirty dog. So you're going to continue using his room?

GRAYLE: Mind your own business.

TETFORD: You haven't been up here once since you quarrelled two days ago. But directly you see him go out you come up and steal his fags.

GRAYLE (incensed): What the hell's it got to do with you? Let go my arm! He told me I could smoke his fags when I wanted to.

TETFORD: Of course I'm no judge, but I should have thought it would be rather undignified to accept favours from a fellow you didn't like. What do you think?

GRAYLE: They aren't for me. They're for Eric and Madame Louis.

TETFORD: Eric? I suppose you mean Rickman.

GRAYLE: I said Eric.

TETFORD: But surely you *meant* Rickman? (*He gives an extra twist to the wrist.*)

GRAYLE: Oh, all right – Rickman, if it pleases you.

TETFORD: Was it Rickman's idea?

GRAYLE: Let go my arm! You can suck up to Conrad if you like and tell him I took his beastly cigarettes. I don't care.

TETFORD: Was it Rickman's idea?

GRAYLE: Mind your own business!

TETFORD (*with an extra twist*). Was it?

GRAYLE: Steady! No, it wasn't.

TETFORD: I thought not. Don't you think you'd better put them back?

GRAYLE (*tearfully*): Let go my wrist!

TETFORD: Because, you see, if Conrad misses them he'll think that I've taken them, and it might be rather awkward.

GRAYLE: I tell you he said I could have his fags, and you can tell him I've taken them. I'll tell him myself if I see him first.

TETFORD (*releasing him*): Mind you do.

GRAYLE (*rubbing his wrist*): You've nearly broken my wrist, you swine. As if Conrad cares tuppence who takes his fags. I can do what I like with him.

TETFORD: You'll go too far one of these days.

GRAYLE: You've got a hell of a cheek, anyway, accusing a fellow of stealing. You'd better mind your own rotten business. You're getting worse than Conrad. Who are you to dictate?

RICKMAN's *voice is heard outside calling* 'Grayle!'

GRAYLE (*going to door*): Hullo!

The door opens in his face and RICKMAN *strides in. He is very exhilarated, chiefly owing to drink.*

RICKMAN (*to* GRAYLE): Well, I'll be goddamned! What's the game, Allan? Didn't know you patronised this shanty still.

GRAYLE (*ignoring this*): I can't find those cards.

RICKMAN: It don't matter. We've stopped playing. That geek Crawley wanted his cards to play bridge with.

GRAYLE: Aren't we going on?

RICKMAN: No. Madame's fed up.

GRAYLE: But, damn it all, that's not fair. I was just beginning to win some of my money back. (*To* TETFORD.) It's all your fault, you fool.

RICKMAN (*laughing*): It don't matter. I lost too.

GRAYLE (*indignantly*): You! You ruddy liar! You've got about three hundred francs of mine!

This seems to amuse RICKMAN, *who*

goes off into paroxysms of mirth, pointing to the discomfited GRAYLE *as an object of derision for* TETFORD.

RICKMAN: Don't make me laugh. It's bad for my constitootion. (*Seriously.*) It's only your way of figurin' it. I play regular, and I've bin made a goat of lately. I'm about evens on to-day's run, with a bit to the good.

GRAYLE: I don't call it fair, anyway.

RICKMAN: It's square enough. You'll make good next time. Perhaps. (*He laughs again.*) Where's Conrad, Harry?

TETFORD: Gone out with Mother Prendergast.

GRAYLE: Have you left Madame Louis all alone, Eric? (*He slightly emphasizes 'Eric' for* TETFORD's *benefit.*)

RICKMAN: She's waitin' on you downstairs. Says you asked her to tea.

GRAYLE: And you too, of course. You must come and help me out.

RICKMAN: Right you are, Bo'. I'll be there.

GRAYLE: But it's only quarter to four.

RICKMAN (*winking at* TETFORD): Tell her to come up here. Conrad won't be back for a bit probably.

TETFORD: He won't be long.

RICKMAN: Never mind. He don't often have visitors. I'd like to see his face when he sees her.

GRAYLE (*after a pause*): We'd better go down to her, Eric. Conrad will only make a fuss.

RICKMAN: I'm waitin' on a telephone call. Bring her up here till I'm through with it.

GRAYLE: But . . .

RICKMAN: Go on!

GRAYLE: Right oh. (*He goes.*)

RICKMAN: We'll pull Conrad's leg, you see. He said he didn't want to be introduced to her, but he won't be able to help himself when he finds her in his room.

TETFORD: You'll only make trouble. What's the good? Conrad's all right when he's alone.

RICKMAN: Shoot that! If he can't take a joke he isn't worth his salt. He ought to go over to Canada. They'd knock some of the buck out of him. He wants settin' up badly.

RICKMAN (*drifting over to the door*): Well, . . . cheer oh!

RICKMAN: Where are you off to?

TETFORD: I've got an appointment.

RICKMAN (*suspiciously*): Who with?

TETFORD: Fellow named Tetford. I don't think you know him very well.

RICKMAN: O scats! Stay and see this through with me.

TETFORD: Sorry, old bean; I don't like your friends.

RICKMAN: Who d'you mean? Madame?

TETFORD: And Grayle.

RICKMAN: He's only a kid. What's wrong with him?

TETFORD: He gives me frost-bite. So long!

RICKMAN (*after a moment's hesitation*): Say . . . Harry!

TETFORD (*turning at the door*): Hullo?

RICKMAN (*taking him by the arm*): You're not peeved, are you? You ain't such a goddamn fool as that?

TETFORD: I hate the little beast, that's all.

RICKMAN: I don't exactly cotton to him, if that's what you mean.

TETFORD: Then why d'you let him hang on? He's Conrad's pal; let Conrad keep him. However, please yourself.

RICKMAN: Well, you're a one-eyed sort of a guy. Aren't you now? Don't you see I'm only learning him to play vingt-et-un?

TETFORD: What? Do you mean . . .?

RICKMAN: Don't let on, will you? You see, it's his idea.

TETFORD: Well, you are the limit!

D'you mean you're simply out to fleece him?

RICKMAN (*with great charm of manner*): Well, that's putting it kind o' crude. He keeps on naggin' at me to play with him, and if I don't learn him someone else will.

TETFORD (*not without admiration*): Well, I think you're the outside edge!

RICKMAN: I figure it like this. If a man's got money and no experience, he'll be robbed as sure as sure. If he's got experience and no money, he'll be able to make money and keep a hold on it. Young Grayle's one of the first lot. He's got money and no experience, so I'm sharing my experience with him and he's sharing his money with me. It's fair do's.

TETFORD: And in the meantime I've got to be bored, eh?

RICKMAN: Come in with us.

TETFORD: Thanks. I haven't got enough experience. (*He opens the door.*) Here they are. Look here, you're having tea with me to-day in the cake shop.

RICKMAN: I promised young Grayle.

TETFORD: So I heard. But you're having it with me. D'you see?

RICKMAN: Well, all right, Bo'.

TETFORD (*masterfully*): And you're coming along with me directly your telephone call's over, and you're not going to wait on here to rag Conrad.

RICKMAN: Right, Steve.

TETFORD: And don't forget it!

Voices are heard outside.

MME LOUIS: In here?

GRAYLE: That's right, Madame.

RICKMAN: Come right inside, Madame.

MADAME LOUIS *comes in, followed by* GRAYLE. *She is a dark, slim woman of about 32, with a pale face and long almond-shaped eyes. Her pallor is enhanced by the mourning she is wearing. She is of the Jewish cast, in the curve of her nose and lips and the arrangement of her hair,* which, parted in the middle, is pulled straight down over her ears to the nape of her neck. Her eyes are dark and restless, and the rings round them are so deep that they have more the appearance of dark brown stains.

MME LOUIS (*observing* TETFORD *at the door*): Here is Mr Tetford. We have had so nice a game of cards. You should have joined us. Why did you not?

TETFORD: I'm too poor.

MME LOUIS (*laughing*): Poor Mr Tetford!

She has a way of shaking her head slightly when she laughs. It does not open her lips much, but affects more her eyes, wrinkling them up and making them appear even more oriental than they already are. Her laugh ripples in a superficial insincere silveryness, which contains no infection; leaves, indeed, no impression of mirth.

GRAYLE (*to* RICKMAN): I've ordered tea downstairs, Eric, for quarter-past four.

TETFORD (*quietly*): Rickman's having tea with me.

GRAYLE: No, he's not. He's having it with me.

TETFORD: Ask him.

RICKMAN (*to* GRAYLE): Sorry, Bo'. Harry's right.

MME LOUIS: What a nice room this is.

RICKMAN: Sit down, Madame.

MME LOUIS (*sitting right of centre table*): Thank you.

GRAYLE (*crossing to* RICKMAN): Look here, you said you were going to have tea with me and Madame Louis. (*He speaks in an undertone.*)

RICKMAN: Sorry, Bo'; I've promised Harry.

GRAYLE: You promised me first. You said you'd help me out. I don't want to have tea alone with her. Tell him you can't come.

MME LOUIS (*to* TETFORD, *who is watching* GRAYLE's *manoeuvring with smiling contempt*): I seem to have brought bad weather with me, do I not, Mr Tetford?

TETFORD: Oh, no. This is rather good weather.

MME LOUIS: Good? You are joking. Mürren has a beautiful climate. So warm.

TETFORD (*looking at the pouring rain outside*): Ah, but this is an exceptional summer, you see. We haven't had such good weather as this for weeks.

MME LOUIS: What do you all do when it rains?

RICKMAN: Same as we do when it doesn't. You must come over to Canada, Madam. God's own country. We can teach you something about weather.

GRAYLE (*to* RICKMAN): Go on, Eric. Tell him you can't go to tea with him.

RICKMAN (*peevishly*): Oh, cut it out. I'm having tea with Harry.

GRAYLE: Why?

RICKMAN: Because I want to.

GRAYLE: Oh, all right. (*There is a knock at the door.*)

RICKMAN: I guess that's for me. Come in!

Enter MARIE.

MARIE: Captain Rickman, sir.

RICKMAN: Yes. Is that the telephone?

MARIE: Yes, sir.

RICKMAN: Righto. Thanks.

MARIE: Thank you, sir.

She goes out, leaving the door open.

RICKMAN: S'cuse me, Madame.

TETFORD: I'll come with you. We'll go on to tea afterwards. (*He smiles sweetly at* GRAYLE.)

RICKMAN: Come on, then. (*He goes out.*)

TETFORD: Shall I cancel one of your teas for you as I pass, Grayle?

GRAYLE (*turning away*): Mind your own business!

TETFORD: I have. Cheer oh, old bean.

(*He goes, and is heard to sing as he descends the stairs.*)

MME LOUIS (*amused*): 'Old bean!' How droll! He is a comique, your friend.

GRAYLE (*surlily*): He's not my friend.

MME LOUIS: Poor Mr Grayle! You are angry, n'est-ce pas? But you do not mind to take tea with me alone?

GRAYLE: Oh, no; rather not. Only he said he'd come.

MME LOUIS: I will not come, if you prefer it. Another day, perhaps?

GRAYLE: Oh, no; we'll have tea together just the same. (*He is rather touched by this sympathy, and looks at her with a new curiosity.*) It's jolly decent of you to think of it, though.

MME LOUIS (*smiling at him*): It was for you, I thought; not for myself. I prefer to take tea with you alone.

GRAYLE (*surprised*): Do you? Why?

MME LOUIS: I do not much like Captain Rickman. He is a little rough. (*Pause.*) But I should not have said that. He is your friend.

GRAYLE: No. He *is* rather rough. He's rather a different class, you know.

MME LOUIS: Ah, yes, I can see that. You have a very comfortable room here, Mr Grayle.

GRAYLE: It isn't mine. It belongs to Captain Conrad.

MME LOUIS: Captain Conrad? I do not think I know him.

GRAYLE (*remembering* CONRAD's *refusal to be introduced*): No, I don't think you do.

MME LOUIS: Then where is your room? You said you had a room upstairs.

GRAYLE (*blushing*): I meant this one. I share it with Conrad, you see.

MME LOUIS: Ah, yes; I see. He is a friend of yours?

GRAYLE: Well . . . er . . . yes.

MME LOUIS: How nice. To have a friend. You are great friends?

GRAYLE: Well . . . hardly. We used to

knock about a good deal together, you know.

MME LOUIS: 'Knock about' . . . it is a droll phrase. (*She smiles at him; he blushes.*)

GRAYLE: Well, he lets me use his room and . . . so forth.

MME LOUIS: Oh, yes. I understand. Why are you not such great friends now?

GRAYLE: I don't know. He's older than me, you know.

MME LOUIS: A little too old, perhaps?

GRAYLE: Something like that. Don't let him know I spoke about him, though, will you?

MME LOUIS: Of course not. I am most discreet.

GRAYLE: You see, he's . . . he's got an awful temper, and he's always trying to pick quarrels. He gets beastly sentimental, too, when he's not cursing you. I hate sentimentality, don't you?

MME LOUIS: Ah, yes; it is not nice.

GRAYLE: But it pays to keep on the right side of him. I don't want to lose this room.

MME LOUIS (*laughing*): Ah, you are diplomatique. Would I like him, do you think?

GRAYLE: No. You might, of course. He doesn't like women, though.

MME LOUIS: Then I should go, perhaps? He might hurt me!

GRAYLE (*laughing*): Oh, no. Don't you worry. You'll be all right with me. (*Pause.*) But we might leave soon, all the same.

MME LOUIS (*pointing to work on table*): Is this your work?

GRAYLE: No, it's Conrad's.

MME LOUIS: Ah, yes. He writes?

GRAYLE: I believe so.

MME LOUIS: And you? Do you write?

GRAYLE: Only letters and so forth.

MME LOUIS: Not books or poetry?

GRAYLE (*scandalised*): Good Lord, no!

MME LOUIS: But you should try. It is a great art. I am sure you could if you tried.

GRAYLE: Do you think so? (*He is pleased. Shyly.*) As a matter of fact, I did write one or two . . . er . . . poems once. (*Hastily.*) I was only a kid, you know.

MME LOUIS: Then I was right. You published them?

GRAYLE: No. I never tried to. They weren't very good.

MME LOUIS (*getting up*): You have a good view of the mountains from here.

GRAYLE: Rather. Come and see it.

MME LOUIS (*stopping by the bookcase*): Your friend has a lot of books. Are they philosophy?

GRAYLE: I expect so. They're very dull.

MME LOUIS: Then we will leave them.

GRAYLE (*opening the verandah windows*): I believe it's stopped raining. No, it's drizzling a bit still. The mist's cleared away.

MME LOUIS (*standing inside the room on the right of the window, looking out*): It is in the valley still. See, there it is. (*She puts her hand across his shoulder to direct his gaze.*) See how it curls up over the edge. Like clouds. Like smoke. Like dreams. (*She rests her hand on his shoulder.*)

GRAYLE: I suppose it'll be blown back tomorrow.

MME LOUIS (*after a pause*): Do you not love this view? I do. It makes me what you do not like – sentimental. Music makes me the same.

GRAYLE (*looking back at her*): Does it?

She is smiling at him, so he looks away again blushing, but makes no attempt to ease his shoulder of her hand.

I don't mind it in a woman. That's different.

MME LOUIS: And it does not affect you a little also? This view?

GRAYLE: Oh, it used to, of course. But

when you live up against a thing for so long you don't notice it at all after a time.

MME LOUIS: You want a change. That is it. Poor old bean!

She laughs much at her successful imitation of TETFORD, *showing all her teeth.* GRAYLE *joins her.*

GRAYLE: I'd like to get away for a bit. We were thinking of going to Interlaken, but it fell through.

MME LOUIS: You must come and stay with me in Lausanne. I have a nice house there, where I live all alone. We would have a good time, n'est-ce pas?

GRAYLE (*trembling*): By jove! I'd love to.

MME LOUIS: We will arrange it. See how the Eiger peeps out now! The mists are leaving him. He is a beautiful mountain, the Eiger; do you not think so?

GRAYLE: They're all about the same, aren't they?

MME LOUIS: Ah, no. You do not think that. He is so handsome, and when he turns red sometimes at sunset he looks so passionate. They say he is a very bad mountain; that is why they called him Eiger. But you have heard all that.

GRAYLE: No, I haven't. What is it?

MME LOUIS: Oh, but you should know. Eiger means Ogre, and this mountain here is the Jung frau or Girl. The one in between the two is the Monk, and the peasants say he was put there to keep the Ogre away from the Girl, for the Ogre had bad intentions to her.

GRAYLE: Really? How funny!

MME LOUIS: Yes. It is droll, is it not? That is the allegory of the three mountains. (*She sighs.*) Ah, I am so sad for the Eiger.

GRAYLE (*looking at her*): Sad? Because of the Monk being in between?

MME LOUIS: Yes. If the Eiger desires the Jung frau, it is nature, n'est-ce pas? (*She smiles at him, and his eyes are full of questions.*) I detest the Monk! Let us shut the window; it is growing cold. (*She comes in. He closes the window and comes down, looking much perplexed.*) Would you think me very bad if I asked for a cigarette?

GRAYLE: Rather not! (*He offers cigarettes from the table.*) My mother smokes. All women smoke nowadays.

MME LOUIS: Thank you. I was longing for a cigarette. How nice and fat they are. (*He holds a lighted match for her.*) Thank you very much.

GRAYLE: No, it's not properly lighted yet. (*Their gazes meet across the flame.*) That's it.

MME LOUIS: You are a nice boy. (*She sits on the sofa.*) What do they call you? 'Allan,' is it not?

GRAYLE: Yes, Allan. (*He draws near to her.*)

MME LOUIS (*repeating it*): Allan. . . . Your English names are pretty names. May I call you Allan? (*Her voice caresses the word.*)

GRAYLE (*drawing nearer still*): Yes, rather! I'd love it – awfully. You say it toppingly. Much better than other people.

He is standing between her and the door. CONRAD *comes in. His face lights up on seeing* GRAYLE.

CONRAD (*like an echo*): Allan! (*He sees* MME LOUIS.) Oh . . .

GRAYLE (*with a false joviality*): Hullo, Jim! You look wet. I brought Madame Louis up to show her the room. This is Captain Conrad – Madame Louis.

CONRAD (*nodding awkwardly and without warmth towards the sofa*): How d'you do. (*He puts no question mark at the end of the phrase, but* MME LOUIS *does not need one.*)

MME LOUIS: I am very well, thank you. Mr Grayle has been very kind to me.

CONRAD (*ignoring her, taking off his mackintosh*): What have I done to deserve this, Allan?

GRAYLE: What?

CONRAD (*now completely controlled*): Your presence here.

GRAYLE (*flushing*): I don't understand. I'm always here.

CONRAD (*hanging his coat behind the door*): On the contrary, you haven't been near me for two days.

GRAYLE: Haven't I?

MME LOUIS: Ah, Allan has been looking after me.

CONRAD (*to* GRAYLE): You don't mean to say you didn't realise it? (*There is a mocking note in his voice.*)

GRAYLE: Do you mind my being here?

CONRAD: Not a bit. (*He takes off his tunic.*) I only wondered why. You haven't come to forgive me, have you?

GRAYLE: Don't be silly.

CONRAD: Well, then – perhaps to ask forgiveness? (GRAYLE *is silent.*) I haven't got any money to lend, if that's what you want. (*Pause. He buttons his blazer on.*) Have you run out of cigarettes?

GRAYLE (*angrily*): I suppose you've been talking to Tetford.

CONRAD (*surprised*): Tetford?

GRAYLE: He said he was going to report (*He sneers on this.*) me to you for 'stealing' your fags.

CONRAD: So you *did* come up for cigarettes? I haven't heard a word from Tetford about it, as a matter of fact.

GRAYLE (*disbelieving*): Then why did you mention it?

CONRAD (*breezily, hanging up his tunic*): My dear fellow, I was only trying to think of different reasons for your presence here. I felt sure it couldn't be for the pleasure of seeing me. And apparently I was right. You say it was my cigarettes.

GRAYLE (*uncomprehensive as usual*): Well, don't make a fuss, anyway. (*With a meaning glance at* MME LOUIS.) I told Tetford that I'd let you know what I'd done. I'll put them back. (*He does so.*)

CONRAD (*transferring pipe, etc., from his tunic to his blazer*): Not at all. Keep them, by all means. They're there for visitors. The room too. I never look upon it as *really* mine.

GRAYLE: I suppose you're trying to be funny?

CONRAD: No, no. Only curiosity. I like trying to follow the workings of your brain. I suppose I had no right to ask really.

GRAYLE (*crossing to him*): I say. For God's sake keep that for afterwards! Don't make a scene!

MME LOUIS: It is not with me you are angry, is it, Captain Conrad?

CONRAD: I'm not angry. Who said I was angry?

MME LOUIS: I thought you did not like me to be here, perhaps. You see, I have heard you do not like much the fair sex. (*She gives him a ravishing smile.*)

CONRAD: The fair sex? Which sex is that?

GRAYLE (*getting off the arm of his chair*): He's not very well today, Madame. Let's go downstairs. Tea must be ready.

MME LOUIS: I must go first to my room to prepare myself.

GRAYLE: Right-oh. (*He opens the door for her.*) I'll be downstairs waiting for you.

MME LOUIS: I shall not be long. Au revoir, Monsieur le Capitaine.

CONRAD *does not answer. He is looking at* GRAYLE. *She goes out.*

GRAYLE: I suppose you think the way you behaved was rather funny? It wasn't.

CONRAD (*his back to the window*): No, it wasn't.

GRAYLE: I don't mind for myself, of course, but you might have waited until she was out of the room.

CONRAD (*like an echo*): I suppose I might have.

GRAYLE: Of course you should. It was very rude. I don't know what she'll think of me now.

Finding CONRAD *so amenable, he has decided to let him off this time.*

Look here. I want to know where I stand.

CONRAD (*who appears to speak with difficulty*): Where you stand . . .

GRAYLE: There's no need to go on repeating what I say. What did you mean about being surprised to see me?

CONRAD: I thought you weren't going to speak to me again?

GRAYLE: I didn't intend to. Every time we meet you grouse at something. I'm rather tired of it.

CONRAD: Then why did you come up?

GRAYLE: I thought we might come to some arrangement.

CONRAD: Why didn't you come alone?

GRAYLE (*evading*): I'm having tea with Madame Louis.

CONRAD (*after a pause – passing a hand over his forehead*): Oh, yes. Er – what were we talking about?

GRAYLE: Can't we come to some arrangement?

CONRAD: Some arrangement?

GRAYLE: Well, do you want me to continue coming to this room? You never treat me as if you do.

CONRAD: Does it matter much what I want?

GRAYLE: Of course it does. It's your room. I propose that if we are to share this room we share expenses too. (*Pause.*) Do you hear?

CONRAD (*as though waking up*): What was that?

GRAYLE: I wish you'd listen. I say that if you don't want me to come here any longer I'll stay away; but if you *do* want me to go on sharing this room with you I must share expenses too. That's fair, I think.

CONRAD: How do you mean?

GRAYLE (*patiently*): Why, that I pay for half the room, of course. Then I shan't be under any obligation to you as I am at present.

CONRAD: I see. And then you can bring up whomsoever you like?

GRAYLE: Yes.

CONRAD: And if we quarrel you can still use the room – conscientiously.

GRAYLE (*detecting a note he doesn't like*): Now don't start that.

CONRAD: And in course of time you'll probably look upon it as entirely yours and just let me use it on sufferance, or not at all. Is that it? (*He is trembling.*)

GRAYLE: I shan't talk to you if you're going to start that sort of thing.

CONRAD (*controlling himself*): I'm sorry. I suppose I'm not well. About the room. . . . You find it comfortable?

GRAYLE: It's better than the lounge downstairs.

CONRAD: Er . . . which half would you like? (*He laughs oddly.*)

GRAYLE: Be sensible. (*There is a pause.*)

CONRAD: Aren't you keeping Madame Louis waiting?

GRAYLE: I shouldn't be if you'd make up your mind.

CONRAD (*rapping on the window behind him*): I'm not very good at riddles today.

GRAYLE (*turning away*): Well, think it over, anyway.

CONRAD (*suddenly*): Come here a moment.

GRAYLE (*turning*): I want to know something.

GRAYLE *moves rather impatiently over to the chair by the table (C.). CONRAD comes down the room, his hands behind him, his eyes fixed on the carpet.*

GRAYLE: Well?

CONRAD (*looking at him from under his brows*): Why did you apologise for me to Madame Louis?

GRAYLE: I didn't.

CONRAD: You said I was ill. Why?

GRAYLE: Well, you are, aren't you? You've just said so.

CONRAD: Come, come! That wasn't it. You were rather ashamed of me, weren't you?

GRAYLE: Well, yes, I was, if you want to know the truth. I couldn't let her go away with the idea that you meant to be rude.

CONRAD: So you apologised for me to that woman!

GRAYLE: You ought to be jolly grateful.

CONRAD (*his voice rising*): You dared to apologise for me! You dared!

GRAYLE: Oh, for God's sake don't start that game! (*He is about to go away.*)

CONRAD (*seizing him by the wrists, his face livid*): You were ashamed of me, and apologised – and then you want to come to some arrangement – some arrangement – about the room . . . only the room . . . just the room . . .

GRAYLE (*wrenching his left hand free*): What the hell! You and your bloody temper! Let go, will you? (*He tries to push him away with his free hand.*)

CONRAD: You apologised . . .

GRAYLE *wrenches his other hand free and staggers back a pace.* CONRAD *hits him heavily in the mouth. He falls and lies there, lies there long enough for* CONRAD *to become suddenly frightened.* GRAYLE *gets up slowly, his mouth bleeding.*

GRAYLE: You swine!

CONRAD: I'm sorry. (*He makes as though to help him.*)

GRAYLE: Leave me alone, you beast! It was a foul blow!

CONRAD: I didn't mean . . .

GRAYLE (*hitting at him*): Go to hell! (*He staggers towards the door.*)

CONRAD: I didn't mean it, Allan. I'm sorry I . . .

GRAYLE *goes out, holding his mouth.* CONRAD *is suddenly overcome by a feeling of faintness, his face pales, and the muscles round his mouth twitch. He staggers, almost falls, but saves himself by clutching the back of the chair beside him.*

ACT THREE

Scene 1

The night of the dance, 30 July.

It is about 9 pm, and CONRAD's *room is in darkness, but the light of a moon turning to its last quarter, gives the mountains outside dim, spidery outlines. The melody of some dreamy, prewar waltz drifts in through the open verandah windows.*

CONRAD, *in a blue mess uniform, comes in and switches on the lights. His first remarks are addressed to* DR Croz *outside.*

CONRAD (*holding the door open*): You can spare me a moment, can't you?

CROZ: Afterwards! Afterwards!

CONRAD: No; now, doctor, please. I really won't keep you a moment.

CROZ (*impatiently*): What ees it? What ees it?

He comes in, a stout, frog-like man, in very old-fashioned evening dress.

CONRAD: I've been trying to catch you all day, you see.

CROZ (*half interrogatively*): Yes, yes?

CONRAD: Do you remember me coming to you two days ago? For something to make me sleep?

CROZ: Yes, yes. I give you someting.

CONRAD: It had no effect. I haven't slept now for about five nights. I want something else.

CROZ: I will give you a leetle more.

CONRAD: Haven't you got anything else? I shall go mad if I don't sleep tonight.

CROZ: No. It ees se best I haf.

CONRAD: Can't you give me an injection of morphia?

CROZ: No, no. I haf none.

CONRAD: Yes, you have. I've seen it in your room.

CROZ: I cannot gif eet you. Don't be so seely.

CONRAD: Why not?

CROZ: I am not allow.

Pause.

CONRAD: You think I'm shamming, don't you? You think I'm swinging the lead for the next Repatriation Board? That's why you laughed at me when I came to you two days ago. I didn't go up for the one that sat today. You know that. I suppose you think I'm laying up a case for myself for the next?

CROZ (*wreathed in smiles*): I did not say eet.

CONRAD: You think it, though, don't you?

CROZ (*beaming*): You sat eet, not me.

CONRAD: Can't you tell a man's ill by his face? Do I look well?

CROZ: You do too moch work, like me. You sit always in here, and write. You must go more into the air. (*Suddenly patting him on the arm.*) You will all be home soon. I say eet.

CONRAD: That's it! That's it! (*The waltz has stopped.*) You think I'm shamming. I suppose you're afraid of being made a fool of. Where's your humanity, man? Give me that, if you can't give me morphia. You don't know what it is to be a prisoner. (*He taps his forehead.*) That's where it takes us, there. If you'd had a spark of humanity about you you'd have got Adelby through the Board today.

CROZ: He ees not ill.

CONRAD: His wife is. I told you so. Over and over again I told you so.

CROZ: But that is not my beezness. Eet is sad, but we cannot help. We haf our orders.

CONRAD: A word from you would have done a lot.

CROZ: Yes, yes, it might. Eet might not. If one is allow to go, others will want to go. You know yourself. (*He pats him again.*) I would send you all to England eef I could, but what am I? Noting. (CONRAD *does not speak.*) Eef you come to me after I will give you a leetle someting for to make you sleep.

CONRAD *says nothing and* DR. CROZ *bustles out.* CONRAD *presses*

his forehead with his hand and turns wearily away into the room.

JELLERTON *appears at the open door. He has taken off his tunic and cap and has on a grey cardigan. He has an envelope in his hand. He taps to attract* CONRAD's *attention.*

CONRAD: Hullo? What is it, Jellerton?

JELLERTON: Beg pardon, sir . . .

CONRAD: Oughtn't you to be in your hotel now? (*He looks at his watch.*) Oh, no; you've still got another half-hour.

JELLERTON: I was jest doing a job of work in your bedroom, sir. One o' your tunics wanted a stitch or two under 'ere. (*He indicates one of his own armpits.*)

CONRAD (*looking at envelope*): What have you got there?

JELLERTON: It's a telegram, sir; for Mr Adelby. Mrs 'Auser give it me 'arf an hour back, and I 'aven't bin able to find 'im.

CONRAD (*to himself*): Adelby.

He takes the envelope and looks at it.

When did it come?

JELLERTON: Couldn't say, sir.

CONRAD: Have you looked in his bedroom?

JELLERTON: No, sir. I dunno which it is.

He rubs his moustache apologetically.

CONRAD: You've tried downstairs, have you?

JELLERTON: Yes, sir. 'e ain't there.

CONRAD: Well, just go and look in his bedroom, will you? It's number 22 on the next floor.

JELLERTON (*going*): Yes, sir.

CONRAD: By the way . . .

JELLERTON: Yes, sir?

CONRAD: You needn't say anything about a telegram. Just ask him if he'll speak to me for a moment.

JELLERTON: Right you are, sir. (*He goes out and returns in a moment.*)

'e was there, sir. Says 'e'll come down at once.

A two-step starts down below.

CONRAD: What was he doing? He wasn't in bed, was he?

JELLERTON: No, sir. 'e was jest sitting there.

CONRAD: Reading?

JELLERTON: No, sir. Jest sitting there.

CONRAD (*turning away*): All right, Jellerton.

JELLERTON: I'll be in your bedroom if you want me again, sir.

CONRAD: All right.

JELLERTON goes. Enter ADELBY. He is looking terribly ill, but his big pipe is in his mouth and his face wears its placid, mild expression. He, too, is wearing blue uniform.

ADELBY (*closing the door*): Your servant said you wanted to see me.

CONRAD (*nervously*): Yes. I didn't disturb you, did I?

ADELBY: Disturb me? No.

CONRAD: Take a pew. (ADELBY *sits.*) Here you are.

He hands him the telegram.

ADELBY (*without change of tone, but with a gap in between*): For . . . me?

CONRAD (*turning away and sitting at his table*): Er . . . yes.

ADELBY opens it quietly and reads the message it contains. His face does not seem to change at all in expression. One would imagine that he knew what it contained before he opened it. Yet he takes a long time to read it. The two-step is heard faintly downstairs. He closes the telegram, puts it back in its envelope and into his pocket. For a moment he stares wide-eyed into space, then he shivers slightly and getting up goes slowly to the verandah.

ADELBY: Aren't you a . . . dancing-man, Jim?

CONRAD: I do sometimes. I don't feel up to anything much tonight.

ADELBY: Do you mind if I shut these windows? That tune . . .

CONRAD: Not a bit.

ADELBY closes them and comes quietly down stage towards CONRAD, who, with his hands clasped backs-downwards upon his forehead, is lying in his chair.

ADELBY (*touching him on the shoulder*): Thank you.

He goes towards the door, but before he gets to it someone knocks. CONRAD springs up and faces the door.

CONRAD: Come in!

It is MRS PRENDERGAST in evening dress.

MRS PRENDERGAST: Well, I declare! Here you both are! The only two deserters. I wondered what had become of you. (*She holds out her hand.*) Good evening, Mr Adelby. You're quite a stranger to me.

ADELBY (*touching it*): Good evening.

MRS PRENDERGAST: I am so sorry you didn't pass the Board. I so hoped you would.

ADELBY: Thank you.

MRS PRENDERGAST: Mr Crawley was the only one, wasn't he? But then I suppose it was only to be expected, and the poor boy is not at all well.

ADELBY (*after a slight pause*): Is it going all right downstairs?

MRS PRENDERGAST: Oh, yes; I think people are enjoying themselves quite a lot, and despite everything. You're coming down after the interval, aren't you?

ADELBY: I . . . think not. If you'll excuse me. I am (*he smiles at her*) not as young as I might be.

MRS PRENDERGAST: Stuff! Of course you must come down. Mustn't he, Captain Conrad?

CONRAD (*looking up*): I beg your pardon?

ADELBY: You must excuse me.

MRS PRENDERGAST (*softly*): Is there . . . is your wife any better?

CONRAD *makes an uncontrolled movement and then is still.*

ADELBY: No . . . I'm afraid . . . she's dead.

He touches the pocket of his tunic where the telegram reposes. His voice seems quite expressionless.

MRS PRENDERGAST (*with a sudden gesture of pity*): Oh . . .

ADELBY (*a curious note in his voice – loudly*): No, no! (*More quietly*) Please!

He goes out, leaving as unobtrusively as he came.

MRS PRENDERGAST (*in a hushed voice*): When did he hear?

CONRAD: Just now.

MRS PRENDERGAST: Through you?

CONRAD: No. It came direct.

MRS PRENDERGAST: How cruel! (*Pause.*) She was quite young and pretty, wasn't she?

CONRAD (*wearily*): Yes. I believe so. (*Pause.*) And he told me he was never going to be unhappy again.

MRS PRENDERGAST: Oh. . . . Isn't it terrible! Poor Mr Adelby! It's just one thing after another. (*Pause.*) I *do* so wish they'd let him go home.

CONRAD: It wouldn't have helped.

MRS PRENDERGAST: Ah yes, it would. It would have made a difference. He'd have been among friends, anyway. He always looks so lonely up here. And now he'll be eating his heart out.

CONRAD: You didn't really expect that to weigh in his favour, did you? Don't you understand yet that we simply have to grin and bear things?

We're no use to anyone. Why should anyone take trouble over us? I suppose half the world thinks of us as pariahs, outsiders, cowards – if it thinks of us at all.

God! Life's a hell of a joke sometimes!

MRS PRENDERGAST (*sitting down on the sofa*): It's hard, I know. You aren't looking well.

CONRAD: I don't sleep.

MRS PRENDERGAST: You oughtn't to be up here brooding. You're becoming an absolute old man, I declare. Why don't you come and dance?

CONRAD: I have been down.

MRS PRENDERGAST: Stuff! You wandered round the room once, looking too miserable for words. You ought to be helping us all to entertain our guests.

CONRAD: I've got this vile neuralgia still. It's like an iron band round my forehead. I keep on wanting to push it off.

MRS PRENDERGAST: Why don't you see the doctor?

CONRAD (*with a mirthless laugh*): I have. He says he doesn't know when the next Board's sitting.

MRS PRENDERGAST: He didn't! Why don't you report him?

CONRAD (*laughing spasmodically*): I don't know. It strikes me as being rather funny now. Besides – what's the good of reporting a Swiss to a Swiss? (*He laughs again.*) It's the same in the Army, you know. Sick-lists are always looked upon with the gravest suspicion. Poor, trustworthy Tommy!

MRS PRENDERGAST: Well, you ought to do something about it. Shall I go down and speak to him about you?

CONRAD: No, thanks. Besides, you mustn't worry him. He's having such a good time downstairs with the Swiss officers of the Repatriation Board. It would be a pity to disturb him.

MRS PRENDERGAST: Stuff! I'm sure he'd come and see you if I asked him to. He's really quite a nice little man.

CONRAD: Oh, yes. I expect so. He's only a fool.

MRS PRENDERGAST: He doesn't spare himself. He works very hard among the Swiss peasants.

CONRAD: Does he? Do you find it very hot in here?

MRS PRENDERGAST: I suppose it is rather warm, but I'm so glad of a rest I didn't notice it.

CONRAD: It seems intolerably hot to

me. (*He pulls at his neck.*) I'll open the windows if you don't mind.

MRS PRENDERGAST: Please do. The air's very heavy tonight.

CONRAD (*opening the windows*): The band's stopped.

MRS PRENDERGAST: It's the interval for refreshments. I expect a good many of them have had quite enough refreshment recently. They say Captain Rickman, Mr Tetford, and Mr Grayle sat up most of last night drinking in order to look ill when the Board saw them today.

CONRAD: I know; I told Tetford he was wasting his time.

MRS PRENDERGAST: It *is* so silly. Of course one expects that of Captain Rickman – drink doesn't affect him much either – but the other two! Ah, well! I suppose it's no good doing or saying anything; but, I declare, it makes me very miserable.

CONRAD: Does it? I've got past that stage. I don't care now, very much.

He comes down the room treading carefully on the patterns.

MRS PRENDERGAST: Have you quarrelled with Mr Grayle? I may ask, mayn't I?

CONRAD: Oh, yes. I don't think we've met once during the last month without friction of some kind.

MRS PRENDERGAST: Isn't that rather a pity? What was it all about?

CONRAD (*vaguely*): All about? I don't know. I suppose we just jarred on each other.

He arrives at the door and leans his forehead against its cool surface for a moment with a sigh of relief.

I did my best to . . . Did I? I don't remember now. (*Desolately.*) I suppose we're just different – like everyone else, and so we jarred on each other.

MRS PRENDERGAST: So you're still at loggerheads are you?

CONRAD (*moving up and down between the verandah windows and the fourth wall*): No. We had a . . .

definite break. He's gone in with Tetford and Rickman, I believe, and I . . . well, I'm alone.

He misses a pattern on this and goes back to step on it again.

MRS PRENDERGAST: Poor boy! What did you quarrel about?

CONRAD: I forget now. I know I lost my temper as usual. I believe it was something to do with that woman who's staying here. . . .

MRS PRENDERGAST: That Jewish-looking widow, I suppose?

CONRAD: Yes. Madame Louis.

MRS PRENDERGAST: And what happened?

CONRAD (*carefully*): I lost my temper and . . . hit him.

MRS PRENDERGAST (*with vigour*): And a very good thing, too!

CONRAD: Oh, no. I can't imagine how it happened. I was sorry. I kept on saying I was sorry. I wouldn't have hit him for anything. Not for anything. He said he'd finished with me – even after I'd told him I was sorry. . . .

MRS PRENDERGAST: So that's how his lip was cut! He told me he'd fallen down or something.

CONRAD: Did he? Then I oughtn't to have spoken. Please don't mention it. . . .

MRS PRENDERGAST (*on edge*): For goodness sake stop walking up and down! You fidget me beyond words.

CONRAD (*apologetically*): I'm sorry. . . . I didn't know. (*He leans against the door.*) This neuralgia makes me rather restless.

MRS PRENDERGAST: You won't improve it by behaving like a caged lion. No, as I said before, I think you were quite right to hit Mr Grayle, and I wish you'd do it again!

CONRAD *says nothing, but goes slowly back to the verandah.*

The way he is carrying on with that woman is positively scandalous.

CONRAD: It's nothing to do with me.

MRS PRENDERGAST: Yes it is. You

used to be his friend, and you're five years older than he is.

CONRAD (*explosively*): You don't understand. It's nothing to do with me. He doesn't speak to me or come near me. I don't exist.

MRS PRENDERGAST: Don't be ridiculous. He liked you once; he can't have changed round as completely as all that.

CONRAD: Yes he can. That's where you're wrong. He can do things like that without another thought. I wish to God I could.

He comes down again on the patterns.

MRS PRENDERGAST: Well, someone ought to look after him.

CONRAD (*wearily*): Then you'd better go to Rickman. He'd probably pay attention to Rickman. (*He laughs.*) I've got a plant to look after now. (*He waves his hand towards it.*) Can't be bothered with anything else. Plants or rabbits; it's the same thing.

MRS PRENDERGAST: Nonsense. Besides, Captain Rickman can't even look after himself, and he's certainly not the proper person to look after that boy. Mr Grayle wants guiding.

CONRAD (*smiling*): With a stick, I think you said?

MRS PRENDERGAST: Certainly! If all else fails, as you say it has. He's only nineteen! Just think of it! Though I've known some boys – even younger – who carried themselves splendidly – like regular soldiers. It's a blessing that he wasn't an infantry officer with other men's lives in his hands as well as his own.

CONRAD: You can't judge by what you see here.

MRS PRENDERGAST: Oh, yes, you can. Mr Grayle has not left school more than a year. But he's had a year in which to learn to be a man and he hasn't succeeded. My boy put on khaki when he was just eighteen and he became a man from that moment.

CONRAD (*surprised*): I didn't know you had a boy.

MRS PRENDERGAST (*with very little emphasis*): I had. (*Pause.*) I like Mr Grayle; that is why I don't like to see him making a fool of himself.

CONRAD: But what's the good of all this? You can't prevent it. You can't criticise it. You aren't *with* us. It's part of the life, the abnormal life we're leading. I find myself hating people sometimes up to the point of murder, and being attracted to others in a way that terrifies me. I don't know what I'm doing half my time. I find myself looking at my watch and putting it back in my pocket without realising what the time is; striking a match and blowing it out before I've lighted my cigarette. I pull myself up sometimes brooding over things I shouldn't be thinking of, and at night I toss about revelling in the same thoughts. I don't sleep. I hardly sleep at all now, and get up in the morning feeling dry and haggard, always with this stabbing in my head.

MRS PRENDERGAST: Will you please come and sit down, instead of fidgeting me out of my wits with that blessed carpet!

CONRAD (*closing his eyes painfully*): Yes, yes; I'll do anything you like. (*He sits.*) So you can't judge us now, you see; for we're a race apart. Temperamentally unsound. I know all my weaknesses and I cherish them. I value them more than my strength. A race part . . .

With an heraldic knock at the door, which jerks CONRAD *up in his chair,* TETFORD *and* RICKMAN *drift in,* TETFORD *still wearing his half-mocking smile,* RICKMAN *looking subdued and sullen. They are both in mess uniforms;* TETFORD *with a silver pilot's badge upon his breast,* RICKMAN *in the gaudy, silver chain epaulets of the 2nd CMRs.*

TETFORD: God's blessing on this house! I hope we don't intrude. (*Indicating* RICKMAN.) I had to get my little friend away from the Swiss doctor, who turned him down this morning. He wanted his blood.

RICKMAN: Dry up, Harry!

MRS PRENDERGAST: Have you both been dancing?

TETFORD: Ra-ther! We zoomed round rather successfully, didn't we, Eric? My last split-air turn was a sight for tired eyes. My partner was still talking about it when we left.

He does a turn or two round the room, humming to himself.

MRS PRENDERGAST: And what's happened to the band lately? Surely the interval's over by now?

TETFORD: Oh, yes. But the band got demobilised during the interval, and the Major's still trying to collect it again.

MRS PRENDERGAST (*getting up*): There! I knew something would happen. I'd better go down again.

To CONRAD, *who is lying with closed eyes in his chair.*

Will you take me down, Captain Conrad? I'm sure you ought to be downstairs taking an interest in things instead of moping here.

CONRAD: I think I'll stay here, if you don't mind.

MRS PRENDERGAST: Now just come down and show yourself again and help me to a little refreshment, and then you can come back.

CONRAD (*getting up and staggering slightly under the pain caused by his change of attitude*): Very well.

MRS PRENDERGAST: Please don't stay up here too long, Mr Tetford. We shall want you all downstairs.

TETFORD: Shan't be long. We'll come down when we've had one of Conrad's fags.

MRS PRENDERGAST *and* CONRAD *go out.* TETFORD *strolls over to the chair by* CONRAD'*s table, taking a cigarette from the centre table on the way.* RICKMAN *stands, inertly, in the middle of the room.*

TETFORD: What's up with Conrad?

RICKMAN (*indifferently*): Search me.

TETFORD (*sitting*): Didn't you see when he got up then? He nearly fell.

RICKMAN: Did he? I guess he's going soft, like the rest of us.

There is a short restless pause.

TETFORD: See Grayle getting off with Madame downstairs?

RICKMAN: Yes.

TETFORD *glances at him.*

TETFORD: Did you notice the way he looked at her as he handed her the coffee?

RICKMAN (*heavily*): He's taken a trick with her all right.

TETFORD: Little fool! He thinks he's rather clever. She's got her knife into you, my son, after what you said to her.

RICKMAN (*sourly*): O – shoot her, anyway!

TETFORD: Grayle's a bit oiled, isn't he?

RICKMAN: Tight as a fool. (*But the swagger has gone out of him.*)

There is another short restless pause.

TETFORD (*reaching for the tennis racket which is lying on* CONRAD'*s table*): Ole Crawford's pretty bucked with himself. I'm glad he's passed, poor devil! TB isn't it?

RICKMAN: B'lieve so.

TETFORD: What are you standing up for?

RICKMAN (*sitting obediently on the sofa*): Are we going to have a drink?

TETFORD: No. Let's wait till we get downstairs.

Dreary silence.

RICKMAN (*suddenly starting upright*): Harry! This is the life.

Silence. TETFORD *gazes at him critically.* RICKMAN *slowly subsides on to the sofa again.*

TETFORD (*quietly*): What's up, Eric?

RICKMAN: That ruddy Board to-day. It's enough to make you choke. Day and night – and nothing to do but drink yourself to death.

TETFORD (*balancing the racket on his nose*): There is a certain sameness about it.

RICKMAN: I guess . . . so. What am I

to do afterwards? That's what worries hell out of me. I've forgotten every darn thing I knew about timber. I'm good for nothing else.

Suddenly brightening.

When does the next Board sit, d'you know?

TETFORD, *balancing the racket, begins to laugh spasmodically; but this sound and the echo of his own question are too much for* RICKMAN, *and he sinks his face abruptly into his hands.*

TETFORD: Well, if that isn't –

Then he perceives the dejected attitude of his friend, rises, quietly puts the racket on the table and goes to him.

Cheer up, Eric.

Sitting on the arm of the sofa, he touches him on the head, and one is reminded of an earlier scene between CONRAD *and* GRAYLE.

RICKMAN (*dropping his hands*): I feel kind o' beat. Sick – homesick, I guess.

TETFORD: Never mind, old son.

RICKMAN: Two years in Germany, and six months in this one-horse city. And how much more to come? That's it – how much more to come?

TETFORD (*slipping his hand on to* RICKMAN's *shoulder*): Maybe it won't be so long.

RICKMAN: Maybe it will.

TETFORD: Well, maybe it won't *seem* so long if we stick together.

RICKMAN (*linking a finger in* TETFORD's *dangling hand*): Yes, I'm glad o' you, Bo' – but that's about all. I feel just cut off from the world in this place. It's like being in the lumber camps out West in that respect – only you don't feel it there! No, by God! you don't feel it there! That's the life, Harry! I've been figurin' it all day. Why – (*He grips* TETFORD's *hand, and the poetry in him, sensed by* TETFORD, *but unsuspected by* CONRAD, *is released.*) – why, a man gets a hunger out there, and there's good food to satisfy it. Not messed-up junk like we get here, but clean food –

that draws the water to your mouth.

There's salmon, for instance, beautiful fresh salmon from BC, and porridge for breakfast. There's no milk, o' course, except you keep your own cows, but we never take it – only with the porridge, and then we use condensed. You drink your tea neat; good tea it is, too; black and green.

A waltz is heard to start below.

Smoked bacon you get, too; and fine steers – fine, big steers from the West, and good white bread – not this brown dope; but sweet bread, the best I ever sunk a tooth in. And you feel a kind o' spread about your chest, and you don't give a hoot for any man. Harry! It's a proud little country!

He ceases, staring before him, tense, visionary.

TETFORD: Eric – I've been thinking. What do you say we both go out there together after this?

RICKMAN (*releasing his hand and looking up*): You? Why, what about that now?

TETFORD: I'm not fixed up in any way. I thought we might start something there on our own. We'd pull along all right together, I guess – and you need me to keep a hold on you.

RICKMAN (*happily*): Oh, that's so, is it? Don't you come pullin' any of that stuff around here! But, that'd be fine, now, wouldn't it? Only . . .

TETFORD: Only what?

RICKMAN: Well, you ain't what one'd call extra tough; and you need to be tough out there.

TETFORD (*scornfully*): Tough! I bet I'm as tough as you – at the moment, I mean. But it's only an idea, you know; if you don't cotton on, well – there's no harm done.

RICKMAN (*almost shyly*): Why, it'd be fine, Harry. Just . . . sooperlative. Will you come? Straight?

TETFORD: As soon as we're out of this. It's a partnership then?

RICKMAN: Why – what do you think?

He thrusts out his hand. TETFORD

takes it. Something passes between them.

And if we don't pass that goddamn Board next time, I'll . . . I'll . . . (*He can't think of anything sufficiently impressive.*)

TETFORD (*happily, keeping him down*): O, chuck it, Eric! It doesn't matter so much now.

RICKMAN: You're right again, Bo'. It don't signify.

So they are sitting quietly contemplating that golden future when CONRAD comes in. He halts a moment on seeing them, remote from their happiness, confused.

RICKMAN (*releasing TETFORD's hand, but without embarrassment*): Hullo, Jim! How are your front feet?

CONRAD: What? Why have you shut those windows? O – they're open. God! I feel hot, don't you?

RICKMAN (*getting up*): Can't say I do. Just cool.

He goes back to the window and stands listening to the music.

CONRAD (*pulling at his collar*): I'm stifling. Stifling.

He sits down heavily by the centre table.

I suppose you haven't got one of those little medicine chests, either of you?

TETFORD: I had one, but I lost it in Germany.

He gets off the arm of the sofa and, softly whistling an accompaniment to the music, sits down at CONRAD's table and takes up the racket again.

I've got some aspirin, if that's any good.

CONRAD: Never mind. It's something in the air. I'll sit and rest a bit.

There is a knock at the door. CONRAD starts.

Who's that? Come in!

It is only JELLERTON.

JELLERTON: Beg pardon, sir. Is Mr Adelby 'ere?

CONRAD (*dimly – his head on his hand*): Adelby? (*Recollecting.*) Adelby? No. Why?

JELLERTON (*indicating a glass of hot milk he is carrying*): It's his 'ot milk, sir; and I can't find 'im anywhere. (*CONRAD stares at him dully.*) Mrs 'auser asked me to bring it up, sir. The maids is all busy.

CONRAD: Didn't he say where it was to go?

JELLERTON: It's reg'lar, sir, for a quarter past nine. It usually goes to 'is bedroom, sir. I think 'e 'as it in bed. But 'e's not there, 'cause I've looked.

RICKMAN, *still at the window, has his back turned. TETFORD has rested the bottom of the tennis-racket on the floor between his legs, and is dreamily working the handle to and fro as though it were the joy-stick of his aeroplane. Neither is paying any attention.*

CONRAD (*getting up*): That's funny! He's not downstairs. I know that. (*In sudden breathless terror.*) No. . . .!

RICKMAN (*turning from the window*): Try Crawford's room. He's often there.

CONRAD: Come with me.

He goes out swiftly, followed by JELLERTON.

RICKMAN: Come on, Steve. Let's quit this shanty. I'm just ripe for a hop, and we'll drink to the noo limited company.

TETFORD *does not answer. Sitting in the chair with the tennis-racket between his legs, he imagines himself back in his aeroplane. He works the different parts of the invisible machine as directed, starting, while RICKMAN is speaking, with the wind-screen in front of him – loosening a screw on his right front, pulling the top of the screen towards him and re-screwing it. RICKMAN watches him open-mouthed.*

What the blue blazes –!

TETFORD: Hop in, Pard! We'll clear off to Canada toute suite. Forgot all about this old bus of mine.

RICKMAN: You're crazy!

TETFORD: Hop in! There's no time to lose!

RICKMAN, *amused, takes an adjacent chair and sits behind him.*

Fresh salmon from BC! You right? Good!

Shouting to an imaginary mechanic.

Petrol on! Switch is off!

(*To* RICKMAN.) Did you hear her snort?

Shouting again.

Petrol off! Switch is on!

He lies back.

She hums! She hums!

RICKMAN (*rocking his chair*): Steady the buffs! How high are we?

TETFORD: Don't talk! We aren't off the ground yet. Where did I get to? Ah, yes, we must open the throttle.

He pushes a lever on his left gently forward.

She's doing maximum now. We must throttle her down.

He moves the same lever back slightly faster.

Now we're ready. The engine's just ticking over.

He waves his hand from left to right.

That's to warn the mechanics out of the way. Now!

He pushes the left lever half-forward.

That speeds her up. We're taxying out of the aerodrome now. . . .

RICKMAN: Mind you don't taxi into a lunatic asylum.

TETFORD: . . . Nose into the wind.

He pushes the left lever right forward and settles back into his seat, moving the tennis-racket gently forward a bit.

Her tail's off the ground now. I can feel it.

He brings racket gently back to his stomach.

Now we're rising.

RICKMAN: Why didn't you do this when the doctors were around? You'd

have got repatriated, sure!

TETFORD: Take a look down? What do you think of that? Pretty good view, what? There's Mürren bang underneath. Blow it a kiss from me, will you?

RICKMAN: You're right! And there's that goddamn hotel on the edge of the precipice. And there's that skunk of a doctor poking his face out of his bedroom window. Heave a spanner at him, will you?

TETFORD: Must be fifteen hundred up now. Engine's conked out.

He pushes the tennis-racket forward to flatten out the machine.

Shall we do a loop?

He pushes the racket forward to dive down about one hundred feet, his eyes fixed on his speed-indicator.

RICKMAN (*getting up*): No, let's land and get a drink.

TETFORD (*to himself as he reads speed*): One hundred . . . one hundred and ten . . . one hundred and twenty. Good enough!

He pulls racket straight back.

She's up on her tail.

He looks up.

See Mürren going back over your head?

RICKMAN: Come off it, you silly stiff. I'm fed up with your ruddy acrobatics.

TETFORD: Wouldn't you like to see me do another stunt?

RICKMAN: Yes – crash!

TETFORD: Crash? Right. We've just come out of a spin. Stick is back. . . .

RICKMAN (*taking him by the hand*): Come on, before I bash you. Sitting there talking a blue streak!

CONRAD *comes in. He looks very frightened.*

CONRAD: He's gone out!

RICKMAN: Who has?

CONRAD: Adelby.

RICKMAN: Well, why shouldn't he?

CONRAD (*moving down in front of the centre table*): I don't know. I . . . (*He stops, glances across at them and goes on again.*) . . . don't know.

TETFORD (*getting up – interested*): What's up?

CONRAD: He's . . . he's burnt a lot of papers in his room, too. On the floor. It's very late for a walk, isn't it?

He stands in front of the table, staring straight before him.

TETFORD: Not for Adelby. He always chooses extraordinary times like this for a walk.

RICKMAN: Dinner time, usually.

TETFORD: Down the railway-line to Grütsch. He always goes the same way.

RICKMAN: D'you think he keeps something down there? A bit of fluff? Wily old bird, Adelby, if you ask me!

TETFORD: Shut up, Eric!

CONRAD (*suddenly turning*): Oh! – but don't you remember? He said . . . he said . . . Quickly! I must go! I must . . .

The right side of his mouth gives, and begins to pull spasmodically from the corner. With a gurgling, inarticulate cry he falls heavily to the ground. His face is deadly pale; his back rigid and arched.

RICKMAN: What the . . . Quick, man! He's chucking a fit!

They throw themselves upon him. His whole body is thrown into a series of jerkings and twitchings. His face is contorted. His tongue flung out from his mouth.

TETFORD (*pulling out a handkerchief with difficulty*): Put that in his mouth quick, before he bites his tongue!

RICKMAN *does so.*

RICKMAN (*straining*): God! We want another! Jellerton! Jellerton!

TETFORD: Mind he doesn't kick you. Hang on to his arms and legs. Never mind his head!

RICKMAN (*to* CONRAD): That's all right, sonny! Take it easy. God! He's strong! Jellerton! Jellerton!

Scene 2

CONRAD'*s room, four days later, 3 August.*

The room is tidy, and a few vases of flowers impart, under the circumstances, an atmosphere of nursing homes and sickness. The centre table has been pushed into the corner, where skis and ski-sticks once stood, and the sofa is backed against CONRAD'*s table so that it commands a view of the door and the verandah. The windows are open.*

It is about 7 pm and the sun is sinking down behind the Sefinen Furgge. The peaks of the Jungfrau and Gletscherhorn and the Ebnefluh-Mittaghorn ridge are pink, and beneath this rosy band the snow seems more white, the rocks more black, and the glaciers more green than is natural. The sky is pale. As the sun sinks the pink flames and creeps further up the summits, shadows taking its place; the sky appears to grow paler, and the green of the glaciers intensifies. Very little of the flame is then seen. A great golden fleecy cloud spreads slowly across from the right. The blue of the sky deepens. The mountains, abandoned, rise like delicate silver points from an ebony sea of pine woods. The moon grows brighter throughout. The golden cloud disperses.

Inside the room sits TETFORD *reading a book. His chair is placed right back against the middle wall near the windows, and he has tilted it back so that it stands upon two legs. Every now and then he looks over his left shoulder towards the verandah, on which a vacant chair can be seen. There is a tap at the door.* TETFORD *gets up quietly and opens it.* MRS PRENDERGAST *comes in.*

MRS PRENDERGAST: They told me you were on duty. Where is he?

TETFORD (*nodding*): On the verandah.

MRS PRENDERGAST: Is he any better? Is there any change?

TETFORD: No, except that he's been rather restless all day. Wandering about the verandah and peering in here at me. But I don't think he knows me.

MRS PRENDERGAST: Poor boy! (*Pause.*) They've found . . . Mr Adelby's . . . body.

TETFORD: No. . . . (*He makes a helpless movement and turns his head away.*) And all along I've been thinking in spite of everything, that there was still some hope of his having . . . simply gone away. Who found it?

MRS PRENDERGAST: Captain Rickman's search party.

TETFORD: Where? Do you know?

MRS PRENDERGAST: Somewhere out near Isenfluh.

TETFORD: Right out there?

MRS PRENDERGAST (*nodding*): They say he must have fallen a hundred feet. Killed outright, the doctor says.

TETFORD: Are they bringing him back here?

MRS PRENDERGAST: No, down to Lauterbrunnen, I think. Isn't it awful?

TETFORD: Poor devil! (*Pause.*) Is there any doubt? It wasn't . . . accidental?

MRS PRENDERGAST: I wish I could think so. The Major says the men are not to know about the telegram he got.

TETFORD: I see. Yes. I'm glad of that.

MRS PRENDERGAST: It's the right thing. I had to tell him about it.

TETFORD: I know.

MRS PRENDERGAST: I didn't want to. But it might have made a lot of difference.

TETFORD: You were quite right.

MRS PRENDERGAST: Poor Mr Adelby!

TETFORD: Four days – it seems like months.

MRS PRENDERGAST: He was the last person I should have thought would do a thing like that. He always seemed so . . . calm. How . . . hurt he must have felt!

TETFORD: He walked such a long way to . . . do it.

MRS PRENDERGAST: I wonder if he

meant to do it when he went out, or made up his mind on the way, or – or if it was really an accident. . . .

TETFORD: His burning all his letters before he went – that's what makes it look . . .

MRS PRENDERGAST: We shall never know for certain.

TETFORD (*gratefully*): No. We shall never know.

MRS PRENDERGAST (*stealing to the verandah doors and looking out*): And he suspected from the beginning?

TETFORD: I think so. I think that's what brought on the fit that night.

MRS PRENDERGAST: He's had no more since?

TETFORD: No, that's the only one. He seemed to be better the next morning, and then he began to go like this. . . .

MRS PRENDERGAST: Is he subject to fits? Three or four of the men here are.

TETFORD: I don't know. I never heard of his having had one before.

MRS PRENDERGAST: He was so nervy and highly strung. He was like a woman in some ways.

TETFORD: He'd been worrying a lot, too, I think. About Grayle and life in general.

MRS PRENDERGAST: Has Mr Grayle been to see him?

TETFORD: Oh, yes. Two or three times, for a few minutes. He's taking the next duty, as a matter of fact.

MRS PRENDERGAST: I'm glad he helps.

TETFORD: He doesn't, very much. He's only been on duty once – and then he got Crawley to keep him company. But he's got to come tonight because we're so short-handed. I think he feels it, though – as much as he's ever likely to feel anything.

MRS PRENDERGAST: May I go out and speak to him?

TETFORD: If you like. But don't touch his plant. He's always afraid that someone is going to steal it.

MRS PRENDERGAST *steps across to the verandah, and then halts abruptly in the doorway. She stretches out a cautioning hand to* TETFORD, *who is behind her, and then retreats into the room.* CONRAD *comes to the threshold. He is dressed in a tunic and khaki shorts, stockings and brogues. The tunic is open, disclosing a white vest. His head is bare. In front of him, in his two hands, he carries the pot of azaleas. He stops, just outside the room, gazing at* MRS PRENDERGAST.

MRS PRENDERGAST: Well, old boy, how are you feeling? (*He makes no sign.*) You're looking heaps better, I declare. Don't you remember me? Old Mother Prendergast? (*He turns his head away, staring before him.*) Of course you do. Old Mother Prendergast?

TETFORD: It's no good.

MRS PRENDERGAST: Won't you come in and talk to us?

TETFORD: No, he won't come in; I've tried.

MRS PRENDERGAST (*to* CONRAD): Isn't it a lovely sunset? Are you warm enough, dear? Shall we come out to you for a little?

She approaches. He notes the movement; his eyes slide round and he carries the bush of azaleas to his left side, away from her. She stops.

TETFORD: It's no good.

MRS PRENDERGAST: Would you like me to come and see you again?

Silence. She shakes her head.

Won't you even say good-bye to me?

She holds out her hand. He clutches his plant more tightly, looks wildly round, and goes back out of sight.

MRS PRENDERGAST (*dabs her eyes*): It makes me so miserable. Why does he like that old plant?

TETFORD: I don't know.

MRS PRENDERGAST: It's dying. It wants watering.

TETFORD: He won't let anyone touch it.

MRS PRENDERGAST: Well – I don't know. (*With sudden vigour.*) O, why are people so cruel to each other? (*Weakly.*) What does the doctor say?

TETFORD: Nothing. I don't think he understands very well. He just comes in and jokes.

MRS PRENDERGAST: He's a kind man, really.

TETFORD: I know. Jim doesn't like him.

MRS PRENDERGAST: Is he quite safe out there?

TETFORD: Oh, yes; quite. He prefers it, too. He never comes into the room until he's brought in. I think he doesn't like leaving the view. We watch him, of course. He's going to be sent away tomorrow.

MRS PRENDERGAST: Where to?

TETFORD: I don't know.

MRS PRENDERGAST: When do you come off duty?

TETFORD: At seven o'clock.

MRS PRENDERGAST: It's after that now. Why isn't Mr Grayle here?

TETFORD: He'll come in a minute or two, I expect. He was a little late last time. Doesn't like the job much. He seems rather nervous of Jim.

MRS PRENDERGAST: Would you like to come and have some dinner with me when you're relieved?

TETFORD (*hesitating*): It's very decent of you. But I don't think I will, thanks, in case Eric comes back. I haven't seen him all day, and he'll want me.

MRS PRENDERGAST: Very well. (*Impulsively.*) Will you give him my love? I think he's been splendid – practically without rest for four days. I . . . well, I suppose I'd better be running along. Is there anything else I can do?

TETFORD: I don't think so, thanks.

MRS PRENDERGAST (*holding out her hand*): Well – goodbye. I think you're all perfectly splendid.

TETFORD: Goodbye.

*He opens the door for her, and then,
coming back into the darkening room,
stands looking out of the window at
the great golden cloud.* GRAYLE
comes in.

GRAYLE: Sorry I'm late.

TETFORD: Have you had dinner?

GRAYLE: Yes. It's a rotten dinner.
Cold stuff. I suppose you know they've
found –?

TETFORD: Sh-h! Yes. But you'd better
not talk about it in front of him.

GRAYLE (*going to the window*): Where
is he? I don't see him. (*Looking out.*) I
say, what's he doing out there?

TETFORD: He's been standing there a
good deal today, looking up at the
mountains.

GRAYLE: Oughtn't he to be sitting
down? He can see just as well from the
chair.

TETFORD: You must let him do as he
likes.

GRAYLE (*after a pause*): I didn't know
he wandered about. When did he
begin to wander about?

TETFORD: He's been rather restless all
day. I'll get down to my dinner now.

GRAYLE (*detaining him*): Does he
wander about . . . much?

TETFORD: Yes, a good deal. But he
won't come in here; I don't know why.
At least, he won't for me. You'd better
try what you can do.

GRAYLE: Does he say anything? Does
he recognise people?

TETFORD: No, I don't think so.
Sometimes he mutters to himself, but
it's very indistinct.

GRAYLE: Why is he so restless? He
didn't get out of his chair once the last
time I was here.

TETFORD: I don't know; but you must
let him do as he likes.

GRAYLE (*detaining him*): Any special
orders?

TETFORD: No. Don't worry him, that's
all.

GRAYLE (*detaining him*): I say!

TETFORD (*impatiently*): What is it?

GRAYLE: You can have your dinner
sent up here if you like. Rickman isn't
back.

TETFORD (*looking at him strangely*):
Thank you. But I don't think I will. So
long.

*He goes out. After a moment's uneasy
hesitation* GRAYLE *crosses back to
the table and takes a cigarette from
the box there. His back is turned, so
he doesn't see* CONRAD *come to the
windows. But the act of taking the
cigarette reminds him of an old scene,
and, as he lights it, he glances over
his shoulder, sees* CONRAD, *and
starts round.*

GRAYLE: Hullo, Jim! Just taking one of
your fags. D'you mind? How are you
feeling? (*With a nervous laugh.*) You
needn't look at me like that. Aren't
you pleased to see me? You always
used to say you wanted to see me
alone, but you don't seem –

CONRAD *murmurs something and
takes a step into the room, which
sends* GRAYLE, *with a sharp 'Now!
Now!' between the sofa and the table.
They stare at each other.* TETFORD
comes in.

GRAYLE (*with great relief, and a false
joviality*): Hullo, Tet! Changed your
mind?

TETFORD (*crossing to CONRAD
without giving GRAYLE a second
glance*): Why, Jim! Anything the
matter?

GRAYLE (*coming from behind his
barrier*): He came in just after you
left. Have you changed your mind?

TETFORD: No. I left my book. What is
it, Jim? Anything I can do?

CONRAD, *his eyes still on GRAYLE,
murmurs something.*

GRAYLE: Do you understand what he's
talking about?

TETFORD (*to CONRAD*): What is it,
Jim boy? Wouldn't you like to sit
down, old man? You've been standing
about such a lot today.

GRAYLE: Isn't it awful? Fancy going
like that! Doesn't it give you the

creeps, being alone with him? It does me.

TETFORD (*hardly*): Does it? I don't mind.

GRAYLE: Who's relieving me?

TETFORD: Rickman – if he's back.

GRAYLE: Come and keep me company after dinner for a bit?

TETFORD: I don't think so, thanks.

GRAYLE (*pettishly*): You'll come and keep Rickman company, I bet.

TETFORD (*quietly*): Yes.

CONRAD (*in a clear voice*): I'm sorry. I'm awfully sorry. I didn't mean to.

TETFORD: What does he mean?

GRAYLE: I don't know. (*But the expression of his face belies his words.*)

TETFORD (*to CONRAD*): What are you sorry about, old boy?

GRAYLE (*quickly*): I don't suppose it's anything. He's just rambling.

CONRAD (*less clearly*): I'm sorry. . . . (*He falls to murmuring.*)

TETFORD (*soothingly*): I shouldn't worry if I were you. (*To GRAYLE.*) Do you think there's anything on his mind?

GRAYLE: I don't know at all.

TETFORD (*picking up his book*): Well, I'm off. (*To CONRAD.*) Good night, Jim! (*CONRAD's lips move.*) That's it! (*Quietly.*) Poor devil! (*To GRAYLE.*) Can't you be decent to him even now?

He goes out.

GRAYLE: Why don't you sit down, Jim? You'll get tired standing up.

He pats the sofa arm against which he is standing.

Come and sit here.

CONRAD *does not move.* GRAYLE, *braver now, goes towards him.*

Shall I help you over there?

He takes him cautiously by the elbow. CONRAD *does not move.*

Don't you want to? What are you sorry about? Because you hit me? Don't let that worry you. I don't mind. I didn't know you were ill. (*He laughs.*) Come on. Don't look so solemn!

CONRAD, *holding his plant against him with his left hand, stretches out his right towards GRAYLE. Suddenly nervous, GRAYLE retreats a step. CONRAD follows, and gazing straight before him touches GRAYLE's sleeve and moves his hand gently up the defensive arm. A very piteous expression settles on his face. His lips move again.*

GRAYLE: What's the matter?

CONRAD's *face becomes expressionless, and clasping the azalea-bush with both hands he goes out through the verandah windows to resume his seat in his easy-chair – a creature obscure, apart, with his plant in his lap and his profile turned to catch the last rays of the setting sun.*